Ikkyū and the Crazy Cloud Anthology

A Zen Poet of Medieval Japan

Frontispiece overleaf:
Portrait of Ikkyū and Mori with an inscription and Chinese poem in Ikkyū's hand at the top and a Japanese poem by Mori in Ikkyū's hand. Courtesy of Masaki Museum, Osaka. The full inscription including the two poems reads as follows:

> Within the circle, appears a whole self,
> The painting expresses Xutang's true features,
> The blind girl's love songs shame Pavilion Master,
> One song before the blossoms equals ten thousand years of spring.

Old monk Jun Ikkyū of the Eastern Sea, formerly of Daitokuji and Seventh Generation Descendant of Master [Xutang] Tianze, composed this himself and gave it to Lay Disciple Tamagaki.

Uta "Song" by Mori Jōro [term of respect for women entertainers]

> Sleep of yearning,
> on this bed of sorrow sleeping,
> I float, I sink,
> but for tears
> there is no consolation.

大貧相裏現全身
畫出雲堂面目真
盲女艷歌笑樓子
花前一曲萬年春

前大德天澤七世裏
順一休老初月題之
玉垣居圡

森上郎□詠

宅安志津
□□□□

SONJA ARNTZEN

Ikkyū and the Crazy Cloud Anthology

A Zen Poet of Medieval Japan

Revised & Expanded Edition

QUIRIN PRESS
Melbourne & Basel
2022

Published by Quirin Press
P.O. Box 4226, Melbourne University, Vic. 3052, Australia
E-mail: enquiries@quirinpress.com
http://www.quirinpress.com

Originally published by University of Tokyo Press in 1986 as part of the Japanese series of the UNESCO collection of representative works

Copyright © 1986 Sonja Arntzen
Copyright © 2022 Quirin Press for this second revised edition

All rights reserved. No part of this publication may be reproduced or transmitted in any form or by any means, electronic or mechanical, including photocopying, recording or otherwise stored in a retrieval system, without prior permission in writing from the publishers.

The National Library of Australia Cataloging-in-Publication entry:

Arntzen, Sonja, 1945– Author
Ikkyū and the Crazy Cloud Anthology: A Zen Poet of Medieval Japan
Foreword by Katō Shūichi
Revised and expanded ed.
ISBN: 978-1-922169-40-2 (pbk.)
Quirin Pinyin Updated Editions (QPUE)

Contains selected poems from Ikkyū's 一休 *Kyōunshū* 狂雲集 with text in Chinese script, Japanese *kundoku* reading in Romanization, and translation and commentary in English.

Includes bibliographical references and indexes.

Zen poetry, Japanese -- Translations into English. | Ikkyū 一休, 1394–1481. | Buddhist monks -- Japan.
895.11

ISBN: 978-1-922169-40-2 (pbk.)

To speak of Ikkyū is really to speak of oneself…. This man will now continue for some time to summon up a new concern among various people. We forget he was a Zen monk. It is a strange and marvelous thing that everyone has the sense of secretly having met him somewhere before. Is he not perhaps the only one of a kind in the history of Buddhism through India, China, and Japan?

—Yanagida Seizan
"Ikkyū no Shisō to Sono Shōgai"

Contents

Preface to Revised Edition	ix
Foreword by Katō Shūichi	xi
Preface	xv
Introduction	
Ikkyū: The Man and His Times	1
Dialectic of Non-Duality	31
Allusion	34
A Note on the Text and Its Organization	53
Translations from the Crazy Cloud Anthology	56
Afterword: Reflections, Realizations, Suggestions for Research Possibilities	
Ikkyū and the Red Thread	193
Literature and Religion	194
Allusion, New Digital Resources, and Other Lines of Approach to Poetic Composition	195
Insights Gained from Preparing the Romanized Texts for the Poetry	197
Imagining the *Kyōunshū/Crazy Cloud Anthology* for the Brave New Digital World	200
Abbreviations	203
Notes	204
Bibliography	217
Index of Poems	223
Glossary–Index	227

Preface to Revised Edition

For this revised edition of *Ikkyū and the Crazy Cloud Anthology*, the Chinese texts for the translated poems have been converted from simplified Japanese kanji to traditional Chinese glyphs, *kundoku* readings in modified Hepburn Romanization have been added for all *Kyōunshū* poems, and Romanization of Chinese terms, titles, and proper names has been converted to Pinyin. Eleven new translations of poems and an afterword have been added

Readers who know the 1986 edition of this work will notice major revisions in the poem translations from the latter half of the *Kyōunshū* "Crazy Cloud Anthology." These corrections and new interpretations were made possible due to the publication in 1997 of modern commentaries for that section by Hideo Kageki in *Kyōunshū*, volume two of the *Ikkyū Oshō zenshū* "Complete Works of Reverend Ikkyū." Volume one in that same series updates Hirano Sōjō's *Kyōunshū Zenshaku* "Complete Commentary for the *Kyōunshū*," which had only been completed up to poem 493 in 1976. Accordingly, this revised edition of *Ikkyū and the Crazy Cloud Anthology* has made the *Ikkyū Oshō zenshū* edition of the *Kyōunshū* its base text instead of the 1972 *Chūsei Zenka no shisō* edition in the Iwanami *Nihon shisō taikei* series. Note that from poem 572 the poem numbers are different by one digit between these editions. Furthermore, Romanizations of the poems follow the *kundoku* readings in the *Ikkyū Oshō zenshū* unless my interpretation has differed, or, on the rare occasion that the poem was not included in that edition.

The preface to the 1986 edition lists the teachers who guided my work. They have all passed on, but my gratitude to them will last until my own dying breath. Indeed my gratitude to all those mentioned in the old edition remains undiminished. There are new acknowledgments to make now. I thank Quirin Press editor Olivier Burckhardt for the quick decision to publish and his prompt responses that were always enlivened with a blithe sense of humour. The keen eye of copy editor Cheryl Hutty corrected many typos in the original edition. She also carefully converted the Wade–Giles Romanization to Pinyin as well as signalling all Chinese glyphs needing conversion to traditional forms. This saved me an immense amount of time and I could never have done it as well.

The reckoning of gratitude would not be complete without mentioning Richard John Lynn, a scholar of Chinese letters and my husband. He was tireless with his help in finding and supplying internet resources, looking over drafts of poems with a critical eye, and occasionally contributing elegant translations of Chinese source poems. The original edition of this work was the result of twenty years of labour, starting from zero of course, but, that this major revision took only six months, owes a lot to Richard's assistance and camaraderie.

The following poems have been reprinted with revisions from the following publications:

Ikkyū Sōjun: A Zen Monk and His Poetry (Bellingham: Western Washington College Press, 1973), poems 13, 14, 15 and 16

words have no meaning: poems and translations from the 2007 Montreal Zen Poetry Festival, Zengetsu Myokyo, ed. (Montreal: Enpukuji Press, 2009), poem 964 in the *Ikkyū Tokushū*

Rethinking the Sinosphere: Poetics. Aesthetics, and Identity Formation, Nanxiu Qian et al., eds. (Amherst, NY: Cambria Press, 2020), poems 491, 492

Foreword

Ikkyū Sōjun is one of the strongest personalities in Japanese history: an authentic Zen master and a provocative poet. He lived in and around Kyoto during a time of social upheaval in the fifteenth century, a period marked by frequent peasant rebellions and by internal wars among different samurai clans. Kyoto, the ancient capital, was burnt; much of the cultural heritage was lost, not only monuments and documents, but also traditional moral values and aesthetic conventions. Freed from stagnant formalities and rigid canons, however, the century of destruction was also one of new possibilities—new personalities, ideas, and art forms. It was during that turbulent period that *renga* verse, Nō theater, Chinese ink painting and calligraphy, and tea ceremony were aesthetically refined. Ikkyū himself was a participant in these creative activities, and in the circle of associates around him were the leading artists, Nō actors, poets, painters, and tea masters. They were his friends, or his disciples. Outside the haven of great Zen temples, Ikkyū, often threatened by wars, fires, and famine, managed to provide for himself an invisible sanctuary.

The large and prosperous Zen temples, notably the Five Temples of the Rinzai sect, received the patronage of the samurai authorities: They were big landowners and money lenders on the one hand, and pursued cultural activities on the other. Inside the temples, scholarship on Buddhist texts as well as on Chinese classical literature was encouraged, libraries enriched, and books published. Some of the monks wrote poetry, others produced ink brush paintings. In a word, the Rinzai sect, to which Ikkyū belonged, was highly institutionalized and secularized through its close link with political power and through its cultural activities, which were not necessarily Buddhist in nature. Ikkyū did not, however, conform to all these trends. He chose a sort of bohemian life, denied himself any worldly concern for fame or comfort, and adamantly stuck to his personal Zen enlightenment.

Not all sects of Kamakura Buddhism took the same path as the Rinzai sect did. Jōdoshinshū, a sect founded by Hōnen and Shinran, which had declined for some time, restored its popularity among farmers during the fifteenth century, with Rennyo as its spiritual leader. Discarding the great temples' authorities, Rennyo preached the doctrine of simple prayers to Amida, effectively appealing to the uneducated people, who often revolted against the samurai rulers. There is reason to speculate that Ikkyū may have been interested in Rennyo's style of Buddhism. However, Ikkyū did not compromise his Zen and, on that account, was not unlike Dōgen, founder of the Sōtō Zen sect in the thirteenth century. Different from most Buddhist monks, both Ikkyū and Dōgen did not incline to any form of syncretism whatsoever, be it between Buddhism and Shintoism or between different doctrines of Buddhism. And neither was prepared to compromise his lifestyle for any worldly convenience. Moreover, it can be noted here that as Zen masters they shared a rather rare capacity in their verbal expression of Zen Truth. Although a kind of immediate, mystic experience, such as enlightenment, tends to defy any description or explanation by words, they both wrote prolifically: Dōgen in prose, leaving us his theoretical writings, *Shōbō Genzō*; Ikkyū in verse, giving us his poetry collected in *Kyōunshū*. If Dōgen was the most powerful theoretician in the history of Japanese Zen, Ikkyū was undoubtedly the most imaginative, the most provocative, and the most controversial poet.

Ikkyū's poetry falls into four categories: first, poems on purely philosophical themes; second, erotic poems on his amorous relations; third, poems relating to his own poetic inspiration; fourth, satires, sharp and biting, denouncing the contemporary mores in the great Zen temples. No Japanese poet has ever combined, as Ikkyū did, such abstract ideas and intense sensuality, such aggressive social criticism and tender lyrical imagery.

Ikkyū's important rhetorical technique was, as the author of this book rightly points out, the frequent use of allusions to classical literature. Allusions, to be sure, had been applied by many other Chinese and Japanese poets to make short poems work at different levels—through images present and those evoked by allusion. For Ikkyū, however, that was not all. Allusion, and indirect suggestions, were most likely for him means by which he could overcome not only social pressures, but also his own psychological inhibitions; for example, to express his anger with particular individuals or to render extremely sensual images of sexual love.

If we dare to compare him with Western poets, Ikkyū was, like François Villon, an implacable non-conformist—almost a poet-outcast, a remote ancestor of modern *poètes maudits*, although unlike Villon, Ikkyū was not hanged but honored, toward the end of his life, by the Imperial court. And like St. John of the Cross, he brought close, in his poetic imagery, the sense of unity with the Absolute in his enlightenment, and the sense of transcendence in his love-union. Different from the Spanish mystic, however, Ikkyū's transcendental experiences included also the union with Nature in his inspired moments, much in the same vein as his beloved Chinese poet, Tao Yuanming. Last, like John Donne, one might say, Ikkyū was a high priest, expected to assume sooner or later the direction of a great temple, Daitokuji, which was the equivalent of a bishop's position in England, and yet did not refrain from describing carnal love in his uninhibited poetry. For their metaphysics of eros, Ikkyū and John Donne did not need to wait for Freud.

I came across Ikkyū's poetry, and his extraordinary personality, in the early 1960s, when I was teaching a survey course on the history of Japanese literature at the University of British Columbia. I was fascinated by him. Although at that time hardly a commentary on *Kyōunshū* or detailed study on the poet was available, I decided to talk about him in my classes. Some students, particularly Ms. Sonja Arntzen, the author of this book, reacted enthusiastically to all that I was saying. I still recall with pleasure those classes at U.B.C.: Sonja's bright eyes when we discussed Ikkyū, and, through the window, a strip of blue water of Vancouver harbor. Without a sensitivity to poetry and a touch of non-conformism in life, no one probably can really enter into Ikkyū's world. This is not a matter of knowledge but of something fundamental and unalterable in a personality. Knowledge, eventually, might follow.

In later years, I have read a bit more about Ikkyū. I have published, with Eva Thorn, a German translation of his poetry (*Ikkyū: Im Garten der schönen Shin*); wrote an introductory essay to Mr. Yanagida Seizan's *Nihon no Zen Goroku: Ikkyū*; and am still working with Mr. René de Berval on a French version of some Ikkyū poems. Meanwhile, however, Sonja Arntzen has done much more. Over twenty years, she has continued to study Ikkyū's life and works in Canada and in Japan, absorbing all the scholarly literature on the subject, which proliferated after those Vancouver years. Knowledge, indeed, joined sensitivity. And here is her book: a brilliant achievement by a born poet as well as a solid scholar. Now it is my turn to listen to Sonja, friend and former student. Other readers will also enjoy her presentation of Ikkyū, as I certainly did.

Katō Shūichi

Preface

From the time in the mid-sixties when I first heard about the fifteenth-century Zen poet Ikkyū Sōjun, I have felt that this poet's work cried out for translation. Responding to that perceived need, translations from the *Kyōunshū*, "Crazy Cloud Anthology," Ikkyū's major poetry collection, form the body of this book. The introduction preceding the translations aims at elucidating that poetry. The first part of the introduction sketches a historical and biographical background for Ikkyū so that the reader will have a context in which to fit the many personal references in the poems. The second part of the introduction explores how the poetry itself works, how it is powerful, first by looking at the philosophical stance that stimulates the poetry and then at the special contribution the technique of allusion makes to the poetry's functioning. A key discovery is that Ikkyū's poetry delivers experiences of Zen rather than statements about it. Hence the analysis concentrates on describing these experiences. While it is true that any poetry realizes itself primarily in the reading rather than in the retroactive appreciation of a message, this point of view is particularly important to keep in mind with Zen poetry, for Zen as a philosophy rejects definition and fixed meaning. The challenge for any poet committed to communicating the experience of Zen is to avoid limiting meaning, indeed sometimes it is to avoid meaning anything at all. The challenge for a critic of such poetry is to open up the possibilities of perception without setting up fixed modes of interpretation.

Underlying my approach as a whole to Ikkyū and his poetry is the conviction that the reading of this poetry can be relevant to a modern audience. For one, his voice is often a troubled one struggling to deal with the insanity of his times; we can find an affinity with his struggle. In this age, when organized religion has in many parts of the world lost its power to both inspire or bind the minds of thoughtful, sensitive people, it is instructive to listen to this poet, who, although he was a monk, strove to transcend the barrier between religion and the secular world. Due to social breakdown, the era in which Ikkyū lived was relatively much freer than periods of Japan's past, which is why Ikkyū was able to carry the dissolution of the forms of his religion so far. This, too, puts him closer to the modern world where the fact of freedom similarly brought about by a breakdown of traditional mores has forced individuals to seek their own equilibrium between limitation and freedom. Ikkyū's balancing of these two poles can mirror our own dilemma.

There are many people to thank who have contributed to this enterprise. I am forever grateful to Professor Katō Shūichi whose eloquent lectures about Ikkyū, long before there were any English translations or commentaries on his work in modern Japanese, lit the spark of enthusiasm that remains with me to this day. Through the years he has taken an encouraging interest in the work as it progressed. Good fortune has blessed me with many fine teachers along the way. The ebullient Professor Iida Shōtarō of the University of British Columbia guided my first faltering steps in research. Professor Leon Hurvitz, also of U.B.C., supervised the dissertation which formed the basis for this book. While professing no interest in Zen or Ikkyū, he was able by virtue of his linguistic genius to illuminate so many difficult passages. Moreover, his example as a scholar in terms of patience, energy, love of learning, and utter fidelity to the words of a text was inspirational. In Japan, Professor Yanagida Seizan of Kyoto University and Professor Hirano Sōjō of Hanazono University contributed generously to my research. Both of them not only shared the wealth of their minds and libraries but also the warmth of their hearts and homes. My debt of gratitude to them is limitless.

Many people have given the manuscript an editorial scan in the course of the eight years or so it has been in preparation; my thanks in this regard to Jan Walls, Ken Bryant, Roy Kiyooka, and most recently

Stan Beeler and Sharon Domier. Thanks must also go to the University of Tokyo Press, which believed sufficiently in the manuscript to keep knocking on the doors of potential funding agencies to obtain a publication subsidy. Indeed, the well-worn expression holds true that if there is anything of merit in this work, it should redound to the credit of those mentioned above; the errors and shortcomings are mine alone.

The debts of gratitude do not end there, however, for gifts of financial support must be recognized as well. The two crucial years I was able to pursue research in Kyoto under Professors Yanagida and Hirano were funded by The Japan Foundation. I thank the Foundation formally for that support here. The Suntory Foundation has provided a publication subsidy for the work without which the book could not have come into being. I acknowledge this vital support.

Finally, I must thank my mother who by caring for my daughter time and time again has freed me to work. In this regard, I would also like to thank my neighbors of Ichijoji in Kyoto who also shared my tasks of motherhood. The time has come to mention my daughter as well who has grown up with this manuscript almost as a rival sibling. The patience and tolerance she perforce acquired to cope with the situation, I thank her for now.

The following poems have been reprinted, with revisions, with the permission of the Center for East Asian Studies, Western Washington University, from the author's *Ikkyū Sōjun: A Zen Monk and His Poetry* (Bellingham, 1973): the enlightenment poem on page 14, the death poem on page 28, and poems number 6, 7, 8, 25, 26, 27, 73, 74, 75, 84, 85, 89, 90, 94, 101, 108, 130, 134, 135, 136, 144, 156, 175, 179, 254, 255, 264, 284, 287, 362, 367, 454, 531, 532, 533, 535, 536, 537, 539, 541, 542, 543, 567.

The following guidelines have been followed with regard to technical matters. [See Preface to the Revised Edition for matters related to Romanization of Japanese and Chinese.] Only years have been converted to the Western calendar, month and day have been left as in the original source; therefore, one should adjust one's seasonal sense approximately one month ahead. Ikkyū's age has been left in Oriental count, which means that he is always a year older than he would be by Western count. Chinese and Japanese names are given in East Asian order, that is, surname first. Chinese names are given in Chinese pronunciation with the exception of the Tang monk Linji, who is referred to as Rinzai, using the Japanese rendering of his name in order to clarify his connection with the Rinzai school of Zen in Japan. As for Chan/Zen, the school of Buddhism to which Ikkyū belonged, Chan will be used in discussions related to China and Zen in Japanese contexts. When the discussion relates to both, Zen will be used in general.

Works from the main Buddhist and Zen canon are cited by their English titles, e.g., *Lotus Sūtra*, *Blue Cliff Record*, when an English translation is readily available. They may be found in the Bibliography under the English title, with the Chinese title in parentheses and references to translations. In the notes, references for quotations from Chinese and Japanese primary sources will give the English translation information and usually the page number in the primary source as well. If only the primary source reference is supplied, it means the translation is the author's. A list of abbreviations for primary sources appears at the beginning of the notes.

Introduction

Ikkyū (1394–1481): The Man and His Times

Ikkyū called himself "Crazy Cloud," a sobriquet rich in connotation. Self-ironic, it declared his craziness to the world. Yet in the paradoxical reasoning of Zen, opposites often trade places. Calling himself crazy also asserted his sanity in a world gone mad. "Cloud" calls up a conventional term for monk, *unsui*, "cloud-water." The term, by way of metaphor, stresses the foremost quality of a monk, that is, his non-attachment to the world. Like a floating cloud or flowing water, he should move through the world with neither material possessions nor the baggage of desire. Thus "Crazy Cloud" can simply mean crazy monk. However, a reader familiar with Ikkyū's writing cannot fail also to hear in the word "cloud," the echo of *un'u*, "cloud-rain," a euphemism for physical love, which abounds in his poetry. Thus, under the surface of his name lies the esoteric meaning "crazy about love"; the crazy monk asserts his loving bondage with the world.

Finally, over and above the name's literary connotations lies the image of a cloud. The man who emerges from this *Crazy Cloud Anthology* assumes as many aspects as a cloud. Sometimes dark and obscure, sometimes flashing with anger, sometimes gentle and enfolding, sometimes a wisp pointing to the moon, he transforms himself from poem to poem. No less prone to change was the time in which he lived, the mid part of the Muromachi period (1338–1568).

It was a turbulent era rife with contradictions. On the one hand, it can be considered degenerate, on the other, dynamic. Certainly, political order degenerated during the period. The shogunate was headed by the Ashikaga clan, but their grasp on the reins of power was never secure. The periods of relative stability for the government depended on the Ashikaga's ability to play one warrior clan against another and thereby maintain a precarious balance. Peace, such as there was, was always uneasy. The Ashikaga's balancing act disintegrated in 1467 with the outbreak of the Ōnin War.[1] Ostensibly fought over the succession to the position of shogun, it was really a struggle to establish a new order of power among the major warrior clans. The fact that it was a war of no gain and so much destruction gives it a curiously nihilistic cast from this vantage point in history. It was fought in the northern part of the capital itself. Here were located the monuments of Ashikaga ascendency, palatial residences and great Zen monasteries. All these were burned and razed to the ground over the course of the war. Indeed, people of old Kyoto families still remark to this day, "Well, there's nothing really old left in the center of the city because of the war, you know." And the war they speak of is not the Second World War, in which Kyoto was mercifully spared, but the Ōnin War. As the struggle dragged on for ten years, the major participants seemed unaware that they were actually destroying themselves. Even though the principal leaders on both sides died, it was still impossible to conclude. In fact, the war came to an end through attrition. Nobody won. While the major warrior factions used up their resources in the capital, enterprising vassal caretakers left at home waxed strong enough to challenge their masters. Thus, in many cases, armies marched home to fight their former comrades.

Because the pattern for political change in the period was the replacement of masters by their former vassals, traditional historians have often referred to the age as one of *gekokujō*, "those below overturning their superiors," a term with decidedly pejorative connotations. In the Confucian world view, social order should mirror the natural order. Thus, inferiors overthrowing superiors is like earth hurling down heaven.

The period was not only prey to political ills but, particularly in the decade preceding the Ōnin War, the home provinces were hard hit by famine and plague. The initial cause was a vicious cycle of unseasonable weather, drought followed by torrential rains. These natural disasters, however, were exacerbated by the lack of a strong central authority that could have organized efforts toward relief. Instead, chaos reigned, and it seems that while thousands died, a fortunate few indulged in extravagance.² Another disturbing aspect of the time was the prevalence of peasant uprisings. These increased in scale and violence as the period progressed. Most often the peasants' demand was for *tokusei*, "act of grace," meaning the cancellation of debts with the moneylenders. (See poem 287.)³ All in all, the pejorative estimation of the period by the old guard of historians seems justified.

Yet, seen from a different angle, the period reveals a more positive picture. The phenomenon of *gekokujō* at least allowed for some kind of social mobility. The peasant uprisings themselves, while perhaps initially prompted by situations of duress, gradually tended to become better organized and were often successful in having their demands met. In fact, a debate rages among modern historians as to whether the uprisings may actually have been the result of increased wealth and a feeling of independence among the rural population rather than desperate acts of the impoverished.⁴ One Japanese historian, on the basis of the increased mobility in the society and the independence gained by rural areas, has gone so far as to call the Muromachi period, a great "people's age."⁵

Moreover, despite the political turmoil of the period, economically the country was growing quite rapidly. Agricultural production actually increased, thanks to advances in agricultural techniques. Burgeoning markets encouraged the diversification of crops, which in turn had a stimulating effect on production.

The proliferation of markets was related to the increasing monetary nature of the economy. Money was called the "big foot" during the Muromachi period because it could go anywhere.⁶ Merchants thrived, and if the domestic scene did not provide enough opportunities for enrichment, an expanding foreign trade was full of them. The trade with Ming China, initiated by the shogunate and assisted by the large Zen monasteries, was actualized by merchant entrepreneurs who profited immensely thereby. The center for this trade, Sakai, resembled nothing so much as one of the Renaissance Italian city states in its wealth and independence.

But most dramatic of all were the developments in the arts. If the positive economic and social aspects of the Muromachi period have only come to be appreciated recently, even the most unbending of traditional historians had to admit and wonder at the cultural brilliance of the era. In the field of letters, two new forms, *renga* ("linked verse") and Nō drama, building on the best of classical literary tradition, realized great heights of perfection. The tea ceremony was just taking form, attended by complementary developments in the arts of pottery and architecture. In painting, monochrome ink landscapes dominated the arena and were in turn mirrored by the austere stone-and-sand meditation gardens. In a word, so many of the arts considered quintessentially Japanese crystallized during the period.

Moreover, these were truly popular arts; both practitioners and audience were drawn from all levels of society. The Nō could draw such huge audiences that subscription performances were used to gather funds for building projects in the capital. *Renga* was the rage throughout Muromachi society from aristocrats to tradesmen. The grand masters of these arts issued from a wide variety of social classes. The *renga* master Sōchō was the son of a smith. The origins of many of the Nō dramatists, tea connoisseurs, and garden architects were so obscure that no one bothered or perhaps dared to record them. The custom followed by artists of assuming a Buddhist name, without formally taking the tonsure, conveniently obliterated family origin. Although the general principle of birth determining position went unchallenged, in actual practice low birth was no hindrance to advancement in the arts. The cultural efflorescence of the Muromachi period must be linked to the absence of social barriers in artistic pursuits.

Thus a degenerate body politic and endemic warfare existed side by side with great cultural achievement which was underpinned by a freedom and social mobility Japan has rarely enjoyed. Interestingly, the arts of the Muromachi are not dominated by a feeling of pessimism but rather a transcendental calm. No one can gaze upon the gardens of the Ginkakuji or the Ryōanji, for example, without experiencing serenity. Nonetheless, the lack of stability and political turbulence of the period must have sorely distressed many living through it. The devastation of famine and war, particularly around the capital in the two decades from 1460 to 1480 took a terrible toll. The positive developments underlying the turmoil may not have been apparent to those swept along, or worse, drowned in the flux. Yet, a vital energy animated this society at every level. In this dynamic mix of negative and positive, one can find parallels to our own age where also peace depends on an uneasy balance and the fragmentation of old values bestows on us a freedom that is at once inspiring and terrifying. In at least one respect, however, Muromachi society is very far removed from our own; that is in the large role played by one religious institution in particular, Rinzai Zen.

Like the great monumental gate at the old entrance to Tōfukuji in Kyoto, the monastic institution of Rinzai Zen loomed over Muromachi society. From the Kamakura period (1185–1334) when Zen had first been introduced to Japan, the Rinzai Zen monasteries, in imitation of Song China, had been organized into a system called *Gozan Jissatsu*, "Five Mountains, Ten Temples." Five Mountains referred to the first five ranks, Ten Temples to the next ten ranks comprising the apex of this pyramid system which during the Muromachi period encompassed thousands of monasteries over the length and breadth of the country. The most important monasteries were the large ones in Kyoto like Shōkokuji, Nanzenji, Tenryūji, Kenninji, and Tōfukuji, which monopolized the five highest ranks, that is, the Gozan proper. In the following discussion, the term Gozan will refer to the *Gozan Jissatsu* monastic system as it existed in the fifteenth century.[7]

The Muromachi Gozan was never fully independent as an economic and social institution since it received its major support from the Ashikaga shogunate. The patron endowed the monastery, and in turn the monastery served its patron. Large estates, tax immunity, and various privileges, mainly of an economic nature, were bestowed upon the Gozan monasteries. In return, the Ashikaga received many benefits, both tangible and intangible. Initially, the most important to the Ashikaga was the prestige derived from patronizing this school which represented the avant-garde of continental, that is, Chinese learning. Ashikaga leaders could look on with satisfaction when even members of the old aristocracy eagerly sought the instruction and company of Gozan prelates. This cultural edifice was a final ornament to their legitimacy as rulers, proving them leaders in culture as well as politics.

However, the rewards of this patronage took more practical forms as well. Zen prelates provided invaluable advice on financial affairs. This was a skill nurtured partly by necessity in the early days of Zen's establishment in Japan when shrewd management of meager resources was essential for survival. Even after becoming wealthy, the monastic institution never ceased to encourage and reward efficient financial management. Indeed, Zen officials were often employed by other Buddhist sects as well as the shogunate as financial advisors.

Foreign affairs was another speciality of Zen monks. For over three hundred years, virtually the only direct contact between Japan and China had been through the study trips of Zen monks to monasteries in China. A small but very influential number of Chinese monks had also made their way to Japan. Thus, information about the state of China was naturally to be had from Zen monks. The intelligence received from monks, and their readiness to serve as emissaries and interpreters indirectly led to the establishment of trade between Ming China and the Ashikaga shogunate, a very profitable venture for monasteries and shogunate alike.

As the Gozan grew wealthy through the profits of the China trade and its considerable land interests, it plowed this capital back into the ever-profitable ventures of money-lending and *sake*-brewing. Wealth produced wealth for the Gozan, and in the process, individual monks, though nominally eschewing material possessions, grew rich as well.

As this monastic protégé prospered, it offered more possibilities for exploitation to its benefactor. The shogunate was not slow to find ways of tapping this source of wealth. Ever increasing fees were levied for the assumption of offices within the institution. If the occupation of those offices could enrich the holder, it seemed only fair for the shogunate to charge its share. Moreover, loans could be had from these monastic banks at a preferred rate of interest with no fear of foreclosure. And when the shogunate was really pressed, it could exact out and out contributions from the Gozan. It is no wonder that when, in response to popular pressure, "acts of grace," that is, cancellation of debts with the usurers, were granted, debts with Gozan lenders were exempt from cancellation. Why throttle the golden goose? It was so comfortable to be able to borrow money within the family, so to speak. It is no wonder, then, that in the anarchy that accompanied the Ōnin War, the major Gozan monasteries should be the chief targets of wildcat incendiarism. Increasingly secular in its concerns, the Gozan became more susceptible to the abuse of its principles. As the stakes associated with superior offices within the monasteries increased, one encounters the open sale of monastic appointments with little concern for spiritual attainment.[8]

Thus, though the prestige of Zen, a by-product of wealth and power, was indirectly responsible for Zen's stimulating influence in art, the position of political dominance sapped the spiritual vigor of the institution. Many monks with a real sense of vocation left the Gozan establishment. Ikkyū himself felt compelled to take this step.

There are no indisputably accurate sources of information about Ikkyū's life. In the archives of Daitokuji and Shūon'an, there exists a handful of documents relating to Ikkyū's abbacy at those two monasteries and the memorial services held following his death. These are the closest to what may be called indisputably accurate sources, but, of course, they have little to tell. His poems in the *Crazy Cloud Anthology* are often preceded by autobiographical notes describing the circumstances of composition. These notes combined with the poems themselves are by far the richest stores of information. Of the works in English on Ikkyū, the earliest one, an article by Donald Keene, entitled "Portrait of Ikkyū,"[9] is based almost exclusively on the *Crazy Cloud Anthology*. The completeness of the picture Keene was able to draw bears witness to the wealth of material about Ikkyū by his own hand.

Although it seems reasonable to consider this material reliable, a contrary viewpoint has been argued quite convincingly by Yanagida Seizan. He maintains that because the *Crazy Cloud Anthology* is a work of literature first and foremost, the information provided therein cannot be taken as literally true any more than the works of Japanese "I-novelists" are accepted as accurate accounts of their lives in a historical sense.[10] While it goes to an extreme to maintain that everything in Ikkyū's poetry is fiction, the insight behind the above argument keeps us from making the mistake of taking Ikkyū's poetry too literally. Literal interpretation nearly always leads astray in literature.

Another major source is the *Ikkyū Oshō Nempu*, "Chronicle of the Reverend Ikkyū,"[11] which is thought to have been composed shortly after Ikkyū's death, by his disciple Bokusai. Written in a ponderous and tortuous style of literary Chinese, hagiographic in character, its goal is to establish Ikkyū's reputation as a superior Zen master. Thus matters of prime importance for the *Nempu* were Ikkyū's legitimacy as spiritual heir in the Daitokuji line, his connections with people of high status, and the respectful regard he was accorded by so many. The *Nempu* scrupulously omits mention of wine shops and brothels, topics which, however, occur frequently in Ikkyū's own poems. Also, Mori, the paramour of Ikkyū's later years, is conspicuously absent. Still, the chronicle is the earliest biographical source for Ikkyū and, while it may be biased, it remains important as a nearly contemporary report.

A major source of misinformation about Ikkyū is to be found in the vast body of popular tale literature which built a legend around him in the Tokugawa period. The most enduring part of this legend is the cycle of stories which portray him as a precocious child. While it is obvious that the Ikkyū tales have much more to say about their own time and authors than about Ikkyū, they nonetheless bear witness to the strength of a personality that was able to spawn such a legend. Some of the earlier tales are particularly interesting for their transformation of materials taken from his poems and biography.[12]

The following biographical sketch presents an outline of Ikkyū's life as recounted in the *Nempu* with augmentation from the *Crazy Cloud Anthology* and other sources. The prime objective has been to use the biographical material to illuminate the poems in the *Anthology* and reciprocally bring to the fore the living, though variable, image of Ikkyū that emerges from his poetry. A thread of concern throughout has been to highlight the ambiguities in Ikkyū's biography, the places where the pieces do not fit together.

The *Nempu* states that Ikkyū was born at dawn on the 1st day of the 1st month of the 1st year of the Ōei era (1394) and that he was the illegitimate child of the Emperor Go Komatsu. Just in what sense he was illegitimate will be explained. His mother was of a branch of the Fujiwara clan connected with the Southern Court,[13] a point of some importance. Fifty-seven years previously, the indefatigable Emperor Go Daigo had led a brief imperial restoration that was aborted by his initial supporters, the Ashikaga clan, once they saw Go Daigo had no intention of catering to their interests. He fled to the mountain fastness of Yoshino and set up what came to be known as the Southern Court. Meanwhile, the Ashikaga crowned a suitably pliable emperor from a collateral line in Kyoto, which came to be called the Northern Court. So, for fifty years, Japan had two emperors and two courts. The very existence of this rival court clearly indicates that the Ashikaga clan's control over the country was less than complete. The Southern Court always provided a convenient cause and cloak, however thin, of legitimacy for other warrior clans to tilt against the Ashikaga hegemony. Indeed, the Ashikaga were never able to solve this problem in a decisive military way and were forced in the end to negotiate a diplomatic settlement. This settlement dictated that the two imperial lines would share the throne by way of alternate succession. The Ashikaga never intended to abide by the agreement and indeed soon violated it, but that is another story, not to be told here. Mention of it suffices to show the temper of the time.

The settlement of the Northern–Southern Courts dispute had been reached a mere three years before Ikkyū was born. Part of the attempt to patch up the differences between the two regimes entailed providing posts for members of the defunct Southern Court in the Northern Court. This was likely the circumstance under which Ikkyū's mother came to serve Emperor Go Komatsu. By the *Nempu*'s account, she served him well, winning his favor. However, jealous people in the empress's entourage slandered her. Given the existing tension, slander was easy to levy. They accused her of sympathizing with the Southern cause, saying she had a knife in each sleeve meant for the emperor. Thus, heavy with the emperor's child, she was dismissed from the court and sent to live with a commoner's family where she bore Ikkyū. Her child, therefore, was not recognized as the emperor's offspring.

Much has been written by Japanese scholars debating the veracity of the account of Ikkyū's parentage. In the Meiji era, the Imperial household itself was sufficiently convinced that royal blood had indeed flowed in Ikkyū's veins to bestow the chrysanthemum emblem on his grave. Ikkyū's close relations with the Imperial Court later in his life seem to support the claim as well. In one of his poems, Ikkyū appears to refer to his royal parentage. (See poem 542.) What has more bearing on his work is how the circumstances of his issue may have effected Ikkyū's feelings toward his mother and women in general. Folk tradition ascribes to Ikkyū a strong attachment to his mother. Though there is no direct mention of her in any of his work, he wrote so often about the sad fate of a court lady losing her lord's favor that one wonders if the legend has some substance. Admittedly, the theme of a court lady falling from her lord's grace is a stock theme in Chinese poetry, the so-called boudoir lament. The image of an elegant woman waiting alone in her chamber for a summons that will never come evoked keen feelings of beauty and sadness in Chinese poets. The related allegorical possibility of representing the frustrated civil official neglected by his lord, also contributed to the long-standing popularity of the theme. Still, Ikkyū's fondness for it is stronger than most poets. One of his first recorded poems, written at age thirteen, is of this genre. It concerns Lady Ban of the Han dynasty, who, having lost the emperor's favor, came to live at Changxin Palace.

Changmen Spring Grass
長門春草 *Chōmon shunsō*

秋荒長信美人吟	*aki wa areru Chōshin bijin no gin*
徑路無媒上苑陰	*keiro ni nakadachi nashi jōen no kage*
榮辱悲歡目前事	*eijoku hikan mokuzen no koto*
君恩淺處草方深	*kun'on asaki dokoro kusa masa ni fukashi*[14]

In autumn's desolation, the lovely lady of Changxin sings.
On the path, no summoning messenger, the garden in shade.
Glory, disgrace, sorrow, joy, these are before her eyes.
Where her lord's favor is shallow,
    the grasses of neglect are deep.[15]

Moreover, Ikkyū's first deep insight into a *kōan*[16] was occasioned by hearing a Japanese version of the same kind of lament.[17] This was a blind *biwa hōshi*'s recital of the Giō section of the *Heike Monogatari*. Therein, Giō, a dancing girl in the service of Taira Kiyomori, persuades him to give an audience to Hotoke, a young dancer who had come without proper introduction, begging to perform. Giō's compassion and generosity bring her grief, for Kiyomori is so charmed by Hotoke's dancing that he decides to cast Giō out and replace her with Hotoke. Giō, along with her mother and sister, retires to a hut in Saga where the three devote themselves to religion. They are surprised one night to find Hotoke at their door. The dancer, having witnessed Giō's fate, realized the vanity of all success in life and resolved to cut off her own attachment to the world.[18]

The recitation of this story helped Ikkyū see into the kōan "Dongshan's Three Beatings":

> When Dongshan came to study under Yunmen, Yunmen asked, "What place have you recently left?"
> Dongshan said, "Chadu."
> "Where did you pass the summer?"

"Baozi Monastery in Henan."

"When did you leave there?"

"The twenty-fifth of the eighth month."

Yunmen said, "I release you from the punishment of three beatings." [That is, three sets of twenty blows of the stick, a common punishment for criminals in Tang China.]

The following day, Dongshan came again and inquired, "Yesterday, the master released me from three beatings, but I do not know what my fault was."

Yunmen said, "You rice bag, from Jiangxi to Henan, for what have you been coming and going?"

At this, Dongshan experienced great enlightenment.[19]

Precisely how "Dongshan's Three Beatings" and the story of Giō coalesced in Ikkyū's mind to give rise to an enlightened realization is, of course, inexplicable. However, perhaps the story of Giō acted as a catalyst precisely because it struck chords deep within him, recalling the burden of chagrin and misery in his own family background. This burden may be what the resolution of the kōan lifted from his shoulders. Moreover, it is possible that when Ikkyū speaks of the famous abandoned women of the Chinese literary tradition, they recall his own mother for him.

Regardless of how close Ikkyū may have felt to his mother, he did not have a long childhood at home, for at the age of six he was placed in Ankokuji, one of the middle-ranking monasteries within the Kyoto Gozan system. About his early training, the *Nempu* notes only that Ikkyū was a precocious child and that by the age of thirteen, he had taken control of his own education by deciding to study Chinese poetry at Kenninji in the Higashiyama district. He began by writing a poem a day and memorizing lines from famous poems.[20] (See poem 210.)

Zen monasteries served as boarding schools and colleges in Muromachi society. An academic education in the period meant a Chinese one. As has already been remarked, the Zen school's initial entrée into the power circle of the warrior elite was by its prestige as a bearer of the new learning from China. Even up until a generation or two before Ikkyū, active intercourse had been maintained between Japanese monasteries and their Chinese counterparts. Many monks had had the opportunity of extended stays in China, perfecting their knowledge of the language and studying firsthand the latest literature and philosophy. It was only in Ikkyū's time that the foreign travels of Zen monks came to have a mercantile rather than intellectual focus.

That Ikkyū wrote in Chinese is a product of his education and situation as a monk. He spent the greater part of his intellectual life in a "China of the mind." It was "of the mind" because he never had the opportunity to go to China or study with a Chinese monk. More importantly, it was a China created in his own imagination with inspiration from literary works. Allusions to the Chinese classics, both Buddhist and secular, animate his poetry. This was because, from long association, certain Chinese figures and phrases had come to hold a concentrated meaning for him. They became part of a kind of shorthand that allowed him to express a great deal in a brief space, as will be elaborated on in the section on allusion.

Ikkyū's first exercise of choice in his education had taken him in a secular direction, the study of poetry. However, by the age of seventeen, he wanted to study Zen seriously with someone he could regard as a personal master. The man he sought out was Kenō (?–1414), a man so eccentrically modest he had refused his own seal of transmission, the document officially certifying a Zen monk's attainment. This cut him off from any chance of advancement within the monastic system, where such pieces of paper were a vital necessity. Kenō is reported to have told Ikkyū after three years of tutelage, "I have already bestowed all my treasures of learning on you, but I have no seal of transmission and cannot therefore give one to you."[21] The following year, Kenō died in such poverty that there were not enough resources for a proper funeral. Ikkyū, still only twenty-one, was set adrift.

The *Nempu* records that at this point, Ikkyū decided to leap into Lake Biwa in order to obtain some sign of the Bodhisattva Kannon's mercy. He reasoned, "If I live, there will be no doubt about the protection of the Bodhisattva Kannon. And even if I end up in some fish's belly, some day I must attain my desire. How could Kannon ever abandon me?"[22] However, he was apparently dissuaded from this course by the timely arrival of a messenger from his mother.[23]

Ikkyū's next step was to seek out another master. He chose the doughty Kasō (1352–1428), a monk of the Daitokuji line, who carried on Zen training of the severest kind in the port town of Katada on the shores of Lake Biwa. A word or two about the Daitokuji monastery will help explain Kasō's particular style.

Daitokuji began its existence as a simple shelter for the monk Daitō (1282–1337) who had studied under Master Daiō (1235–1308), the spiritual heir of the Chinese master Xutang (1185–1269).[24] After achieving enlightenment, Daitō was cautioned not to seek a position at any of the great temples of the land, but rather to nurture his spiritual awareness in poverty and obscurity for twenty years. Accordingly, Daitō went to Kyoto and lived in poverty close to Gojō Bridge. (See poem 8.) Though he made no attempt to advance in the world, his spiritual integrity drew followers to him and admiration from the populace at large. A provincial warrior family built him a more substantial hermitage. He also attracted the notice of two emperors, first Hanazono (d. 1348), then Go Daigo (d. 1339). Eventually, in 1324, Go Daigo provided the land and money to transform the hermitage into a proper monastery with a position of special eminence at the head of the Gozan. It is noteworthy that right from the beginning, Daitokuji drew its support not from the shogunate but rather from smaller provincial warrior families and the Imperial household. Also, a reputation for a pure, uncompromising Zen was the source of its success.

However, patronage from the Emperor Go Daigo was not without its drawbacks. This, of course, was the same Go Daigo whose Southern Court at Yoshino became a thorn in the Ashikaga side for some fifty years. It is no wonder that the Ashikaga did not look kindly upon a monastery so closely associated with the Southern Imperial cause. Daitokuji steadily lost ground, being demoted from the Gozan ranks down to the lower levels of the Jissatsu and finally by its own choice separating from the system entirely. By Kasō's time, the monastery was struggling in relative penury. Nonetheless, by virtue of its necessarily austere regime, Daitokuji preserved the strict training and spiritual orientation of the original Zen monasteries. Such was Kasō's background. In Katada, he developed a reputation for maintaining an old-fashioned rigorous kind of Zen. The *Nempu* account of Ikkyū's petition to study with Kasō bears out this reputation. By that report, Kasō brusquely refused to interview Ikkyū. So he sat down by the gate to await either an interview or death by starvation, whichever came first. After four or five days, Kasō came out to attend a service in the village. Seeing Ikkyū steadfastly at the gate, he told his attendants to give him a good dousing and chase him away with a stick. But when he returned, Ikkyū was still there, refusing to leave. Only then did Kasō relent and bring him in.[25]

Although life at Kasō's was no more luxurious than at Ken'ō's hermitage, Ikkyū studied hard for seven years. His first breakthrough on the path to enlightenment, which came with his insight into the kōan "Dongshan's Three Beatings," has already been discussed. At the passing of that kōan, Kasō is reported to have bestowed Ikkyū's name. Two years later, his full and complete enlightenment is said to have come one summer night when the raucous call of a crow pierced his meditation and pushed him through whatever barrier remained. According to the *Nempu*, Ikkyū rushed to demonstrate his understanding before Kasō, but Kasō would have none of it. "You have only reached the level of an Arhat (adept), you are not a Master yet." "Then I'm happy to be an Arhat," said Ikkyū, " I despise Masters." "Now you are a Master," said Kasō.[26]

It was customary for a monk to express his first experience of enlightenment in a poem. The following is recorded as Ikkyū's enlightenment poem.

十年以前識情心　　jūnen izen shikijō no kokoro
嗔恚豪機在即今　　shin'i gōki sokkon ni ari
鴉笑出塵羅漢果　　a wa warau shutsujin no rakanka
昭陽日影玉顔吟　　Shōyō nichiei gyokugan no gin

For ten years, heart consumed by passions,
Raging, angry, the time is now!
Crow laughs, I leave the dust, end up an Arhat;
Zhaoyang Palace in the sun, a fair jade-like face sings.[27]

The last two lines allude to a Tang poem by Wang Changling (698–757), which laments the fate of Lady Ban, who has already appeared in the poem Ikkyū wrote at age thirteen. When the emperor's affections were stolen away by the infamous Zhao sisters, Lady Ban became a serving maid to the dowager empress. To express her grief, she wrote a poem comparing herself to a white silk fan that was treasured by its owner only for one summer season and then forgotten on the shelf once autumn arrived. (See notes to poem 293.) Wang's poem expresses Lady Ban's feelings.

奉帚平明金殿開
且將團扇共徘徊
玉顏不及寒鴉色
猶帶昭陽日影來

She starts to sweep in the dawn light, the Golden Hall opens;
Taking up her fan, she wanders aimlessly awhile.
Her fair jade-like face is no match for the color of the wintry crows
Coming forth, still bathed in the sun at Zhaoyang Palace.[28]

The "Golden Hall" is the emperor's quarters; Zhaoyang Palace is the residence of the younger of the Zhao sisters, Zhao Zhaoyi. Wang Changling pictures Lady Ban performing her serving maid duties in the morning, watching the Zhao sisters, referred to as "wintry crows," parading their lord's favor, likened to the sunlight, as they commute between his quarters and their own. Ikkyū has obviously incorporated some of the elements from Wang Changling's poem but what does he intend them to mean? While the tone of Wang's poem is sorrowful, Ikkyū's is triumphant. The crow is a positive image in Ikkyū's poem, negative in Wang's. The fair jade-like face sings in Ikkyū's poem even though Zhaoyang Palace is still graced by the sun, her lord's favor. The alchemy of the poem melts good and evil, transforms sadness to joy. The "abandoned woman" in the poet's heart transcends sorrow.

The connotation of Arhat further complicates the effect of the poem. The term designates the adept in Hinayana "Small Vehicle" Buddhism. From the Mahayana "Great Vehicle" point of view, the Hinayana adept's goal of eliminating all desire to obtain enlightenment for oneself seems life-denying and selfish. In opposition, Mahayana Buddhism asserts the ideal of the Bodhisattva, the enlightened being who remains in this world to deliver all sentient beings before he claims release for himself. Not immune to the passion and suffering of this world, indeed through them, he brings solace to all beings. The crow laughs at the Arhat for leaving the world, but did he? In the last line, it seems he is back. Injustice still exists, Zhaoyang still basks in the sun, yet Lady Ban and, with her, Ikkyū sing.

Ikkyū's enlightenment poem as presented here, exists only in the *Nempu*. A different version of it appears in the *Anthology*. There it comes in the middle of the series of love poems to Mori, the paramour of his later years. This leads one to speculate that Ikkyū rewrote his enlightenment poem after meeting Mori. The alternate form is:

> Hearing a Crow, Attaining Realization
> 聞鴉有省 *karasu o kiki sei ari*

豪機嗔恚識情心	*gōki shin'i shikijō no kokoro*
二十年前在即今	*nijūnenzen sokkon ni ari*
鴉笑出塵羅漢果	*a wa warau shutsujin no rakanka*
奈何日影玉顔吟	*nichiei gyokugan no gin ikan sen*

> Raging, angry, heart consumed by passions
> For twenty years. The time is now!
> Crow laughs, I leave the dust and end up an Arhat.
> How about it? In the sun, a fair jade-like face sings.
> (Poem 538)

Significantly the mention of Zhaoyang Palace is absent. The specter of neglect has ceased to haunt the poet.

The discrepancy between the two versions and the absence of the first one in the *Crazy Cloud Anthology* itself had led Yanagida to doubt the authenticity of the first. He suggests that the first one was the creation of the *Nempu* author to answer the need for an enlightenment poem. This argument is linked to the proposition that Ikkyū's true enlightenment came with the passing of the Dongshan kōan, that even the name he received then, Ikkyū (literally, "one pause"), implied "all at rest," "nothing left to do."[29] When was he really enlightened? Did he rewrite his enlightenment poem later or was the second version the only one to come from his hand? Are either of them truly enlightenment poems at all? On these crucial points, Ikkyū's biography is not clear.

The issue of Ikkyū's seal of enlightenment also occupies a great deal of the *Nempu* author's attention. He records that Kasō bestowed one on Ikkyū but that Ikkyū rejected it. So Kasō had to leave it in safekeeping with a woman lay follower with instructions to give it to Ikkyū once he had mellowed.³⁰ Thereafter, mention of it appears time and time again. Ikkyū tears it up and orders it burned, but his disciples piece it together and preserve it.³¹ Finally he burns it himself.³² The anxiousness with which the chronicler asserts over and over that there was a seal to destroy tells us something about how important these pieces of paper were in Muromachi monastic society. If Ikkyū's own followers were so attached to the notion of a seal, it is abundantly clear how the material symbol of enlightenment had outstripped in importance the reality of the experience. This is what Ikkyū battled so strongly against.³³ His poems were his true certificates of enlightenment.

Ikkyū continued to serve Kasō after experiencing enlightenment, and although the *Nempu* records Ikkyū nursing Kasō through bouts of illness, he was not in attendance when Kasō died. It seems he had begun to come and go, embarking on the wandering style of life that he continued until old age. Ikkyū often mentions a "straw raincoat and hat," the traveler's costume, in his poems.

Some of the anecdotes from Ikkyū's wanderings in his thirties give a sense of the wit and humor that must have made him an engaging guest. Once Ikkyū is reported to have visited the house of a lay follower where he saw an old ox in an enclosure. He wrote the following poem from the perspective of the ox and stuck it on one of its horns:

Ox
牛 *ushi*

異類行中是我會	*irui gyōchū kore ware katsute seri*
能依境也境依能	*nō wa kyō ni yori kyō wa nō ni yoru*
出生忘却來時路	*shusshō bōkyakusu raiji no michi*
不識當年誰氏僧	*shirazu tōnen taga shi no sō zo*

Come among the beasts to teach,
    this is what I have done.
What you can do, depends on where you are;
    where you are, depends on what you can do.
We are born and forget the path by which we came;
No one knows in those times what monk's name I had.³⁴

(Poem 73)

The poem alludes to a kōan of Weishan (d. 853) in which he challenges his followers to determine which is which, if a hundred years later, a water buffalo bull were to turn up with the words "Monk Weishan" on his flank. "If you say it is Weishan, it is a buffalo. If you say it is a buffalo, it is still Weishan."[35] Ikkyū imagines the ox to be Weishan's reincarnation. The anecdote goes on to relate that during the night the ox died. So the next day the owner teased Ikkyū, saying "Your poem killed my ox." Whereupon Ikkyū laughed. Here we seem to see a glimpse of the jesting, carefree Ikkyū that plays such a large role in his later legend.

In another place, the *Nempu* tells of him in Sakai strutting about with an enormous wooden sword strapped to his side. Accosted by passers-by who thought it strange to see a monk with a sword, he would draw it to reveal a blade of wood, saying, "You don't know it yet, but these days the world is full of false wisdom that is just like this wooden sword. As long as it is kept in the scabbard, it looks as good as a real blade, but if it is drawn out from the scabbard, it is seen to be only a sliver of wood. It cannot kill people, much less make them live."[36] Such were the novel ways Ikkyū taught Zen. There are several portraits of Ikkyū that depict him with a huge sword in a red scabbard, leaning against his chair that seem to confirm the authenticity of this incident.[37]

The site of Sakai is also important. This thriving port town, just a little southeast of present-day Osaka, represents the positive dynamic forces underlying the turmoil of Muromachi Japan. To all intents a free self-governing city, it steered a delicate neutral course in the country's stormy political sea, specializing in foreign trade and, among other things, arms manufacture, the products of which were sold to all comers. Home of the nouveaux riches, it teemed with a pleasure-loving, open-minded populace. Here if anywhere was a place where the novel and original would find a receptive audience.

Because it was the major depot for foreign trade, Sakai abounded in Gozan branch temples, but their support was not drawn from the city itself. The citizens preferred to patronize disaffected members of the Zen monastic community who found the confines of Gozan society too restrictive.[38] Often these monks were poets, painters, or connoisseurs. In many ways, Sakai was the cauldron where Zen began to be melted down and mixed with popular culture.

Ikkyū's writings indicate that as with so many things in his life, he was torn in two ways by this development. On the one hand, he was bitterly opposed to anything he saw as a bastardization of Zen. This was the false wisdom that was no more than a wooden sword. At the same time, he despised the aristocratic Zen that catered only to the seats of power for the sake of wealth and advancement. Judging from his poetry, his sympathies were with plain folk, the brothel girl, the fisherman, the sandal maker. Thus, he was drawn into expressing Zen in ways understandable to everyone. He is credited with being one of the first to popularize *kana hōgo*, the writing of Zen sermons in colloquial Japanese.[39] Presumably to his own mind, this was not a dilution of the teaching, but simply a transmutation into a more effective medium. However, when he saw others attempting the same strategy with ulterior motives of self-advancement and greed, he became enraged.

This appears to have been the principal bone of contention between Ikkyū and his elder brother in the Kasō lineage, Yōsō (1376–1458). The *Crazy Cloud Anthology* bristles with attacks on Yōsō and his followers. The *Nempu* devotes much attention to the conflict as well. Eighteen years Ikkyū's senior, Yōsō had been a student of Kasō's long before Ikkyū arrived. This alone was probably enough to make relations difficult between them, particularly if the *Nempu* is correct in inferring that Ikkyū quickly usurped the elder's position of chief disciple.[40]

After Kasō died, Yōsō tightened his connections with the head temple by taking up residence at Daitokuji, then at the nadir of its material prosperity. However, he also staked out territory in Sakai and thus secured new wealthy patrons for the head temple. If we judge by Yōsō's deeds, it seems that the rebuilding of Daitokuji's fame and prosperity was his primary concern. All the new resources from patronage were put toward that end. In the late 1430s, he was made abbot of Daitokuji and embarked on an ambitious program of building. Whether justified or not, it was Ikkyū's opinion that Yōsō was building up the prosperity of the monastery by catering to the masses rather than enlightening them, by "selling Zen" to increase the monastery's material status. At least, this is what we infer from the account in the *Nempu* of the first open conflict between Yōsō and Ikkyū. The entry is for the year 1440 and relates how Ikkyū had been invited to become the abbot of Nyoian, a subtemple within the Daitokuji compound, on the occasion of the thirteenth anniversary of Kasō's death. Yōsō, who was abbot of the entire monastery, may have issued this invitation as a way to bring the wayward son back into the fold.

The *Nempu* account of this event implies that Ikkyū took offense at the vulgar, noisy, and extravagant nature of the memorial service. "People from Izumi," that is, Sakai, were very much in evidence; we can take this to mean merchants puffed up with the pride of patronage. Ikkyū had arrived at Daitokuji on the twentieth; the service for Kasō was on the twenty-seventh; on the twenty-ninth, he wrote two poems. One he pasted on the wall of his residence, tacked to the end of an official accounting of monastery property. It was customary for each monk quitting a monastery to fill out such a document to keep track of what articles had been broken or lost during his residency. Ikkyū's poem refers to this prosaic document:

Account List of Nyoian Property, Appendix
題如意菴校割末 *Nyoian kyōkatsu no matsu ni daisu*

將常住物置庵中	*jōjūmotsu o motte anchū ni oki*
木杓笊籬掛壁東	*mokushaku sōri hekitō ni kaku*
我無如此閑家具	*ware ni kaku no gotoki kankagu nashi*
江海多年簑笠風	*kōkai tanen saryū no fū*

Take the everyday things, place them in the hermitage.
Wooden ladles, bamboo baskets hanging on the east wall,
I have no need of these idle things.
Over river and sea, these many years,
    straw raincoat and hat have been my style.[41]
(Poem 84)

The other poem, the more outrageous of the two, he apparently sent to Yōsō in person.

Addressed to Reverend Yōsō upon My Retiring from Nyoian
如意庵退院寄養叟和尚 *Nyoian taiin Yōsō Oshō ni yosu*

| 住庵十日意忙忙 | *jūan jūnichi i bōbō* |
| 腳下紅絲線甚長 | *kyakka no kōshisen hanahada nagashi* |

他日君來如問我　　*tajitsu kimi kitte moshi ware o towaba*
魚行酒肆又婬坊　　*gyokō shūshi mata inbō*

Ten days as an abbot and my mind is churning.
Under my feet, the red thread of passion is long.
If you come another day and ask for me,
Try a fish shop, tavern, or else a brothel.[42]
(Poem 85)

And with this, he took his leave. Yōsō likely thought that building up the prestige and wealth of Daitokuji was a noble task, but to Ikkyū, it looked like grasping for name and profit. What was gold to one was dross to the other.

The nature of the conflict between the two can be clearly seen in the *Nempu* entry which recounts their final break with one another. It happened in 1454 when Yōsō and his disciples were firmly in control of Daitokuji. Ikkyū came to visit Yōsō, who berated Ikkyū for throwing slop water in Kasō's face through constant mention of Baizhang's starvation and Tettō's "Admonition to Disciples Given to Worldly Self-Glorification." Baizhang (749–814) was the monk who instituted the first monastic code for Zen monasteries of which the cardinal rule was " a day of no work is a day of no eating." When Baizhang himself grew old, his disciples wanted to spare him work in the fields, so they hid his farming tools. Stubborn Baizhang refused to eat until his tools were returned. (See poem 180.) Tettō's admonition is directed against concern for fame and wealth in the world. (See poem 33 and the following notes.) Presumably Ikkyū used these two texts when preaching to his followers in order to discredit Yōsō's success in turning Daitokuji into a prosperous temple. Ikkyū countered Yōsō's accusations that Kasō would not have approved of the use of such texts by saying that Kasō had spoken of such things every day. He went on to accuse Yōsō of diluting Zen practice by giving up *sanzen* interview.[43] Yōsō retorted that as he held Kasō's certification, Ikkyū had no right to insult him so. Ikkyū said, "I was certified too, but it is not to be compared with yours." Yōsō replied, "Well, I don't dare to say you were not certified."[44]

A year later, we find him writing a collection of poems and prose pieces which, though entitled *Jikaishū* (Self-Admonition), is actually an impassioned diatribe against Yōsō, Yōsō's disciples, and the direction of Daitokuji under their leadership. He assuages his anger against them by imagining them dying of leprosy[45] and declares at one point that he is finished with Zen and has gone to become a Jōdo Shinshū monk.[46] Most of the poems are composed with rhyming words, *sen* ("boats"), *sen* ("money"), and *zen* ("Zen"). They vilify the monastery's connection with trade.

What are we to make of this feud between Yōsō and Ikkyū? Surely the rights and wrongs of it in objective terms are impossible to sort out from this point in time. In the *Crazy Cloud Anthology*, Ikkyū's case is clear. Yōsō was selling Zen. He was following the lead of the Gozan temples, confusing wealth with spiritual advancement. That is why it was natural that Ikkyū's most vitriolic criticisms should be directed at Yōsō and his disciples rather than at the Gozan establishment, for Yōsō was selling out the one lineage that had remained true. Betrayal within the family cut the keenest.

"If you come another day and ask for me / Try a fish shop, tavern, or else a brothel" went Ikkyū's parting poem to Yōsō, nor is it the only poem to speak of brothels. Many poems suggest that Ikkyū spent a good part of his ramblings in the demi-monde of the entertainment districts of Kyoto and Sakai. The *Nempu* mentions several of Ikkyū's temporary lodgings, one tumbledown hut that others thought unlivable, one unused residence of a friend. In his late fifties, a patron built him a more permanent hermitage, the Katsuroan, "Blind Donkey Hermitage." The name of the residence alludes to Rinzai's dying words, "When I die, my teachings will perish with blind donkeys...."

A *Nempu* entry from about this time is apropos here.

> One day, the master met a monk on the street who asked him "Are there hermits in the city?"
> The master said, "Yes."
> The monk said, "How can there be hermits in the city?"
> The master said, "Well, how?"
> The monk had nothing to say, so the master retorted, "You're a rascal with a dragon's head but a snake's tail."[47]

Ikkyū didn't spend all his time in the city, however. As one of his poems begins "Morning, in the mountains, evening, in the city." (See poem 93.) Ikkyū had a peripatetic relationship with town and country. Off and on, he maintained a hermitage at Yuzuriha in the mountains to the southwest of Kyoto. For the most part, his poems written there do not express a euphoria at being beyond the worldly realm of dust. Rather, they reject eremitic tradition and reveal a longing for the warm atmosphere of the cities' pleasure quarters. (See poems 89, 90.) Still, in some poems written to encourage his disciples to bear the hardships of country living, one can sense a kind of joy in the adventure of it. (See poem 91.)

Later in his life he found a country retreat that brought true peace and contentment. This was at Takigi, midway between Kyoto and Nara. There in 1456, he came upon the remains of an old hermitage established by Daiō, founder of the Daitokuji line. It felt right to resurrect the ruins since the karmic affiliation gave the place a deep resonance for him. Later to be known as Shūon'an, it was the closest to a permanent residence that Ikkyū ever had. When the capital became a dangerous place to live, it was to Shūon'an that he repaired.

The period of 1459 to 1462 brought disasters to the Kyoto area. A vicious cycle of drought followed by floods visited crop failure and plague upon the area. Tens of thousands are reported to have died within Kyoto alone; the corpses of the unburied dead dammed up the Kamo river.[48] (See poems 640, 641, 642.) The difficulties were compounded by the indifference of the shogunate to the widespread suffering.

No sooner had the area begun to recover when, in 1467, the Ōnin War erupted out of a conflict over the succession to the position of shogun. Ikkyū warned his followers the previous year of the danger of war. (See poem 648.) He himself retreated to Shūon'an. His Kyoto residence, Katsuroan was burned down during the war along with Daitokuji and virtually all of the northern part of the city. Even Shūon'an did not remain a safe haven. In 1469, Ikkyū was forced to flee to the Nara area, thence to Sakai, and finally to Sumiyoshi.[49] It seems that while he was at Sumiyoshi he met or renewed acquaintance with Mori, the blind singer and attendant who was the love of his later years.[50] A prose introduction dated 1470 says, "I traveled to Yakushidō and heard the blind girl sing love songs" (poem 541). The poem itself indicates he felt some ambivalence about the feelings she aroused in him. Another prose introduction dated the following year suggests that Ikkyū and Mori knew one another from Takigi and together with the poem signals a resumption of their relationship (poem 542). Here, as with so many aspects of Ikkyū's life, the poems themselves are vivid, while the actual events or people involved are obscure. Mori lives a shadow existence; we know little about her despite her strong presence in a series of poems.

A portrait of her and Ikkyū together testifies that she was not a figment of his imagination.[51] Furthermore, her name turns up on documents at Shūon'an and Daitokuji as a participant in memorial services thirteen years after Ikkyū's death. This is problematical because one poem speaks of "my late attendant Mori."[52] It is a case in point where the question of fiction with respect to the *Crazy Cloud Anthology* comes to fore. If these poems are like an "I-novel" as Yanagida has suggested, fact and fancy are likely mixed.

Surely, this is an unusual group of poems to be written by a Zen monk. It is one thing to write about brothels, using the subject for shock value. At least that falls into line with the iconoclastic streak in Zen, but it is quite another to write love poems, songs of shameless attachment to the gentle, sentimental side of life. When Ikkyū in his seventies writes of love with the fresh ardor of an adolescent, he is unique in Zen literature. The time Ikkyū and Mori spent together was the troubled time of the Ōnin War. They moved from place to place and suffered from hunger. (See poems 531, 532.) Yet there were periods of calm. Intermittently, it was safe to return to Shūon'an in Takigi.

Interspersed among the *Nempu* entries noting the movement of warring troops and flight, are the mention of various art works, some brought to Ikkyū for inscriptions, some his own pieces of calligraphy. The bestowal of poems on the Nō dramatist Komparu Zenchiku indicates that this was the period he received instruction from Ikkyū.[53] We know that the *renga* poet Sōchō was a regular visitor at Shūon'an from 1476 on. The tea master Murata Shukō was associated with Shūon'an from the beginning. Even during the Ōnin War then, Shūon'an was a salon for a wide range of cultural leaders. When one looks at the artists, poets, and so on who were in one way or another members of Ikkyū's circle, it is an impressive array; there were also several painters of the Soga school, Bokusai, Bokkei, and Jasoku.

The Soga painting school produced Muromachi's most original

works in monochrome ink, the portrait of Ikkyū by Bokusai being one of the masterpiece of that style. Sōchō participated in both the Minase and Yuyama linked-verse sessions, which set the standard for serious *renga* composition for years to come. Even more importantly, he led in the composition of comic linked verse, *haikai*, from which a century or so later *haiku* would be born. Komparu Zenchiku, second in importance only to his adoptive parent Zeami, pushed the Nō form to new heights of creativity and sublimity. Murata Shukō originated the "grass hut" style of tea ceremony, the style that was passed on to Sen no Rikyū and thence handed down as the classical form of tea. Monochrome ink painting, *renga*, Nō, tea ceremony—the leaders in these most vital forms of Muromachi art all studied Zen with Ikkyū.

We can surmise that Ikkyū's influence on these artists was significant. Yet, to pin down exactly where and how such art was influenced by Ikkyū is not an easy task. One could point to the Soga painter's ability to capture the essence of Song-style ink painting without being enslaved by its forms; one could hold up the free, sometimes ribald spirit of Sōchō's comic linked verse and say that these were lessons learned from Ikkyū. Zenchiku's debt reveals itself in his theoretical writings so imbued with Zen dialectic. One is reminded, too, of his play *Eguchi*, where a prostitute metamorphoses into a Bodhisattva. In fact, Nō plays often deal with situations in which dualities, such as sacred and profane, are transcended. Here is a poem of Ikkyū's that expresses appreciation for one of Kan'ami's most famous plays *Matsukaze* "Pine Wind."[54] In the dance at the climax of this play, the brine gatherer Pine Wind, crazed with longing for her past lover, an exiled courtier, dons the court robe he left as a keepsake and fuses with his spirit. Since all the actors on the Nō stage were male, this is a scene where a male actor performs a female character who becomes her male lover for a brief moment. In the first line of this poem, Ikkyū seems to recognize that the performance style itself of Nō effects a radical non-duality with the blurring of gender.

可憐男女一身吟	*awaremubeshi danjo isshin no gin*
但仰神扶波上心	*tada kami no tasuke o aogu hajō no kokoro*
惱亂秋風戀草露	*akikaze ni nōran su koigusa no tsuyu*
烟波萬里淚痕深	*enpa banri namida no ato fukashi*[55]

> How moving, man and woman singing in one body!
> Only gazing upward for divine aid, heart on the waves.
> Troubled mind in the autumn wind,
>   dew on love's rank growing grass,
> Ten thousand miles of misty waves, deep are the tracks of tears.

Then again, one might surmise that Murata Shukō found some inspiration for his *wabi cha*, "the tea ceremony style of poverty" from the austerity of Ikkyū's material existence and perhaps in such lines as:

> I believe man's bill of fare is fixed,
> One bowl of mutton gruel with citrus rind tea.
>   (Poem 33)

More important, perhaps, was Ikkyū's example, the demonstration of what it was like to live Zen outside the confines of a monastic institution. After all, he was hardly a monk at all since he observed so few of the regulations that set a monk apart from society. Yet having stripped himself of the outward forms of his religion, he bore witness to its core. That is why he found himself at the forefront of a general movement during the Muromachi period that transmuted Zen into art. On the one hand, this represented a growing secularization of Zen, perhaps to its detriment as a religion. On the other hand, it meant that the basic ideas of Zen could be absorbed deep into the culture. Through art, Zen became an integral strand of the Japanese cultural fabric. Interestingly, it was an eccentric like Ikkyū, someone on the fringe of his society, who should be instrumental in introducing new ideas into the heart of the culture.

In 1474, the middle of the Ōnin War, Ikkyū was asked to accept the abbotship of Daitokuji, which had been reduced to a field of ash in the conflict. All Yōsō's splendid building projects had been destroyed. The monastery's very continuance was in doubt. In these circumstances, Ikkyū found it impossible to refuse the post. Yet the poem he wrote on the occasion indicates that after so many years of tilting against the establishment, he felt somewhat embarrassed to become its head. He refers to the purple robes that were bestowed on him by the emperor as a mark of the high rank.

大燈門弟滅殘燈	Daitō no montei zantō o metsushi
難解吟懷一夜氷	tokegatashi ginkai ichiya no kōri
五十年來簑笠客	gojūnenrai saryū no kyaku
愧慚今日紫衣僧	kizansu shi'e no sō

Daitō's descendants destroyed his remaining light.
Hard to melt the heart in song on an icy night.
For fifty years, a wanderer with straw raincoat and hat,
Shameful today, a purple-robed monk.
   (Poem 568)

Once the war was over, Ikkyū dutifully and energetically set about collecting the contributions necessary for the rebuilding of Daitokuji. Generous donations were forthcoming. The war, a terrible futility in many respects, also had some positive, purgative aspects. The old order of the shogunate was virtually swept away, and with it withered the Gozan system. None of the great temples could afford to rebuild in the grand style they had known previously. Meanwhile Daitokuji's sources of support, the smaller warlord families and Sakai merchants, were in an even stronger position after the war. The years Ikkyū had spent consorting with all manner of people produced an unexpected benefit when Daitokuji was in need. Ikkyū's charisma brought forth donations from a broad range of people. Indeed, his influence in this respect lasted long after his death. In 1525, for example, one of his students, the poet Sōchō, was moved to sell a priceless treasure, his manuscript copy of the *Tale of Genji* in the hand of Fujiwara no Teika, in order to rebuild the great Sanmon gate at Daitokuji.[56] Ironically, after preserving the spiritual integrity of the Daitokuji lineage for so long, the crowning achievement of Ikkyū's career was to reestablish the material existence of the monastery as well.

Throughout the rebuilding, Ikkyū continued to reside at Shūon'an. Then, in the winter of 1481, at the age of eighty-eight, after suffering from an acute ague for a couple of months, he passed away sitting in meditation, seemingly asleep. Sometime during the last illness, he wrote his death poem, a copy of which in his own hand still remains in the possession of Shinjuan, his memorial temple within Daitokuji. In the traditional four character line form of the death poem, it has the feeling of being written quite close to his actual passing. The brush strokes are still marvelously bold, but he obviously forgot one character in the first line and so had to add it small in the margin.⁵⁷ Somehow the effect is more poignant than a faultlessly written poem would have been.

須彌南畔　　　　shumi nanban
誰會我禪　　　　tare ka waga zen o esu
虛堂來也　　　　Kidō kuru mo
不直半錢　　　　hansen ni atarazu

South of Mount Sumeru,
Who meets my Zen?
Even if Xutang comes
He's not worth half a penny.⁵⁸

Even though eccentrics abound in Zen literature, Ikkyū cuts an unusual figure. In the context of the Zen of his own time and place, he was certainly an anomaly. The Rinzai Zen, which was imported into Japan during the Kamakura period, was the full-blown institution of the Song dynasty, comprised of a rigid discipline, regularized study of the kōans, and an elaborate hierarchy of ranks for monks. It was quite removed from the Zen of the Tang dynasty when the masters had been independent eccentrics. Their practice was wild and free; they invented kōans as they spoke. In the Song dynasty, while Zen leaders were anxious to preserve the spirit of those early masters, the increase in numbers of adherents and state patronage forced the monasteries to adopt a bureaucratic structure in order to function. This was the form of Zen that Japanese monks experienced when they studied in China and once they returned to Japan, they sought to emulate it in their own organization. A well-defined structure in the monasteries promoted their credibility as a serious religious movement.

Much of the institutional side of Zen went against Ikkyū's grain. In spirit, he identifies himself with the original Tang masters. A fundamentalist, he keeps harking back to the essential principles of the school. Yet, his insistence on "old-time Zen" made him an iconoclast among his contemporaries. He was even out of step with other monk poets in that his poems are almost exclusively about Zen. By contrast, the focus of the flourishing school of poetry in Chinese within the Gozan was quite secular.⁵⁹

One aspect of Ikkyū sets him apart not only from his contemporaries but also from all Zen masters of the past. He is the only Zen monk to have broached the subject of sex in a religious context. The Tang masters may have had unfettered intellects, but they never approached the subject of the relations between men and women. This is not to say that Zen monks never broke the precept of celibacy. Particularly in Muromachi Japan, discipline within the Zen monasteries was lax. The practice of pederasty was widespread, and apparently even the secret keeping of concubines was not unheard of.[60] However, Ikkyū is unique in treating physical love as a part of his spiritual discipline. For Ikkyū, sex as the principle "desire" was a kind of touchstone for his realization of the dynamic concept of non-duality that pivots upon the essential unity of the realm of desire and the realm of enlightenment. It is as though he tested his own sense of enlightenment against this primary experience.

Ikkyū was well aware that by traditional standards his attitude toward spiritual discipline was highly irregular. The breaking of the monastic code was conventionally thought to bring karmic retribution in its wake, and Ikkyū occasionally had doubts about his own conduct, notably when he was ill. Consider the following poem, one of two entitled "Composed When Ill."

破戒沙門八十年	*hakai no shamon hachijūnen*
自慚因果撥無禪	*mizukara hazu inga hatsumu no zen o*
病被過去因果果	*yamai wa kako no inga no ka o kōmuru*
今行何謝劫空緣	*ima wa nani o gyōjite gōkū no en o shasen*

A monk who has broken the precepts for eighty years,
Repenting a Zen that has ignored cause and effect.
When ill, one suffers the effects of past deeds;
Now how to act in order to atone for eons of bad karma.
(Poem 250)

Ikkyū challenges the norm of Zen enlightenment. The poems where he speaks of the pleasure he finds in love contradict the monk's conventional commitment to non-attachment. Even more perplexing are poems such as the above where Ikkyū unabashedly confesses doubts about his own attainment. Fear of karmic retribution resists reconciliation with the standard conception of an enlightened man as much as attachment to physical pleasure. There is a kōan that Ikkyū frequently alludes to known as "Baizhang's wild fox,"[61] which centers around this puzzling relationship of the enlightened man to karma. The kōan relates the story of an encounter between the Zen master Baizhang and a man who had been coming to listen to Baizhang's sermons. The man said to Baizhang, "I am not a man. Once, years ago, I was a teacher on this mountain who, when asked, 'Does a man of great training (an enlightened man) fall into the chains of karma?' replied, 'No, he does not fall into the chains of karma.' Then, after that, I was reincarnated five hundred times as a wild fox. Now I ask you, for my sake, say a word of enlightenment that I may be released from my fox body." Baizhang said, "The man of great training does not ignore karma." These words enlightened the questioner, who was the spirit of the former teacher who had been reincarnated so many times as a fox.[62] In the poem above, Ikkyū speaks of his fear that his own Zen was one that ignored karma.

The formula of the *Heart Sūtra*, "That which is form is emptiness; that which is emptiness is form," implies the same unity for all opposites, including desire and release, but this particular interface in the realm of truth is a dangerous path to tread and is usually shunned in the name of caution by those following the religious path. It is to walk the wire between "impurity in one's daily life" and an enlightened compassionate perception that can gaze with equanimity upon weakness, whether it be in one's self or other beings. One may fall from this intangible wire unaware.

This is the crux of Ikkyū's moral dilemma. Even though the ultimate insight of Zen is beyond the distinction of moral and immoral, Ikkyū knew that breaking the established precepts entailed the danger of sinking into the degeneracy of a Zen that ignored cause and effect. He lived at the edge of profligacy and enlightenment, and thus met the challenge to "give rise to knowledge and deliverance without destroying ignorance and the thirst for existence."[63] So much of his poetry is directed toward re-creating the experience of the ultimate insight of Zen because, having chosen such a difficult and dangerous path, he had a deep need to constantly renew it. A dividing line cannot be drawn between Ikkyū's grappling with his own strong emotions and his concern with the philosophical problem of non-duality.

From the mixture of the two emerges a poetry that is at once lyrical and metaphysical, sensual and abstract.

Dialectic of Non-Duality

白居易問鳥窠和尚、如何是佛法大意。窠曰、諸惡莫作、眾善奉行。白日、三歲孩兒也解恁麼道。窠曰、三歲孩兒雖道得、八十老人行不得。靈山和尚每日、若無鳥窠一語、我徒盡泥乎本來無一物、及不思善不思惡、善惡不二、邪正一如等語、以撥無因果、而世多日用不淨之邪師也。故餘作此偈、以示眾云。

Bai Juyi asked Master Bird Nest, "What is the broad meaning of Buddhism?" Bird Nest answered, "Do no evil, do much good."[64] Bai Juyi said, "But a three-year-old child could understand a teaching like that." Bird Nest replied, "A three-year-old child may be able to say it, but there are eighty-year-old men who cannot practice it."

Old Master Ryōzen used to say: " If it were not for this one phrase of Bird Nest, our followers would all get bogged down in precepts like:

'From the Beginning, not one thing'
'Not thinking of good, not thinking of evil'
'Good and evil are not two'
'False and true, are one and the same'

and all the rest, so that in the end they would ignore karma and the world would just be full of false teachers, impure in their daily lives."

So now on this topic, I (Ikkyū) have composed a poem and presented it to a congregation.

學者撥無因果沈	gakusha inga o hatsumushite shizuman
老禪一句價千金	zenshi no ikku atai senkin
諸惡莫作善奉行	shoaku makusa zen bugyō
須在先生醉裏吟	subekaraku sensei suiri no gin ni arubeshi

> Students who ignore karma are sunk.
> That old Zen master's words are worth a thousand pieces of gold,
> Do no evil, do much good.
> It must have been something the Elder sang while drunk.
>   (Poem 205)

In this prose introduction and poem, a dialectic unfolds that sets the duality of good and evil against a transcendental view that sees the two as one. Following the composition through as it unfolds reveals the movement from one position to the other. The prose introduction is comprised of two quotations. The first is from a Chinese Zen text, the *Chuan Deng Lu*.[65] The passage describes an encounter between the famous Tang poet, Bai Juyi (772–784), and the Zen master, Niao Ke (741–824) or "Bird Nest," so named because he was fond of sleeping in a large pine tree. Ikkyū jokes in another poem about the Zen master: "His nest must have been cold, that old Zen codger up in the tree."[66] He was well aware of the humorous image conjured up by the name and uses it to set a light mood for the following encounter.

Bai Juyi queries in the conventional manner of a seeker addressing a Zen master, "What is the broad meaning of Buddhism?" In such confrontations, the master's answer in never predictable and usually characterized by a purposeful obliqueness. Thus, Bai Juyi is taken aback by Bird Nest's apparently straightforward reply. "Do no evil, do much good," coming from a Zen master, is too simple to satisfy a questioner like Bai Juyi, and so he counters by saying, in effect, "Do you take me for a child?" Bird Nest neatly replies to Bai Juyi's objections, asserting that, although such a teaching may be easy to pronounce, it is difficult to practice, thereby reasserting that "Do no evil, do much good" is the beginning and the end of the meaning of Buddhism.

The simplicity of that reply dissatisfies Bai Juyi and for that matter any hearer grounded in Zen Buddhism because it is a reply in terms of duality when the idea of non-duality is fundamental to Zen. Consider for example, this passage from the *Vimalakīrti Sūtra*:

> "Good" and "evil" make two. To seek to do neither good nor evil …
> is to penetrate into non-duality.[67]

Bird Nest's pronouncement flies in the face of that orthodox position.

Seen from this perspective, the exchange stands as a kōan, a case that presents a problem to the rational, distinguishing mind.

Ikkyū quotes the Japanese Zen master Ryōzen (1295–1369) to clarify the problem, and the light mood of the initial encounter changes to one of serious consideration. Ryōzen preceded Ikkyū by only four generations in their spiritual lineage. Because of his reputation for uncompromising moral rectitude, it is fitting that he should welcome Bird Nest's pronouncement. He explains why the instruction in terms of duality is not out of place as the concept of non-duality can itself become a trap, something one clings to and is caught in, rather than a key to liberation. Much worse, it can become an excuse for those false of heart to indulge themselves in evil behavior. Even though the ultimate truth is beyond the distinction of good and evil, it is far better to encourage the earnest to do good rather than to allow the misguided to practice evil under the guise of non-duality.

The exchange between Bird Nest and Bai Juyi and Ryōzen's interpretation of it having been presented, Ikkyū now gives us his comment on the case in the form of a poem. He begins by paraphrasing Ryōzen's words followed by adulation in the second line. We might assume, therefore, that praise and celebration will be the order of the poem from here on. However, the subsequent quotation of Bird Nest's words suggests that we reinterpret the second line as also referring to Bird Nest, seeing him as the "old Zen master whose words are worth a thousand pieces of gold." We are thus caught thinking retrospectively as we read, "It must have been something the elder sang while drunk." "Elder" is a term of address applied only to a layman, therefore neither of the old Zen masters is meant here. "Drunkenly singing" is a sobriquet of the poet Bai Juyi, whose question opened the dialogue, so it is he who is introduced into the poem, and he who must have sung, "Do no evil, do much good," while he was in his cups. When we read the third line, we heard these words of wisdom as issuing from the lips of Bird Nest and being echoed by Ryōzen. Now they issue from a tipsy Bai Juyi. From the solemn moral pronouncements of Ryōzen we have come to drunken song. Where the ground was solid, now it slips and shakes.

But that is how it should be. The goal of Zen is not to answer questions but to dissolve questioning. One of the ways in which this is accomplished is to bewilder the student with questions, or with statements that amount to questions, until he finds his own way out of his reasoning mind. That is the art of the kōan, the Zen problem. It is also the art of Ikkyū's poetry. The majority of Ikkyū's poems are not simply about Zen, they are the realization of Zen principles in the form of poetic experience. The basic nature of that experience may be called dialectical, in the sense in which that term has been used by Stanley Fish in his book, *Self-Consuming Artifacts*: "A dialectical presentation … is disturbing, for it requires of its readers a searching and rigorous scrutiny of everything they believe in and live by. It is didactic in a special sense; it does not preach the truth but asks that the readers discover the truth for themselves…."[68]

Truth, in terms of Zen, is beyond dualistic constructs. On the other hand, language is rooted in the propensity of human thought to distinguish between "this" and "that" or "positive" and "negative." Ikkyū's triumph is his ability to use this problematic tool in order to transcend its inherent limitations.

One technique he uses to short-circuit language's dualistic tendencies is to juxtapose opposites in such a way that the distinction between them melts away. This technique is dynamic; he does not present opposites frozen in juxtaposition; rather, as the reader's mind flows through the poem, contradictory elements manifest themselves and in turn dissolve into one another. On the surface, the poet says one thing, but a suggested undercurrent, often brought into being by allusion, says the opposite and cancels the surface theme out. It is in this way that the poems offer experiences rather than pronouncements. In the end, Ikkyū's poems of this kind obstruct any deductive analysis seeking to extract meaning from them as gold is extracted from ore. There is nothing solid in these poems to be extracted. They succeed in the measure that they leave the reader suspended with "not a tile overhead nor an inch of ground below."

Allusion

To Chinese eyes, Ikkyū's poetry is not technically perfect, for he bends and breaks the rules of Chinese prosody at will. His handling of rhyme is unusual and he disrupts the syntax of the seven-character line in audacious ways.[69] It must be kept in mind, however, that Ikkyū was not writing for a Chinese audience. Although they could read Chinese and appreciate the conventions of language and prosody enough to know when those conventions were being violated, his audience lacked an ear for Chinese sound, and those aberrations did not offend their aural sense. I suspect rather that Ikkyū's departures from convention would strike his audience as novel and original. The term *hadaka no gengo* ("naked language") has been used to describe the language of modern Japanese free verse.[70] In Ikkyū's hands, Chinese has a similar naked quality. Yet, from the rawness, the crudeness even, issues a power that makes his poetry compelling reading. His rigorous personality with its rough edges is at one with his mode of expression. The better-mannered compositions of the Gozan poets pale in comparison.

Nonetheless, there is a subtle side to Ikkyū's poetry. Though the niceties of tonal harmony, decorous diction, clever parallelism may be absent, one literary device works a complicated pattern into the plain cloth of Ikkyū's verse: that is allusion. The notes accompanying the translations in this volume will bear witness to the frequency with which he employs this technique. Allusion is often associated with pedantry, but Ikkyū makes it serve much more serious purposes than mere display of erudition. Through its use, he enriches a poem's content and lends grace to his statements. Moreover, it is his principle means for bringing the opposite of any proposition into a poem and thus creating the dialectical experiences his poetry abounds in.

By incorporating allusions into his poems, Ikkyū is able to say a great deal in few words. Ikkyū wrote virtually all his poems in the short *shichigon zekku* form, a four-line poem with seven characters in each line. Its very brevity demands concentrated expression. It was mentioned earlier that for Ikkyū certain Chinese names and famous poems were charged with a wealth of meaning. In his poetry, he uses them almost like a symbolic shorthand. Invoking them, he is able to draw a wealth of story and connotation into his short poems. For example, the single mention of the fifth-century poet Tao Yuanming summons forth all that he stood for: transcendental wisdom, the charm of a simple rustic life, a thumb of the nose to artificial convention, and a love for chrysanthemums. When it is a case of alluding to a specific poem, often he draws in the meaning of that poem to amplify or increase the complexity of the meaning in his own. For example, take the following poem expressing the poet's distress upon witnessing the devastation and suffering caused by typhoon and flood in the year 1460. (See p. 23 and poems 640, 641, 642.) Someone in the midst of the general woe was having a party and the callousness of such gaiety in the face of the suffering disturbed Ikkyū.

大風洪水萬民憂　　taifū kōzui banmin ureu
歌舞管絃誰夜遊　　kamai kangen ta ga yayū zo
法有興裏劫增減　　hō ni kōsui ari kō ni sōgen su
任他明月下西樓　　samo areba are meigetsu no seirō ni
　　　　　　　　　　　　kudaru o

Typhoon, flood, suffering for ten thousand people;
Song, dance, flutes, and strings, who sports tonight?
In the Dharma, flourishing and decay; in the eons,
　　increase and decline.
"Let it be, let the bright moon sink behind the Western Pavilion."
　　　　　　　　(Poem 203)

In Ikkyū's poem, once the first two lines have set the situation, he turns to consider the perspective of eternity, the rise and fall of the eons, which makes this time of suffering the chimera of a moment. After this, the statement "Let it be, let the bright moon sink behind the Western Pavilion" conveys resignation and acceptance.

However, the last line is borrowed whole from a poem by the Tang poet Li Yi apropos a quite different situation. He had traveled a long distance in order to rejoin his beloved and found to his sorrow that she had died during his absence.

On this smooth bamboo mat, water-patterned,
　　my thoughts drift far away.
A thousand miles to make the tryst, now in one night, it is over.
From here on, I have no heart to enjoy the lovely night;
Let it be, let the bright moon sink behind the Western Pavilion.[71]

Here, the same line conveys inconsolable grief. While Ikkyū speaks of public calamity from the perspective of a cyclical eternity, Li Yi speaks of private disaster while caught in the agony of finite time where things end irrevocably. The Li Yi poem becomes a shadow double to Ikkyū's poem. The juxtaposition thus created of two opposed emotions, resignation and grief beyond solace, evoke the state of conflict in Ikkyū's heart. The allusion is the vehicle through which half of the poet's feelings are expressed.

Thus, in myriad ways, reference to key figures, scriptures, and poems widens the scope and meaning of Ikkyū's poems. Each individual case may be different, but, for the sake of discussion, the roles allusion plays in Ikkyū's poetry can be divided into two general categories: the rhetorical and the dialectical. Here, rhetorical use means that allusion is employed in a way that accords with convention. Allusions are made that the reader will not only recognize but also understand in a familiar and thus ultimately satisfying way. Such use generally serves two interrelated purposes. One is to embellish. The other is to make statements indirectly. This also serves an aesthetic purpose since indirect expression is generally felt to have a decorous effect; witness its universal use in polite language. This mode of allusion is common and thus needs no more explanation here. Specific examples of it in Ikkyū's poetry will be examined in the analyses below.

The dialectical application of allusion requires a more detailed explanation, for it is not so common. An allusion is used dialectically when it breaks the contract of conventional understanding between poet and reader, and is based on personal and eccentric interpretations of literary works. Employed in this fashion, allusion disturbs and shocks the reader, forcing him to re-evaluate his sense of what the poem is about. Coming in the last line, it often introduces a contradictory element that collapses the established frame of reference. At other times, opposites are brought together in such a way that the distinction between them is obliterated or, at least, left problematical and unclear. In the confusion, one glimpses a knowing beyond dualistic distinctions.

This particular utilization of allusion owes much to the way tags of poetry and scriptures are used in the Zen dialogues. An example will further the explanation here. Ikkyū often mentions "the little love song" in allusion to a story involving Yuanwu (1063–1135) from the *Wu Deng Hui Yuan*, an anthology of kōan and Zen dialogues. In the dialogue, a prefect comes to Wuzu, Yuanwu's teacher, for instruction. Wuzu asks:

> When you were young, was there not a little love song you used to recite? There are two lines in it that are very close to Zen:

> She often called her maid for no reason at all,
> Just so her lover would recognize her voice.

This implies that the girl calls her maid often so that her lover waiting outside will be comforted by the sound of her voice and guided as to where to steal in to see her. However, when Wuzu says the lines are close to Zen, they are turned into a statement of the philosophical truth that words can often convey something other than their conditionally limited meaning. "Maid" need not simply be a summons, it can also say, "I'm here; come this way," to the person with ears to hear it. The prefect fails to grasp Wuzu's point, and Wuzu sends him away to work on it some more. Then, Yuanwu comes in to inquire about the prefect's progress. Wuzu alludes to the little love song again, saying "He (the prefect) only recognized my voice." Yuanwu gets caught up in the specific meaning of the words, saying, "But she just wanted her lover to recognize her voice. He recognized your voice, why was that incorrect?" Wuzu said, "What was the meaning of Bodhidharma coming from the West? The oak tree in the garden" [itself a famous kōan]. His sudden interjection of this non sequitur enlightened Yuanwu.[72]

Underlying this form of discourse is the notion that language itself has only a conditional value and that its meaning is always tied to the context in which it appears. This employment of tags of secular and sacred literature in new contexts which change their meaning is used time and time again throughout the kōan literature. This, after all, is the material Ikkyū meditated upon for years, and thus it is no wonder his poetic technique is so powerfully influenced by it.

The following series of analyses will trace the warp of allusion through a number of poems in order to acquaint the reader with the variety and complexity of the ways in which Ikkyū employs this technique. The analyses are arranged in an ascending order with respect to complexity of allusion, and alternate irregularly between examples in the rhetorical and dialectical modes.

近代久參學得僧	*kindai kyūsan gakutoku sō*
語言三昧喚爲能	*gogon sanmai yonde nō to nasu*
無能有味狂雲屋	*munō ajiwai ari kyōun no oku*
折腳鐺中飯一升	*setsukyaku sōchū meshi isshō*

> These days accomplished monks of long training
> Are mesmerized by their own words and call it ability.
> At Crazy Cloud's hut, there is no ability but a flavor;
> He boils a cup of rice in a bent foot cauldron.
> (Poem 107)

This poem, which on the surface is simple and direct, can be appreciated without understanding the allusion embedded in the last line. Lines one and two establish and develop the theme, the monks of today and their superficial enlightenment. In line three, the subject becomes the poet himself, "Crazy Cloud," in opposition to the monastic rabble. Line four describes the poet's actual state, poor and cooking with an old, battered pot, with the implication that this is truly virtuous. If one takes the poem without the allusion, it seems to be a rather modest expression of the poet's self-confidence. It says, in effect, "I may be one of no ability but I have a style of my own, and find virtue in frugal living." However, the "bent foot cauldron" in the last line alludes to the "Last Admonition of Master Daitō" (founder of Daitokuji and an important patriarch in Ikkyū's lineage), where Daitō says, "If there is one who practices righteousness in the wilds, who in a little hut passes his day eating vegetables boiled in a bent foot cauldron … such a one, day by day, looks this old monk in the eye and returns the favor of my teaching."[73] Recognition of that allusion subtly changes the effect of the poem. Ikkyū is no longer simply describing his poverty, and his statement of self-confidence is no longer so modest; through the allusion he is saying, "I am the one who looks our Master in the eye, the one who is worthy to receive his teaching, while the rest of you at Daitokuji are charlatans." The statement is all the more subtle for being made indirectly. Here then, is an example of the rhetorical use of allusion.

The Plum Ripened
梅子熟 *baishi jukuseri*

熟處年來猶未忘	*jukusuru tokoro nenrai bōsezu*
言中有味孰能掌	*genchū ni ajiwai ari tare ka yoku namen*
人斑初見大梅老	*ninban hajimete miru Daibai rō*
疎雨淡煙青已黄	*so'u tan'en ao sude ni ki*

Its ripening, over the years, is still not forgotten.
In the words, there is a flavor but who can taste it?
When his spots were first visible, Big Plum was already old.
Sprinkle of rain, fine mist, that which was green
    had already turned yellow.

(Poem 57)

This poem celebrates a former Chinese master, Damei (752–839), whose name literally means "Big Plum." Damei's teacher Mazu was the first to play with the literal meaning of the name. The *Chuan Deng Lu* records how Mazu acknowledged his student's attainment with the phrase, "Ah, the plum has ripened."[74] The title of the poem alludes to this. Note the degrees by which the allusion becomes obvious. The title cues the allusion, but, at the beginning, the content of the poem remains general enough to allow different interpretations. The question in line two gives a twist to the movement of the poem, and begins to suggest because of the reference to "words" that the subject is not an actual plum tree. The appearance of Damei's name in the third line assures our recognition of the allusion. Line four rounds out the poem by coloring, albeit with the monochromes of rain and mist, the vaguely suggested image of a plum tree, and by elegantly embroidering in one more allusion to the original passage in the *Chuan Deng Lu*. Damei answered the question, "How long have you been here?" with "Four times only have I seen the mountains turn green and then yellow."[75] Now the expression is turned to describe a plum, not mountain foliage, no other plum than the old master himself. Knowledge of the original enables one to appreciate how the poet has transformed the allusion in the poem. First he puns on Damei's name, much as Mazu did, then he turns Damei's own words around to describe him. The seasons involved have also been playfully switched. Whereas Damei meant he had seen summer turn to autumn four times, Ikkyū, in referring to a plum, means spring has turned to summer.

The allusions to the monk's biography complement the intent of the poem to praise him. It reworks familiar material within a predictable framework and, because of this, the strategy of cueing the allusion early in the poem and then making a more direct reference at the end is particularly effective. It is pleasurable to pick up the hint of an allusion and then have the supposition of the poem's direction verified by the arrival of a more explicit reference. It is like the fulfillment of a promise, and one's joy at the fulfillment lies in the recognition that earlier a promise was made. The degree of complexity in the application of allusion has increased but it remains rhetorical in its effect.

The following poem is very similar in strategy to the preceding one, except that here the allusion produces a dialectical effect:

餘誠會裏徒日、喫酒必須用濁醪、餚則其糟而已。遂名之曰乾一酒、仍作偈以自咲云。

I admonished my followers saying, "If you are going to drink *sake*, then you must always drink muddy *sake*, and for tidbits just have the dregs. This is why the latter are sometimes called 'dry *sake*.'" Thereupon I made a poem, laughing at myself:

醉裏眾人奈酒腸	*suiri shujin shuchō o ikansen*
醒時伎盡啜糟糠	*samuru toki gi tsukite sōkō o susuru*
湘南流水懷沙怨	*Shōnan no ryūsui kaisha no urami*
引得狂雲咲一場	*hiki etari Kyōun ga warai ichiba o*

Men in the midst of their drunkenness,
    what can they do about their wine-soaked guts?
Sober, at the limit of their resources, they suck the dregs.
He cast himself into Xiangnan river,
    his "Embracing the Sands Lament"
Draws out of this Crazy Cloud a laugh.
              (Poem 206)

In "The Plum Ripened," allusions to a single source are sprinkled throughout the poem. In poem 206, the source of the allusions is a single passage from the *Records of the Grand Historian of China* concerning the suicide of Qu Yuan (third century BC). The following is a paraphrase of that passage.

Disappointed and sorely grieved, Qu Yuan, the slandered but virtuous official, resolved to throw himself into the river. As he stood on the bank of the river preparing to carry out his resolve, a fisherman drew him into conversation. Qu Yuan declared, "All the world is muddied in confusion, only I am pure! All men are drunk, and I alone am sober." The fisherman countered Qu Yuan's lament with some salty wisdom, "A true sage does not stick at mere things .... If all the world is a muddy turbulence, why do you not follow its current and rise upon its waves? If all men are drunk, why do you not drain their dregs and swill their thin wine with them?! Qu Yuan rejected the advice and, after composing the rhyme prose poem "Embracing the Sands Lament," cast himself into the river.[76]

It should be remarked that mention of Qu Yuan in Chinese poetic tradition normally elicits profound sympathy. He represents the pure uncompromising man who is misunderstood and betrayed by his moral inferiors. Indeed, in other places, Ikkyū himself empathizes strongly with him. One does not expect Qu Yuan to appear in a poem of jocular intent. That is why, despite a few key words in the prose preface like "muddy" and "dregs," a reader would be unlikely to think of Qu Yuan. However, upon perceiving the opposition of "drunkenness" and "sober" in the first two lines of the poem one would likely recall Qu Yuan's famous remark, "All men are drunk, I alone am sober." Yet it is probably only upon recognizing the title of Qu Yuan's lament, "Embracing the Sands Lament," that the reader would be quite sure Qu Yuan was being alluded to. Then the allusions in line one and two would be affirmed, and in retrospect the introduction as a whole would appear to have led up to the Qu Yuan reference. For example, the words "dregs" and "muddy" in the introduction would then appear somewhat loaded.

As in the preceding poem, "The Plum Ripened," the allusion is made explicit in the third line by a proper noun, in this case, the title of Qu Yuan's rhyme prose composition. Though the strategy of gradually broadening the hints of allusion and then assuring its recognition with a proper noun in the third line is thus common to both poems, on the level of content, the effect yielded by that strategy is very different. In the poem about Damei, there is a harmony between the intent of the poem, celebration of a former master, and the material alluded to, his biography. In the "muddy *sake*" poem, coming from a monk, the theme of praise for *sake* is unexpected to begin with. Added to that is the incongruity of the allusion to Qu Yuan that gradually becomes apparent in the poem. In Chinese literary rhetoric, it verges on the sacrilegious to make fun of Qu Yuan. This is not to say that it is out of place or fails to work in this particular instance. The jarring quality of the allusion fits the poet's goal in this poem, which is to shock and unsettle the reader, thereby producing laughter. This is the first of many instances where we see Ikkyū using allusion as a vehicle for bringing into the poem something quite opposite or contradictory to the theme apparent on the surface, and thereby creating a dialectical effect.

Arhat Chrysanthemums
羅漢菊 *rakan giku*

茶褐黄花秋色深	*chakatsu no kōka shūshoku fukashi*
東籬風露出塵心	*tōri no fūro shutsujin no kokoro*
天臺五百神通力	*Tendai gohyaku no shintsūriki*
未入淵明一片吟	*imada Enmei no ippen no gin ni irazu*

Tea-brown golden flowers, deep with autumn's color.
Breeze and dew on the east hedge, a heart that has left
    the dust behind.
The miraculous powers of the Five Hundred Arhats
    of Mount Tiantai.
Cannot touch one fragment of verse from Tao Yuanming.
(Poem 77)

We are still dealing with a poem in which only one allusion figures. The title announces a Buddhist subject, chrysanthemums seen as Arhats, that is, monks in the Hinayana tradition. This title raised a question in at least one commentator's mind as to whether there might have actually been a variety of chrysanthemums with that name in the Muromachi period, but the first line provides the answer to that question. It is their color that makes them Arhats, their golden brown color is the same as that of a Hinayana monk's robes. "Breeze and dew on the east hedge" is the key to the allusion. The fifth-century poet Tao Yuanming and chrysanthemums are virtually inseparable in the iconography of Chinese poetry; the expression "east hedge" in a poem on chrysanthemums immediately calls to mind Tao Yuanming's famous line, "Picking chrysanthemums by the east hedge."[77] But why, apart from the chrysanthemum connection, the reference should be made is not yet clear. The next phrase, "a heart that has left the dust behind," is a conventional epithet for Arhat: he who starts on the Path must first leave the dust of the world behind. This phrase is particularly Buddhist in flavor and, therefore, is not an epithet one would normally think of applying to Tao Yuanming, who was many things, but not a Buddhist.[78] For this reason, the allusion to Tao Yuanming remains a small question mark as one proceeds. The next line begins with a grand-sounding Buddhist subject, "The miraculous powers of the Five Hundred Arhats," (we wait the split second in suspense because it is the end of the line) "Cannot touch ... Tao Yuanming." The poem ends with praise for Tao Yuanming and a thumb of the nose for the Arhats.

We have the bringing together of opposites, in this case Buddhist and non-Buddhist. The poem overtly proclaims a Buddhist theme, but the allusion first suggests and then reveals the counter-theme that a pure enlightened heart is more to be found in Tao Yuanming's poetry than in a self-consciously religious Arhat.

Yet, the end result is only mildly dialectical here for two reasons. One is that in the context of Mahayana Buddhism (of which Zen is a part) the term "Arhat" has ambivalent connotations. While meaning "spiritual adept" in general, it also carries a pejorative sense when used specifically to refer to the kind of monk who spurns the world and seeks enlightenment for his own sake alone. This is how Mahayana Buddhism perceived the ultimate goal of practice in the Hinayana Buddhist tradition and, in opposition to that, stressed the Boddhisattva ideal, that is, the enlightened being who immerses himself in the dust of the world in order to save others. To a Mahayana way of thinking, then, the Arhat is fair game for ridicule. Therefore, to say the spirit of Tao Yuanming's poetry is superior to the supernatural powers of Arhats is not contrary to the expectations of Ikkyū's readers. The second and most important element that diminishes the dialectical effect of this poem is that a clear statement has been made. We are in no doubt as to where we stand at the end of the poem. If the reference to Tao Yuanming in the second line was puzzling at first, once the reader gets to the final statement, it is quite comprehensible. One feels, "Yes, of course," rather than being left in a quandary.

The following poem reworks a similar theme in a more dialectical manner.

To Hear a Sound and Awaken to the Way
聞聲悟道 *monshō godō*

擊竹一朝忘所知	*gekichiku itchō shochi o bōzu*
聞鐘五夜絕多疑	*monshō goya tagi o zetsusu*
古人立地皆成佛	*kojin ritchi mina jōbutsu*
淵明端的獨顰眉	*Enmei ga tanteki mayu o hisomu*

Striking bamboo one morning he forgot all he knew.
Hearing the bell at fifth watch, his many doubts vanished.
The ancients all became Buddhas right where they stood.
Tao Yuanming alone just knit his brows.
 (Poem 49)

We have moved up a step in the number of allusions in the poem. Here there are three. "To hear a sound and awaken to the Way" is a standard phrase in Zen that expresses one of the paradoxes beloved by the school. While the senses must be considered obstacles to awakening, it is possible to be awakened to the Way by a sound. This reference encourages the anticipation of a laudatory verse in the same style as the poem about "Big Plum." For the first three lines, one's expectations are satisfied. First comes Xiangyan (ninth century), one of the most famous of the masters enlightened by a sound. One morning, as he was sweeping the garden, the sound of a pebble striking bamboo awakened him. In the words of the *Chuan Deng Lu*, "He forgot all he knew."[79] Then comes Master Fu (ninth century), whose enlightenment by the sound of a bell tolling the fifth watch is recounted in the *Blue Cliff Record*.[80] "The ancients all became Buddhas ..." comes as a kind of summation; if one wonders anything, it is where the poem can go from here. At this point, the name of Tao Yuanming comes as a great surprise. Even when the allusion is recognized, "Ah yes, Tao Yuanming also realized something when he heard a sound—hearing the temple bell, he realized he did not want to become a Buddhist,"[81] a perplexity remains. Is Ikkyū praising or damning? Is he saying Tao Yuanming was the odd man out because he never awakened to the Way? Or is he saying, Tao Yuanming, right where he stood, became a Buddha for not becoming a Buddhist? If he is praising Tao Yuanming, then what of Xiangyan and Master Fu? Were their realizations false? This ambiguity is encouraged by the word rendered "just" in the translation. It can also mean "justly," "correctly," or "rightly so." This second reading would encourage the interpretation that Tao was the only enlightened Buddha of the three, but it is the confusion over which reading to accept which makes the poem engaging. Ikkyū has used the final allusion to unsettle the reader by bringing in something opposed to his expectations.

The poem above has three allusions packed into four lines of verse. The following poem also has three allusions, but two of them occur simultaneously in the same line and phrase.

> Gathering Horse Dung to Cultivate the Mottled Bamboo
> 拾馬糞修斑竹 *bafun o hiroi banchiku o shūsu*
>
> | | |
> |---|---|
> | 煨芋懶殘舊話頭 | *wai'u wa Ranzan no kyū watō* |
> | 不求名利也風流 | *myōri o motomezu mata fūryū* |
> | 相思無隙此君雨 | *sōshi gekinashi shikun no ame* |
> | 拭淚獨吟湘水秋 | *namida o nugu'ute hitori ginzu Shōsui no aki* |
>
> Baked yams is Lancan's old story.
> He did not seek fame and fortune, that too was fūryū.
> Mutual longing without end, This Lord's rain,
> Wiping away the tears, singing alone, autumn by the Xiang river.
> (Poem 493)

The title of this poem brings together the vulgar and the sublime. Bamboo always intimates the sublime in a Sino-Japanese cultural setting; of dung, no more need be said. Yet in practical horticulture (as in Zen), it is salutary that the two be brought together. The first line takes up the theme of dung by alluding to Lancan who baked his yams with dung for fuel.[82] In the original story, the use of dung for fuel is a minor detail which nonetheless adds to the overall earthiness of the account. Here, mention of dung is the link between the title of this poem and the mention of Lancan. The second line develops the material introduced in the first line by making it clear that Lancan stands for uncompromising spiritual integrity. The term "fūryū" here means something between "transcendentally sublime" and "lovely in a rustic way."[83]

"Mutual longing" starts the allusion to the legend about the origin of mottled bamboo. It was said that the splotches on the bamboo stalk were the marks of tears shed by Lord Shun's wives as they waited in vain on the bank of the Xiang river for him to return.[84] The Palace of Mutual Longing is one of the place names on the Xiang river that is associated with Lord Shun's wives. The phrase "mutual longing" followed in the next line by "Xiang river" would immediately suggest the legend to Ikkyū's contemporaries. That is why the reference can be as oblique as it is; it merely suggest the story of Lord Shun's wives and then follows it with another allusion that serves a double purpose. In the context of the mottled bamboo legend, "This Lord" implies Lord Shun for whom the tears that mottled the bamboo were shed. The reader would also recognize it as a term for bamboo, originating in a separate literary source. The source is the *History of the Qin Dynasty*. Therein, Wang Huizhi, when queried why he was planting bamboo even before furnishing his house, replied, "How can I live a day without This Lord?"[85] The statement was such an eloquent expression of the universal sentiment Chinese literati felt toward bamboo that it became an epithet for the plant. "Rain," so often a cliché for tears, binds the two allusions together. "This Lord's rain," an image of rain falling on the bamboo, overlays the sense, "the tears shed on this lord" or "the tears shed for their lord." I suggest that an intended reading of that line registers the two senses and allusions simultaneously. Sensual image and literary reference commingle. The last line continues the allusion to Lord Shun's wives: "tears" and "Xiang river" make the reference explicit. Here, then, is another example of the previously mentioned technique of saving the most explicit reference for the end.

The allusions serve to tell us a great deal about the poet himself in an indirect way. They allow him to be intimately personal without mentioning himself, beyond the title that announces what activity of his occasioned the poem. The reference to Lancan tells us, "When I handle dung, I feel at one with the spirit of Lancan, who turned his back on the world." Line three tells us, "I love bamboo as much as Wang Huizhi, who could not bear to live a day without it, or as much as the two wives loved Lord Shun." Line four implies "In the autumn of my life, I am as lonely as Shun's wives." This, then, is a more complex example of what was found in the first poem of this series, no. 107, namely, use of allusion for indirect expression. The elegant way in which image and literary reference are woven together in line three of this poem also recalls line four of "The Plum Ripened." The various allusions in the "mottled bamboo" are in harmony with the theme of the poem. One might say line three is ambiguous because of the doubling of the sense of "This Lord," referring both to Wang Huizhi's bamboo and to Lord Shun, and because of the layering of the image "rain on the bamboo" over the allusion "tears on the bamboo," but it is ambiguous for aesthetic effect, an elegant confusion, if you will, rather than for the sake of disturbing the reader's sense of meaning. This stands as an example of the complex application of rhetorical allusion.

Now let us look at a poem which stands at the apex of both a hierarchy based on complexity of allusion and one based on intensity of dialectical experience.

雲門示眾云、古佛與露柱相交、是第幾機、自代云、南山起雲、北山下雨。

Yunmen addressed a gathering saying: "The old Buddha and the bare post commune with one another. This is opportunity number what?" Then, answering for himself he said: "On the south mountain, clouds arise; on the north mountain, it rains."

小姑緣底嫁彭郎	Shōko nani ni yotte ka Hōrō ni kasu
雲雨今宵夢一場	un'u koyoi yume ichijō
朝在天臺暮南嶽	ashita ni Tendai ni ari kure ni Nangaku
不知何處見韶陽	shirazu izure no tokoro ni ka Shōyō o min

How did the Little Bride marry Master Peng?
Cloud-rain, tonight, a single dream.
In the morning at Tiantai, in the evening at Nanyue,
No one knows where to see Shaoyang.
(Poem 45)

The introduction to this poem is the quotation of a kōan by the Tang monk Yunmen (d. 949).[86] In this kōan, two phenomena which are quite unrelated interact, and the audience is asked into what sort of category can this be placed. The question is not so interesting when shorn of its imagery. The picture of an old Buddha statue having a conversation with a bare post is much more stimulating to the imagination and, as such, very important to the poem.

Yunmen deigns to answer his own question. He does so by ignoring the demand to categorize, and merely presents another case where two seemingly unrelated phenomena interact. How can clouds on the south side of the mountain make it rain on the north side? It is a restatement of the original question posing as an answer in the form of a declarative sentence.

Another question, "How did the Little Bride marry Master Peng?", opens the poem. "The Little Bride" is a small island in the Yangzi river; "Master Peng" is a large boulder on the south bank of the Yangzi. How did these two features of the Chinese landscape, unrelated but for a spatial proximity, come to be married? Thus we have another restatement of the philosophical question broached in the kōan. The mention of marriage cues a suggestion that something else might have gone on between the old Buddha and the bare post besides simple conversation. The word translated as "communes with" can also mean to "have relations with" in the sexual sense. If the mention of marriage only barely suggests that, then the next line in which "cloud-rain" and "dream" figure renders it obvious.

"Cloud-rain" is a euphemism for physical love that originates in a passage from the "Gaotang Fu" by Song Yu. The wording of the passage becomes important to the interpretation of the third line.

> Long ago, a former king was amusing himself at Gaotang. Feeling weary, he slept and in a dream he saw a woman. She said, "I am the woman of Wushan, 'Sorceress Mountain,' and a guest at Gaotang. I heard you were visiting Gaotang and wish to serve at your pillow. The King thereupon favored her. When she rose to leave, she said, "I dwell on the south slope of Wushan and the Steeps of Gaoqiu. In the morning, I am the cloud, in the evening, I am the rain; morning upon morning, evening upon evening beneath Yangtai." In the morning, the King saw it was as she said and so he constructed a temple and called it "Morning Cloud."[87]

"Cloud-rain" furthermore signals that the poet takes the cloud and rain in the original kōan in an erotic sense. The kōan as a whole takes on a ribald cast, and one is left to imagine what the old Buddha was doing to the bare post or vice versa that could produce cloud and rain.

Line three runs all the elements of the poem together through a maze of allusion. "In the morning…," because of the preparation of line two, now immediately brings to mind the Gaotang passage, "In the morning, I am the cloud, in the evening, I am the rain." The poet's erotic interpretation of the kōan becomes clear beyond doubt. But then one's sense of where the poem is going is jolted by the appearance of Tiantai, the name of a mountain sacred to Buddhism as the seat of the Tiantai school. The erotic turn the poem had been taking is halted momentarily. "In the evening" reestablishes it because it reminds us of "In the evening, I am the rain," but then the mention of Nanyue takes us back to a more religious atmosphere. It is the name of another mountain sacred to Buddhism, the home of the monk Huisi, teacher of Zhiyi, founder of the Tiantai school. Tiantai and Nanyue are thus related; they represent two mountains and two people, one the master, the other the disciple. But what do they mean here? Hirano sees this line as related to a remark that appears in the *Xutang Lu*. There a monk, in reply to the question "What do you do when you cannot say anything?" says, "If I am not at Tiantai, I shall be at Nanyue."[88] Yanagida, on the other hand, sees it as an allusion to two other sayings of Yunmen's:

> In the morning, I arrive at the Western Heaven (India),
> In the evening, I return to the Land in the East (China).
>
> In the morning, I sport at Dandaka (a mountain in India).
> In the evening, I arrive at Luofu (a mountain in China).[89]

These both refer to the self-sufficiency and supernatural powers of an enlightened sage. Then Yanagida, in his interpretative commentary to this poem, suggests that Ikkyū may have been making a connection between Yunmen's kōan and a kōan of Master Daitō. It will be remembered that Master Daitō was an important patriarch in Ikkyū's lineage. Daitō was enlightened by the act of understanding a kōan of Yunmen's and was credited by his teacher with being a reincarnation of Yunmen. The kōan of Daitō's that Ikkyū may have in mind here is what became known as the "Three-Pivot Phrases of Daitō":

In the morning, entwining eyebrows, in the evening, shoulder to shoulder, how about me? The bare post exhausts the day coming and going. Why is it, I do not move?[90]

The "bare post" surfaces again, and there appears another variation of "In the morning … In the evening" that can also be interpreted in an erotic way. Are we looking at another possible source of allusion? Is Ikkyū alluding to Daitō who is alluding to Yunmen? The last line closes this poem with "No one knows where to see Shaoyang (Shaoyang is another name for Yunmen).[91]

In this sequence of kōan and poem, questions have been answered with questions, distinctions between sacred and profane have been blurred, and allusions have been cross-referenced to the point of confusion. It is this kind of poem that has earned Ikkyū's poetry a reputation for difficulty. While teasing with the logic of question and answer, it frustrates comprehension in a logical manner. But, as one reads it, one experiences a marvelous melting together of separate categories of thought. The focal point for the fusion is the enigmatic third line. It is impossible to distill a "meaning" out of that line. Through a welter of allusions, it brings together the sacred and profane, the King and the sorceress, masters and disciples, Tiantai and Nanyue, Yunmen and Daitō; if one follows the trail of allusion as far as Daitō's kōan, even the old Buddha and the bare post are there. There is some familiar ground here. Once again, it is the allusion that brings the unconventional, the opposite of what one expects, into the poem. Also the way in which "In the morning … In the evening" has two or possibly three referents reminds one of how in poem 493 "This Lord" refers to Lord Shun and to Wang Huizhi's bamboo. It is just that here the density of possible allusions has been magnified until one loses track of where they end. Ikkyū wants his reader to lose track of where he is. Here, the allusions are vehicles for running the poem off the dualistic rails of rational consciousness.

The preceding analyses were meant to demonstrate the specific functioning of allusion in individual poems; however, the last poem raises a general problem. The cited commentators differed in their opinions as to the sources of the allusion. All commentators, the present author included, base their opinions on assumptions regarding what works Ikkyū and his audience were familiar with, but even within those perimeters, there is much room for differences of opinion and even error. One may over-read; similarity between a phrase appearing in Ikkyū's poetry and one appearing in another may be purely coincidental. Sometimes, one may miss an allusion, and, given the crucial role allusion often plays, this will hamper one's understanding of a poem.

Part of the difficulty stems from the nature of allusion itself which is, after all, to refer covertly. Some ambiguity and obscurity are inevitable. For example, in the last poem, there is justification for all the commentators' suggestions. Precisely which source Ikkyū had in mind (and it need not have been only one) is unknowable. However, the unknowability does not frustrate in this instance because each of the commentators' views enrich our perception.

This leads us to another aspect of the interpretation of Ikkyū's poetry in general terms as well as with specific regard to allusion, namely that a certain amount of subjectivity will necessarily be present in the commentator's appreciation. Any work of literature requires some participation of the reader's imagination; works which revel in multiple meanings require even more than usual. As a result of all this, we must simply accept the uncertainty and feeling of hidden meanings that allusions bring to these poems. Indeed, these qualities have a poetic function themselves.

An analogy may be drawn here to the way some modern poets use allusion, particularly T.S. Eliot in "The Waste Land." Eliot refers to a large number of sources; quotes from Shakespeare, the Bible, Verlaine, and the Upanishads rub shoulders. The juxtaposition of their original context and the new context in the poem give rise to mixed and unsettled feelings in the reader. Furthermore, it is not necessary to recognize all the allusions nor know precisely what they stand for. Along with compelling images, they become symbols with no definite referents; they summon up the indefinable.

Similarly, Ikkyū uses allusions in unexpected contexts. The meanings of the allusions are often multifaceted and ambiguous. It appears Ikkyū would prevent his reader from easily understanding his poems. Rather, his poems induce questioning.

Nonetheless, one difference between Eliot and Ikkyū with respect to allusion is the underlying message it carries. In "The Waste Land," use of the technique emphasizes the disintegration of culture in the modern world; as he says, "These fragments I have shored against my ruins,"[92] a sense of profound disturbance and despair underlies the work. While Ikkyū's employment of allusion is often disturbing, its ultimate purpose is to short-circuit ratiocination, to knock the mind out of dualistic habits. Underlying this is a sense of wholeness existing necessarily beyond duality.

A Note on the Text and Its Organization

The majority of the poems translated here are from the two-volume edition of the *Kyōunshū* in the *Ikkyū Oshō zenshū* (IZ). Like most modern editions, it is based on the Okumura manuscript, the most superior of all the extant manuscripts for the *Kyōunshū*. A holograph indicating that it was compiled under Ikkyū's direction and Ikkyū's handwriting in two places verify that it is the earliest manuscript. Moreover, it contains the largest number of poems (881) and the fewest copier's errors.[93] The numbers assigned to the translations are the numbers of the poems as they appear in IZ and therefore represent the order of the poems in the Okumura manuscript. A few of the poems come from other sources such as the *Nenpu* or inscriptions on paintings and are so noted. The *Ikkyū Tokushū* collected all poems available in extant manuscripts and reached a total of 1,060. When a poem was only available in *Ikkyū Tokushū*, it is noted and given the number in the *Tokushū*.

The 881 poems of the IZ *Kyōunshū* edition are divided into three sections: a first part comprising 678 poems which are, for the most part, on religious themes and designated as *ge* "religious odes," a second part of 49 *gō*, poems that commemorate names Ikkyū bestowed upon his disciples, and a third part bearing the section heading *shi* "poems." The *shi* designation distinguishes it from the *ge* "religious odes." The difference is content determined; *ge* are expected to treat religious subjects and *shi* secular topics. In formal respects they are the same.[94] The division is not absolute. Many poems in the *shi* section have Zen themes, some poems in the *ge* section seem more secular than religious. Nonetheless, the vast majority of poems in the anthology have some connection with Zen. Occasionally, there are sequences of poems under the same title, which form a unit and often reveal an internal order of progression. One such series is the four poems on "Rinzai's Four Propositions," nos. 13, 14, 15, and 16. There are also series of poems that do not share a title but appear to have been written around the same time and form an autobiographical narrative. This sporadic occurrence of poems that can be dated to events in the poet's biography reveals a loose chronological order underlying the anthology. While the majority of poems cannot be dated, those that can generally fit a chronological order.

In the translation section, the selected poems are kept in the same order as in the anthology. Despite the gaps, keeping the poems in the original order creates an impression of randomness punctuated by occasional sequences of related poems, quite akin to the effect of the anthology as a whole. Such an order lends a serendipitous quality to the reading experience; each poem tends to unexpected.

A mixture of objective and subjective considerations have determined the selection of poems for translation. On the objective side, the concern has been to make the selection as representative as possible. This work endeavors to adequately reflect the range of subject matter, tones, and treatments in the original *Anthology*. On the subjective side, personal predilection has guided the choice. For whatever reasons, either related to content or mode of expression, certain poems have radiated a charm. One always wants to translate poems one likes; moreover, they seem easier to translate. That brings up a third consideration in which both the subjective and objective perspectives conjoin: namely, judgment as to whether the poems translate well into English or not. Generalizations are difficult to apply here, for, in actuality, it is a case-by-case decision. However, it often has to do with the presence of a certain simplicity. Paradoxically, this can occur in very complex poems. Take for example Poem 44, certainly one of the most convoluted poems in the translation section. Yet, the third line of that poem, "One, two, three; ah! three, two, one" slips so easily into English and conveys in a very concrete way the mirror image quality of duality that is so crucial to that poem. The presence of even one line as felicitous as this in a poem makes it a likely candidate for translation.

The translations are accompanied by notes which indicate the sources of allusion, identify proper names, explain special terms, and upon occasion provide interpretation. An effort has also been made to include the opinions of the Japanese commentators Hirano Sōjō,[95]

Yanagida Seizan,[96] and Kageki Hideo[97] where they seemed especially revelatory. The uneven distribution of the commentary is due to the nature of the poems themselves. Some need extensive commentary; some are self-explanatory, and others defy explanation although they remain powerful in their obscurity. Despite their length in individual cases, these commentaries should not be considered exhaustive. The intention has been to include only that material which truly aids appreciation.

Translations from the Crazy Cloud Anthology

Poem 6

Face to Face with the Beautiful One on the Eve of Daitō's Commemoration Ceremony

大燈忌宿忌以前對美人 *Daitō ki shukuki izen bijin ni taisu*

宿忌之開山諷經　　*shukuki no kaizan fugin*
經呪逆耳衆僧聲　　*kyōjū mimi ni sakarau shusō no koe*
雲雨風流事終後　　*un'u fūryū koto owatte ato*
夢閨私語笑慈明　　*Mukei shigo Jimyō o warau*

They are intoning the sutras on the eve of the Founder's ceremony,
The incantation grates on my ears, voices of many monks.
Cloud-rain, fūryū, after it is over,
Mukei in intimate conversation laughs at Ciming.

Notes
the Beautiful One: The word used here, *bijin*, most often means a beautiful woman, but from Qu Yuan on it has been common for Chinese poets to petition the ruler as though he were a lover. "The Beautiful One" may be none other than Daitō himself

Daitō: (1282–1337) Founder of Daitokuji and thus also of the Zen lineage to which Ikkyū belonged. (See pp. 13–14.)

Commemoration Ceremony: Special ceremonies were performed to honor the spirit of important deceased monks within the lineage. This occasion may have been the ceremony for the one-hundredth anniversary commemorating Daitō in 1436.

incantation: When Chinese sutras are chanted by Japanese monks, due to the excess of homophones, they are not understandable to the listeners. They are to all intents and purpose the incantation of magical but meaningless syllables.

Cloud-rain: Euphemism for sensual love originating in the legendary parting words of the Wushan Goddess to the King, her lover, "In the morning, I am the cloud; in the evening, I am the rain." (See pp. 48–50.)

fūryū: This very difficult term to translate is one of the most frequently occurring expressions in the *Anthology*. It has several different meanings therein, not to mention the many meanings it has had in the hands of other poets in other times.[1] Its component characters are *fū*, "wind," and *ryū*, "stream" or "to flow." If we concentrate on the different meanings of fūryū that appear in these selected translations, three meanings can be singled out. The first is the beauty of a simple rustic life. Fishermen, woodcutters, anyone living far away from the artificiality and compromise of the vulgar busy world epitomizes this kind of beauty. (See poem 216.)

The second meaning of fūryū found often in the *Anthology* is still a variation on the idea of beautiful and good but with erotic or, at least, romantic connotations. This is its sense in the poem at hand. The poem entitled "Night Conversation in the Dream Chamber" (poem 545) presents another good example of that usage. Perhaps the difficulty of translating fūryū stems from the fact that it really has very little "meaning" but a wealth of connotation depending on the context in which it appears.

This leads to the third way in which the term is used, which is as a slang word with virtually no meaning at all but powerful connotations that escape neat definition. The closest equivalent in English is "far out," itself slightly passé slang. It is characteristic of slang that one needs to acquire a feeling for what it means in order to understand it. It is true of slang what Louis Armstrong said in response to the question, "What is jazz?" "If you have to ask, you'll never know." Fūryū obviously expresses approval, but when one tries to specify the grounds for that approval, one is in the mental quicksand of the kōans. In poem 52, for example, an adept having passed the kōan would know why Zhaozhou's leaving with his sandals on his head was both so appropriate and amazing—in other words, "far out." Poem 140 is a similar case. Sometimes, usages overlap, as in poem 493 (p. 46), where Ikkyū applies it to Lancan. Lancan's not seeking fame and fortune as the act of a "free spirit" was "far out," yet the picture of him roasting his potatoes in the open air is also fūryū in the rustic sense. Fūryū has been left without translation in the hope that the reader will acquire a feeling for the word as it is used in different contexts.

Mukei: "Dream Chamber," a sobriquet that Ikkyū used later in life. (See poems 820–823.)

Ciming: (987–1040) Two of his students went on to found important schools of Zen. The Daitokuji lineage traces itself back to Yangqi, one of those pupils. Ciming is known for being a monk of ferocious discipline. For example, one story about him stabbing himself in the thigh to keep awake for meditation is still used to encourage students of Zen during long *zazen* sessions. However, in Ikkyū's personal mythology, Ciming had quite a different image. Whenever Ikkyū thought of Ciming, he thought of him tripping out to meet his "old woman" who lived just outside the gate to the monastery. The source for this view of Ciming is unclear, but Yanagida has suggested one early Zen history which mentions that Ciming installed his mother in a cottage outside the gate of the monastery to be able to care for her. Somehow, when this story came into Japan, Ciming's "mother" had been transformed into a comely woman.[2] A kōan based on an exchange between Ciming and Yangqi contributed to the misinterpretation. Yangqi asked Ciming, "If two people meet on a narrow path, what happens?" Ciming said, "You back up and I'll go over there."[3] Narrow path has been understood to mean a narrow alley of a brothel district and hence the amorous aura that came to surround Ciming. Certainly there is no doubt that in Ikkyū's private mythology he was a lusty old man with a woman just outside the gate.

This poem has always been held up as one of the most flagrant examples of Ikkyū's "wild fox" brand of Zen. The poet seems to declare that while the other monks were piously chanting the sutras, he was making love with a beautiful woman, laughing at Ciming who had to go outside the temple to meet his woman. Even as an attack against the empty formality of ritual, it appears to go too far. No one seems to have doubted that the poem should be taken literally.

Yanagida refutes that assumption. In a brilliant exposition of this poem, he puts forth the thesis that the theme of this poem is entirely the spiritual intimacy Ikkyū felt for Daitō, the founding patriarch of his monastery.[4] The poem challenges the monks caught up in the formal expressions of respect for

Daitō. It says, "While you mouth incantations you don't understand, I have been sitting face to face with the founder at one with his spirit." Yanagida points out how certain phrases in the overtly erotic vocabulary link up with utterances of Daitō's. For example, the phrase, "face to face" recalls Daitō's "Separated for an eternity, they are not apart for a second; face to face all day, they are not face to face for a second." Even the cloud in "cloud-rain" may be seen as an allusion to Daitō since he was thought of as a reincarnation of Yunmen, literally "Cloud-gate." Also, we have seen a poem in the section on allusion where Daitō and Yunmen, cloud and rain, have all been conjured into one.

Yet, if most people have been led astray by this poem, then the poet intended it so. The erotic suggestion is very strong; he did not want the allegorical interpretation to be obvious. Were there no ambiguity, it would not challenge the reader as it does. Moreover, Yanagida's thesis about the allegorical intent of the poem has come at just the right time, for it has become too easy for modern audiences to accept the fact that Ikkyū might have been making love with someone while a commemoration ceremony was going on. His thesis forces us to re-evaluate not only this poem but all the others where iconoclasm is achieved through erotic suggestion. Thus, it furthers what might be called the dialectic of interpretation.

Poem 7

Praising Monk Xutang

贊虛堂和尚 *Kidō Oshō o sansu*

育王住院世皆乖　　*Ikuō Shūin yo mina somuku*
放下法衣如破鞋　　*hōe o hōgeshite hoai no gotoshi*
臨濟正傳無一點　　*Rinzai no shōden itten nashi*
一天風月滿吟懷　　*itten no fūgetsu ginkai ni mitsu*

The Master of Yuwang turned his back on the whole world.
He abandoned his monk's robe as though it were a broken sandal.
Of Rinzai's Correct Transmission, not a jot;
Whole heaven clear, wind and moon fill a singing heart.

Notes:

Monk Xutang: (1185–1269) The Chinese patriarch in the Daitokuji lineage, since he was the master to instruct Daiō. Ikkyū felt a special affinity for Xutang, often signing himself as the "Seventh-Generation Descendant of Xutang." Later in his life, because of dreams his followers had upon the installation of a portrait of Xutang at Shūon'an, it came to be believed that Ikkyū was a reincarnation of Xutang. What seemed to impress Ikkyū most about the man was his independent stance with respect to monastic and state authority. At one point late in his life, his defiance of authority actually resulted in his imprisonment. His death poem gives a hint of the personality Ikkyū admired:

> Eighty-five years
> Knowing nothing even about the Patriarchs,
> Rowing with my elbow, serving, going,
> Erasing my tracks in the Great Void.[5]

Yuwang: A mountain monastery where Xutang was abbot after 1258.

Poem 8

On the Topic of *The Venerable Master Daitō's Conduct*

題大燈國師行狀末 *Daitō Kokushi no gyōjō matsu ni daisu*

挑起大燈輝一天	*Daitō o kakage okoshite itten o kagayakasu*
鸞輿競譽法堂前	*ranyo homare o kisou hōdō no mae*
風餐水宿無人記	*fūkin suishuku hito no kisuru nashi*
第五橋邊二十年	*daigokyōhen nijūnen*

Raise high the Great Lamp, let it light the whole sky.
The phoenix carriages compete in praise before the
    Dharma Hall.
Wind-eating, water-dwelling; no one records
The twenty years he spent around Gojō Bridge.

Notes:

Daitō: See pp. 13–14 and note to poem 6.
The Venerable Master Daitō's Conduct: The title of a book written by a contemporary of Ikkyū. Ikkyū was offended by the absence of any mention of the hardships Daitō endured.
the Great Lamp: A literal translation of Daitō's name.
phoenix carriages: The vehicles of the rich and powerful.
Wind-eating, water-dwelling: conventional phrase describing the life of a beggar.
Gojō Bridge: Fifth Avenue Bridge in Kyoto, long a haven for beggars and other cast-offs of society. After recognizing Daitō's enlightenment, Daiō told him not to set about teaching right away but to nurture his understanding in obscurity for twenty years. This he did by living in a small hermitage close to Gojō Bridge. The term "twenty years" appears often in Zen texts meaning an extended period of training. It need not be taken literally.

Rinzai's Four Propositions—four poems

臨濟四料簡　四首 *Rinzai no shiryōken—yonshu*

Poem 13

Take Away the Person Without Taking Away the Environment

奪人不奪境 *datsunin fudatsukyō*

百丈溈山名未休	*Hyakujō Isan na imada kyūsezu*
野狐身與水牯牛	*yakoshin to suikogyū*
前朝古寺無僧住	*zenchō no koji sō no jūsuru nashi*
黃葉秋風共一樓	*kōyō shūfū tomo ni ichirō*

Baizhang, Weishan, names not yet laid to rest,
Wild fox body and water buffalo bull.
In the old temples of former dynasties, no monks dwell,
Yellow leaves and autumn wind share a single pavilion.

Poem 14

Take Away the Environment Without Taking Away the Person

奪境不奪人 *datsukyō budatsunin*

臨濟兒孫誰的傳	*Rinzai no jison dare ka tekiden*
宗風滅却瞎驢邊	*shūfū mekkyakusu katsuro hen*
芒鞋竹杖風流友	*bōai chikujō fūryū no tomo*
曲㮈木床名利禪	*kyokuroku mokushō myōri no zen*

Who among Rinzai's descendants got the transmission?
The teaching perished with a blind donkey.
Straw sandals, bamboo staff are friends of fūryū,
Ornately carved chairs betoken the Zen of fame and gain.

Poem 15

Take Away Both Person and Environment

人境俱奪 *ninkyō gudatsu*

雉翳亀焦身迍邅	*chiei kishō mi chunten*
幷汾絶信話頭円	*Hei Fun shin o zetsushite watō madokanari*
夜來滅却詩人興	*yarai mekkyakusu shijin no kyō*
桂折秋風白露前	*kei wa oru shūfū hakuro no mae*

Pheasant gone to cover, tortoise scorched, one is obstructed.
All word cut off from Bing and Fen, the story is complete.
Night comes extinguishing the poet's inspiration,
The cinnamon tree lies broken before autumn wind
    and white dew

Poem 16

Take Away Neither Person nor Environment

人境俱不奪 *ninkyō gufudatsu*

莫道再來錢半文	*iukoto nakare sairai zeni hanmon to*
婬坊酒肆有功勲	*inbō shūshi ni kōkun ari*
祇緣人話相如渇	*tada hito no shōjo ga katsu o kataru ni yotte*
腸斷琴臺日暮雲	*chō wa danzu kindai nippo no kumo*

Don't say, "That comeback's not worth half a copper,"
Brothels and wine shops have their own merit,
It is just for that people tell of Xiangru's thirst,
Heartrending, the zither terrace, clouds at sunset.

Notes:
Rinzai's Four Propositions: These four poems are responses to a teaching of Rinzai (Linji) that came to be known as "Rinzai's Four Propositions." They have been interpreted as Rinzai's elaboration of the Indian formula of logic called *catuṣkoṭikâ* otherwise known as the "tetralemma" or "four-fold negation," the stages of which can be summarized as: affirmation, negation, both affirmation and negation, neither affirmation nor negation. Rinzai complicates the development of this logical pattern by introducing two terms, literally 人 *nin* "person" and 境 *kyō* "environment," into each stage of the formula. In the *Rinzai Roku* (*Linji Lu*) Rinzai frames his propositions as "Sometimes, one takes away the person without taking away the environment," and so on implying that these are four ways of perceiving reality. When Rinzai was asked what each of the four statements meant, he answered with poetic couplets.[6] Paul Demiéville translates the two terms at their most abstract level of possible signification as "subject" and "object." Ruth Sasaki translates them as "person" and "surroundings." Didier Davin, in an article entirely devoted to the background and interpretation of these four poems, cites evidence that during the medieval and Tokugawa periods, Rinzai monks understood "person" to represent ordinary, shallow, and biased understanding, while "environment" represented wise, deep, and universal understanding.[7] In other words, both terms were understood to refer to states of consciousness. Nonetheless, three of Ikkyū's poems end with concrete natural images, so I would argue that Ikkyū's interpretation of the term

kyō included a sense of the natural environment. Accordingly, I have opted to translate the two terms as "person" and "environment."

[13]

Baizhang: Baizhang Huaihai (720–814) An early Zen master in the Rinzai school lineage, famous for drawing up the first set of monastic rules designed particularly for Zen communities in which the cardinal rule was: "A day of no work is a day of no eating."
Weishan: Weishan Lingyu (777–852) A student of Baizhang.
Wild fox body: Reference to "Baizhang's wild fox" kōan. See introduction p. 30 for a translation of the episode. Baizhang's pronouncement that the enlightened person does not "ignore karma" liberates a being who had been reincarnated five hundred times as a wild fox for having declared that the enlightened man does not fall into the chains of karma when he was a teacher on the same mountain years ago.
water buffalo bull: Weishan's kōan in which he imagines a water buffalo showing up a hundred years later with Weishan's name on its flank. He challenges his students to declare whether the creature is a buffalo or Weishan. See introduction pp. 17–18.

[14]

teaching perished with a blind donkey: Just before he died, Rinzai asked his follower Sansheng what he would say when people later on asked about Rinzai's teaching. Sansheng gave a shout in the style of his teacher, whereupon Rinzai said, "Who would have thought that my True Dharma Eye would perish with this blind donkey!"[8] Ikkyū took "Blind Donkey" as the name for his hermitage in the city from this story.
straw sandals, bamboo staff: Symbols of an itinerant life.
fūryū: Here meaning something close to enlightened consciousness. See notes to poem 6.
Ornate carved chairs: Elaborately carved chairs provided a seat of honor for presiding masters at lectures and ceremonies at temples. Formal portraits of Zen masters both in China and Japan show them seated in such chairs. There are several portraits of Ikkyū seated in just such a chair.

[15]

Pheasant gone to cover: No definite source has been identified for this expression and the present translation is forced. The second character refers more likely to a blind used for hunting pheasants. Davin cites a possible source in a story about a hunter who became so angry at missing his pheasant that he destroyed his blind. Davin concludes that although the exact source is uncertain, it is clear that the expression is intended to convey frustration with hitting one's target,[9] so, I have taken liberties with the translation to suggest that.

tortoise scorched: Refers to the ancient Chinese practice of applying hot irons to tortoise shells and ox scapula in order to divine the future from the cracks thus formed.

one is obstructed: This may be an allusion to *Zhun* 迍 "Birth Throes," Hexagram 3 of the *Yijing*, particularly the commentary to the second *yin* line in the hexagram which speaks of impasse in the throes of birth. Davin, however, has made the intriguing suggestion that Ikkyū may actually have taken this expression from the one of the Chinese rhyming dictionaries available to him. Davin surmises that Ikkyū's process of composition probably involved coming up with one line ending in a rhyme word, and then trolling a rhyme dictionary to seek possible endings for the other two lines required to rhyme. Both dictionaries that Davin mentions as candidates for dictionaries available to Ikkyū cite this same example from the *Yijing* for the word 迍 *ten*, "impasse, obstruction."[10]

Bing and Fen: Names of two commanderies that rebelled and cut themselves off from the Tang dynasty. Rinzai mentioned them in the couplet he offered as an illustration of this proposition:

> "Bing and Fen are cut off from news,
> Isolated, each in their corner."[11]

[16]

"*That comeback's not worth half a copper*": Both Hirano and Davin identify this as an allusion to Yuan Wu's sub-commentary to the first kōan in the *Blue Cliff Record*.[12] The kōan tells of Bodhidharma's arrival in China when he was interviewed by Emperor Wu of the Liang dynasty (r. 503–549), who was known for endowing many monasteries and commissioning devotional statuary. Emperor Wu asks, "What is the cardinal meaning of the holy truth?" Bodhidharma replies, "Vast emptiness, no holiness." Emperor Wu, puzzled, inquires, "Who are you?" Bodhidharma responds, "I don't know." At which point, Yuan Wu's sub-commentary appears to mock Bodhidharma with: "Bah! That comeback's not worth half a copper."[13] The point is that this line invokes the very beginning of the Zen tradition and places the discourse of the poem within the slippery rhetoric of the kōan.

Brothels and wine bars: Hirano and Davin identify this as an allusion to a story handed down about the three places Buddha's disciple Mañjuśrī spent his summer retreat.[14] Although the story has an earlier antecedent, Davin cites its rendering in the *Chanlin Leiju* as the version Ikkyū would have known. In the presence of Buddha, another disciple, Mahākāśyapa, asks Mañjuśrī where he spent the three months of the summer retreat. Mañjuśrī replies that he spent one month at Jetavana temple, one month at a boy's school, and one month in "brothels and wine shops." Mahākāśyapa chides him for staying the last month in places "out of accord with the dharma" and requests permission from the Buddha to censure Mañjuśrī, to which the Buddha replies, "Do as you wish." But when Mahākāśyapa takes up the mallet to sound the wooden block summoning the assembly for the chastisement, suddenly one hundred thousand trillion images of Mañjuśrī appear, and even exhausting all his supernatural powers, Mahākāśyapa is unable to raise the mallet. The Buddha then asks him, "Which of these Mañjuśrī do you plan to censure?" Mahākāśyapa had no answer.[15] Here, then, is a foundational story in Buddhism that interrogates easy assumptions about the holy and profane.

Xiangru's thirst: Sima Xiangru (178–117 BCE) has a substantial biography in the *Records of the Grand Historian* (*Shiji*). He was famous as a poet of *fu*, a long form noted for extravagant expression and flights of lyricism. The episode from his life that achieved legendary status was the story of his marriage to Wenjun, the daughter of wealthy Zhuo Wangsun. It happened when Xiangru was out of office and living on the charity of a friend. He was invited to a banquet at the Zhuo residence. Xiangru knew of the recently widowed daughter Wenjun and that she loved music. Persuaded to play the zither upon which he was known to be a master, he poured his heart into his music in order to win hers. Wenjun fell so deeply in love with him at first sight, that she eloped with him that very night to Xiangru's hometown, Chengdu. Wenjun's father was enraged and refused to give his daughter even "a copper." This mention of small coin in the account links Xiangru's story to the first line in the poem. Life in Chengdu was not easy because Xiangru's home had become "four bare walls with nothing inside." The couple moved again and borrowing money from her relatives opened a wine shop. Wenjun minded the counter and Xiangru in workman's loincloth "ran errands … or washed wine vessels at the well in the market place." The romantic notion of a talented literary gentlemen adapting to such lowly circumstances with seeming enjoyment impressed generations of readers in the

Chinese cultural sphere. Eventually, Wenjun's father was shamed into settling a proper dowery on his daughter and Xiangru's official career rebounded with the growing fame of his poetry. His later career included literary and political achievements, but none of them captured the popular imagination to the degree of his winning Wenjun with playing the zither and cheerfully taking up a bar owner's life. Xiangru is also recorded to have suffered from the disease of "thirst," now assumed to have been diabetes, which afforded him the excuse to "live a life of retirement" from a relatively young age.[16]

With each poem, this set increases in the density and multi-faceted quality of meaning. A recapitulation of the poems and their relation to each other and "Rinzai's Four Propositions" may be of use here.

The first poem calls up two Zen masters who have been taken away as "persons" by time and who, in their recorded teachings, raised the issue of reincarnation from human to animal form, another way in which "person" is taken away. This, in turn, raises the large question in Buddhism of what is reincarnated if the self is an illusion. The question remains ultimately unanswered and perhaps unanswerable; as Weishan intimates in his own answer to the conundrum he set his followers, "If you say, 'What is it?,' then you get it." Thus, three ways in which "person" can be taken away are broached. Whereupon the viewpoint of the poem pans out to consider the vicissitudes of history during which temples may be built and later emptied of their people, their buildings left to be inhabited by what does endure, the natural environment as represented by the passing of the seasons and the movement of air.

The second poem in accordance with not taking away "person" dwells on subjectivity, in this case the transmission of wisdom, the very foundation of the Zen tradition, the transmission of mind to mind beyond words. It also deals with value judgments. Always, when cogitating human beings are in the foreground, deciding what is right, what is wrong, is important. A free spirit wandering around with empty pockets is good; richly endowed temples are bad. Who did get the correct transmission from Rinzai? Did it perish with that blind donkey as Rinzai himself predicted? Or was the blind donkey the one with real understanding? So often in Zen rhetoric, damnation is delivered with faint praise and praise offered as mocking condemnation. And, as for the natural environment, it has simply been left out of this poem.

The third poem illustrates a thorough-going negation. All human efforts, whether to hit a target or second-guess the future are for naught. Political order, one form of the collective subjectivity of human beings, is broken. Even poetic inspiration is exhausted. The natural world lies wasted too, broken by autumn storms, and withered by cold dew. One can see this poem as an expression of the first noble truth of Buddhism: "Life is suffering." Nothing escapes sickness, aging, and death. It is the negative statement of the truth of reality.

The fourth poem runs the "neither affirmation nor negation" position through a labyrinth of allusions that encompass the beginning of Zen with Bodhidharma's arrival in China, the interrogation of ordinary assumptions about morality, and the beguilement of romance as it has been played out in human lives like that of Xiangru over millennia. The fourth line begins with a phrase that occurs often in Ikkyū's poetry, literally "tearing the guts," but it can be used to express the feeling of having your breath taken away by the beauty of something. Or it can express unbearable sadness, gut-wrenching pain. Or, it can express both at the same time, which is what I think it does here. We are left to imagine Xiangru suffering from thirst but playing the zither marvellously on a terrace accompanied not only by his beloved but by a symphony of colour in the sunset clouds. We are left in the moment, the only place ever to be.

I have advanced this running interpretation of the four poems in the spirit of offering one possible entry to their appreciation but aware that Rinzai would likely shout in derision, not to mention the possible reactions a modern textual scholar of careful philological disposition. I only hope Ikkyū would laugh indulgently.

Poem 17

Straw-Sandal Chen

陳蒲鞋 *Chin ho'ai*

賣弄諸人瞞諸方　　*shonin o mairōshi shohō o azamuku*
德山臨濟沒商量　　*Tokuzan Rinzai motsu shōryō*
拈槌竪拂非吾事　　*nentsui juhotsu waga koto ni arazu*
只要聲名屬北堂　　*tada yōsu seimei no hokudō ni zokusen koto o*

> Putting on a sales pitch to the people, out dealing them
>   right and left.
> Deshan and Rinzai have no way to haggle.
> Wielding the stick and raising the fly whisk are not for me.
> My fame need only belong to the north hall.

Notes:
Straw-Sandal Chen: (780–877) A monk who returned to lay life after achieving enlightenment and took up the occupation of making straw sandals in order to support himself and his aged mother. He was thus an example of a gainfully employed and filial Zen adept. Ikkyū imagines him to be a skillful flogger of his wares.
Deshan: (780–865) Tang master noted for his use of the stick in Zen training. "Thirty blows if you can answer, thirty blows if you can't answer"[17] sums up his style of teaching.
Rinzai: (d. 866; Ch. Linji) Founder of the Rinzai school of Zen to which Ikkyū belonged.
Wielding the stick and raising the fly whisk: The motions of teaching formalized Zen.
north hall: Traditionally the part of the house where women resided, hence a reference to Chen's mother.

The intrusion of the first person pronoun in the third line renders the poem slightly ambiguous. Either Chen is speaking in quotation or Ikkyū is speaking of himself. Some commentators have interpreted the last line as a veiled reference to Ikkyū's own mother.

Xutang's Three Pivot Phrases—three poems

虛堂和尚三轉語　三首 *Kidō Oshō santengo—sanshu*

Poem 25

One's Eyes Are Not Yet Clear; How Is It That You Make Trousers to Wear Out of Empty Air?

己眼未明底因甚將虛空作布袴着

畫餅冷腸飢未盈	gabyō reichō ue imada mitazu
娘生己眼見如盲	jōshō no kogan mite mō no gotoshi
寒堂一夜思衣意	kandō ichiya e o omou i
羅綺千重暗現成	raki senjū an ni genjō

Painted rice cakes are cruel, they never satisfy hunger.
Born of woman with eyes of flesh, seeing as though blind.
In the cold hall, one night, think of clothes;
Figured gauze, a thousand folds, appears in the darkness.

Poem 26

Draw a Line on the Earth, Make a Cage; How Is It That You Penetrate But Do Not Pass Through?

劃地爲牢底、因甚透者箇不過

何事春遊興未窮	nani goto zo shun'yū kyō imada kiwamarazu
人心尤是客盃弓	jinshin wa mottomo kore kyūhai no yumi
天堂成就地獄滅	tendō jōjushi jigoku metsusu
日永落花飛絮中	hi wa nagashi rakka hijo no uchi

Why is my enthusiasm for spring revelry never exhausted?
People's minds are just like "the bow in the guest's cup."
Heaven attained, hell disappears,
All day long amid falling flowers and flying willow fluff.

Poem 27

Go to the Sea and Count the Sands; How Do You Stand Tiptoe on the Point of a Needle?

入海算沙底、因甚針鋒頭上翹足

撒土算沙深立功	tsuchi o satsushi isago o kazoete fukaku kō o tatsu
針鋒翹脚現神通	shinpō ashi wo tsumadatete shintsū o genzu
山僧者裏無能漢	sanzō ga shari munō no kan
東海兒孫天澤風	Tōkai no jison Tentaku no fū

Scatter the earth and count the sands, it builds up great merit;
Super-human powers appear, you stand tiptoe
　　on the point of a needle.
This mountain monk is a fellow of no ability,
Yet, son of the Eastern Sea, he is of Tianze's style.

Notes:
Xutang's Three Pivot Phrases: The first Chinese patriarch of the Daitokuji lineage. (See poem 7.) By Song times, it was customary for masters to compose a set of three pivot or turning phrases. "Pivot" implies that they have the power to turn the mind around and break its customary patterns of ratiocination.

[25]
Figured gauze, a thousand folds: The phrase connotes heavenly robes worn by immortals.

[26]
the bow in the guest's cup: A proverbial expression for deluded perception. The

source is in the *Jin Shu*, roll 43, the biography of Yue Guang:

> Yue Guang had a friend who for a long time had not come to visit. Yue Guang asked why. He said, "The last time I sat here you gave me a cup of wine, and as I was about to drink, I saw a snake in the cup. Thinking it bad to mention it, I drank it and got sick." At that time, Yue Guang had a famous Hunan bow on the wall, painted like a snake. Yue Guang thought the snake in the cup was the reflection of that bow. He put the wine cup in the same place as before and asked the guest if what he saw before was in the wine again or not. The guest said, "Yes, it is just as before." Yue Guang then explained what it was, and the guest was much relieved.[18]

[27]
son of the Eastern Sea: That is, a son of Japan, here meaning Ikkyū himself.
Tianze: Another name for Xutang.

Prose Introduction to Poem 33

凡參禪學道之輩、須日用清淨。不可日用不淨。所謂日用清淨者、究明一則因緣、到無理會田地、晝夜工夫不怠、時時截斷根源、佛魔難窺處分明坐斷。往往埋名藏迹、山林樹下舉揚一則因緣、時無雜純一矣。謂之日用清淨人也。然而稱吾善知識、擎杖拂集眾說法、魔魅人家男女、心好名利, 招學者於室中、道悟玄旨、使參者相似模樣閑言語、使教者片箇情也。這般輩非人也。寔日用不淨者也。以佛法爲度世之謀、是世上榮衒之徒也。凡有身無不着、有口無不食。若知此理豈衒於世哉、豈諛於官家哉。如是之徒、三生六十劫、入餓鬼入畜生、可無出期。或生人間受癩病苦、不聞佛法名字。可懼可懼。右靈山徹翁和尚示榮衒徒法語。題其後云、

All those who would study Zen and learn the Way must be pure in their daily lives. Impurity in one's daily life is not allowed. The person who can be called pure in his daily life will be one who by clarifying even one case of karma will arrive at the realm of understanding beyond reason. Day and night, he practices his skill without tiring. As the occasion arises, he cuts off the sources of delusion and decides with clarity and finality matters which even the Buddhas and the Devils have difficulty in glimpsing. He repeatedly buries his name and conceals his traces; under a tree in a mountain forest, he raises up a case of karma for study. At all these times, he is unadulterated and pure. This is one who may be called pure in his daily life. However, take the example of one who says of himself, I am a Good Friend, who raises up the staff and fly whisk, gathers a congregation, preaches the Dharma and thus bewitches the sons and daughters of others; who, in his heart, coveting fame and profit, invites students to his cell and says he will enlighten the profound mystery for them, thus causing the students to be guilty of specious and idle chatter and the master in turn to be trapped in biased feelings. This type is not even human. This is truly one impure in his daily life. One who takes the Buddha's teaching and makes of it a scheme for succeeding in the world is a fellow given to worldly self-glorification. Everyone who has a body has to wear clothes; everyone who has a mouth has to eat; if you understand this truth, how can you boast of yourself in the world; how can you adulate high office? This sort, for three lives or sixty eons will be a hungry ghost or a beast; there will likely be no fixed term for release. And if by chance he is born as a human being he will suffer from leprosy and never hear even the name of the Buddha's teaching. Oh, terrible, terrible!

What precedes is Master Tettō Ryōzen's sermon delivered to those given to self-glorification. Taking it for a subject, as an epilogue, I say:

Poem 33

工夫不是涅槃堂　　*kufū kore nehandō ni arazu*
名利耀前心念忙　　*myōri mae ni kagayaite shin'nen isogashi*
信道人間食籍定　　*shinzu ningen no shokuseki no sadamareru koto o*
羊虀一椀橘皮湯　　*yōbi ichiwan kitsupi tō*

If your skill cannot work in the Nirvana Hall,
Confronted with the glitter of fame and profit,
    your mind will be busy.

I believe man's bill of fare is fixed,
One bowl of mutton gruel with citrus rind tea.

Notes:

situation: Literally, one case of cause and conditioning, here equivalent to the term kōan.

Good Friend: Good friend in the religious sense, a term applied to virtuous monks, meaning one who is fit to preach the Dharma and who can stimulate enlightenment in others.

three lives or sixty eons: Three lives is the shortest period to become a Buddha; sixty eons is the longest. "Eon" is used here to translate the Buddhist term "kalpa," which denotes an unimaginably long period of time. A metaphorical expression of its length alludes to the time it takes for a block of granite a mile square to be worn away from being brushed once every hundred years by the gossamer robes of an immortal. The compound "three lives or sixty eons" appears frequently in Ikkyū's poems with the meaning of simply a very long time.

hungry ghost or a beast: In Buddhist cosmology, two of the *rokudō* (six courses) through which sentient beings transmigrate according to the dictates of karmic retribution. The *rokudō*, in descending order, are god, human being, asura (warrior or titan), beast, hungry ghost (creatures of insatiable desire), and denizen of hell.[19]

Master Tettō Ryōzen's sermon: Master Tettō Ryōzen (1295–1369) was the first abbot of Daitokuji to succeed the founder Daitō. In addition to the fact that Tettō was a direct forebearer in the Daitokuji line of transmission and due veneration as such, Ikkyū was particularly drawn to Tettō's stern style of Zen. It is noteworthy that this sermon does not appear in the *Tettō Roku*, the official record of his pronouncements. The only extant text for it other than the several manuscripts of the *Crazy Cloud Anthology* is a scroll in Ikkyū's hand kept in the Shinjuan repository at Daitokuji. Mention of the sermon also appears in the *Nempu*. There, Yōsō, the senior disciple of the same master as Ikkyū and often the subject of complaint in the *Anthology*, accuses Ikkyū of throwing slopwater in their master's face because he instructed his students with Tettō's sermon and the story about Baizhang dying of starvation. Ikkyū seems to think Yōsō is implying that he invented them, for he retorts, "I did not make up the story about Baizhang dying of starvation. You can clearly see reference to his 'a day of no work is a day of no eating' in the record of Patriarch Xutang. And as for Tettō's sermon, it was something our former master [Kasō] used to speak of every day."[20] (See p. 21.) This leaves room for speculation that this sermon, if not Ikkyū's invention, may be his transcription of it as remembered from oral presentation.

Nirvana Hall: The monastery infirmary, where, willing or not, one may have to experience Nirvana, which is extinction as well as enlightenment. Metaphorically, it means a life or death situation.

Poem 35

Peach Blossom Waves

桃花浪 *tōka rō*

隨波逐浪幾杠塵	*zuiha chikurō iku kōjin zo*
又值桃花三月春	*mata tōka sangatsu no haru ni au*
流恨三生六十劫	*urami o nagasu sanshō rokujū kō*
龍門歲歲曝腮鱗	*Ryōmon saisai sairin o sarasu*

"Following waves, chasing waves," how much red dust?
Once again meeting the peach blossoms,
    spring in the third month.
Futile regrets flowing down stream, three lives to sixty eons;
At the Dragon Gate, year after year,
    gills and scales parching in the sun.

Notes:

Peach Blossom Waves: A stock expression for the early part of the third month in the lunar calendar when the peach blossoms scatter over the waves of the flooding rivers. Legend also designates this as the time when carp gather at a river called the Dragon Gate to attempt to climb the falls. Those that succeed turn into dragons.

"Following waves, chasing waves," how much red dust?: The phrase "following waves, chasing waves" came to be known as one of the "Three Pivot Phrases" of Yunmen. This line is a synopsis of the last two lines in a poem of Ikkyū's entitled "What is it like, the Yunmen school?" "The One Word Barrier and the Three Phrases/How many people have red dust in their eyes?" Hirano offers an explanation of the sense there as, "The three phrases are difficult kōans, how

many people have been led astray?"²¹ Aside from the water imagery inherent in this oblique phrase of Yunmen's, why he should be alluded to becomes clear in the last line.

At the Dragon Gate, year after year, gills and scales parching in the sun: As well as calling up the legend about the carp turning to dragons, this line alludes to kōan no. 60 in the *Blue Cliff Record*:

> Yunmen raised his staff and said: "This staff turns into a dragon that swallows up heaven and earth. Then where will you find the mountains, rivers, and great earth?"

Superimposed over the legend of carp turning into dragons, then, we have Yunmen turning a staff into a dragon. The specific allusion, however, is to the first four lines of the appreciatory verse that caps the kōan:

> The staff swallows up heaven and earth,
> In vain do you speak of running the peach blossom rapids.
> Those with sun-burned tails are not catching the clouds
>   and seizing mist,
> Those with bleached gills, why must they lose their livers
>   and their souls?²²

The poem describes the feeling of failure encountered when striving to transcend one's limitations. Yet, built into the poem through the allusion is also the triumphal image of Yunmen's staff turning into a dragon and swallowing up the mountains and the rivers, that is, the obstacles to be overcome.

Poem 37

Addressed to an Assembly on the Winter Solstice

冬至示眾 *tōji jishu*

獨閉門關不省方	hitori monkan o tozashi hō o kaerimizu
這中誰是法中王	kono uchi tare ka kore hōchū no ō
諸人若問冬來句	shonin moshi tōrai no ku o towaba
日自今朝一線長	hi wa konchō yori issen nagashi

Alone, closing the gates and passes,
    not going on tours of inspection.
In this, who is King of the Dharma?
If people ask for a phrase about winter's coming.
I say, from this morning, the day is one thread longer.

Notes:
Addressed to an Assembly on the Winter Solstice: Of the importance of the winter solstice celebration in Zen temples, Hirano says, "Zen schools, from olden times, have made the yearly festivals occasions for a master to mount the lectern and hold dialogues with his students. Because the winter solstice is the shortest day of the whole year and from the next day the days lengthen, it is called the return of the *yang*. When *yin* reaches extremity it turns into *yang*: this is compared to the fact that at the bottom of the greatest doubt there is great satori. Therefore this day is celebrated as the most auspicious of the whole year. It is a day of deep meaning."[23]

Alone, closing the gates and passes, not going on tours of inspection: An allusion to the winter solstice hexagram of the *Yijing*, no. 24, "Return." The comment on the image of that hexagram is:

> Thus the former kings on the day of solstice, closed the gates, merchants and travelers did not go about, and the ruler did not make tours of inspection.[24]

In that hexagram, one straight (*yang*) line appears at the bottom of five broken (*yin*) lines. The import is the same as explained above by Hirano, just when the dark forces of *yin* become strongest, the *yang* element reenters from beneath.

King of the Dharma: A person of ultimate self-possession. The expression can be traced back to the *Lotus Sūtra* where it is the words of the Buddha:

> I am the Dharma King
> With respect to the Dharma acting completely at will.[25]

Poem 40

The Buddha's Nirvana

佛涅槃 *Butsu nehan*

滅度西天老釋迦	*metsudosu Saiten no rō Shaka*
他生出世到誰家	*tashō ni shusse shite ta ga ya ni ka itaru*
二千三百年前淚	*nisen sanbyaku nen mae no namida*
猶洒扶桑二月花	*nao Fusō nigatsu no hana ni sosogu*

He crossed over to extinction in India, old Śākyamuni.
In another birth, he emerged into the world,
    to whose house did he go?
The tears of two thousand three hundred years ago
Still sprinkle in Japan, the blossoms of the second month.

Notes:
The Buddha's Nirvana: The death of Śākyamuni, the Buddha's incarnation as a man.
Still sprinkle in Japan, the blossoms of the second month: The Buddha's Nirvana is celebrated on the fifteenth day of the second month. In the old lunar calendar, the second month was usually closer to March of the solar calendar, so that by that time the peach blossoms were already in bloom and falling.

The ambiguity of the last two lines makes the poetry here. Do the tears sprinkle on the blossoms, perhaps a figurative way of saying it rained this year on the celebrations for the Buddha's Nirvana, that it was as if the tears of two thousand years ago were sprinkling on Japan? Or are the blossoms of the second month, that sprinkle and fall every year in the second month, Japan's tears for the death of the Buddha?

Prose Introduction to Poem 44

僧問岩頭云、古帆未掛時如何。頭云、小魚吞大魚。僧云、掛後如何。頭云、後園驢喫草。

A monk asked Yantou, "What is it like when the old sail has not been hoisted?" Yantou said, "The small fish swallows the big fish." The monk asked, "And after it is hoisted, what is it like?" Yantou said, "In the back garden the donkey eats grass."

Poem 44

寒溫苦樂愧慚時	kan'on kuraku kizan no toki
耳朶元來兩片皮	jida ganrai ryōhen bi
一二三兮三二一	ichi ni san san ni ichi
南泉信手斬猫兒	Nansen te ni makasete myōji wo kiru

Cold, hot, pain, pleasure, time to be ashamed.
Ears from the beginning are two pieces of skin.
One, two, three, ah! three, two, one.
Nanquan trusting his hand cuts the cat in two.

Notes:
A monk asked ... the donkey eats grass: The introduction to this poem is a kōan. The lead personage is Yantou (827–887). Different versions of this kōan appear in several places in the Zen canon. That which appears in the *Chanlin Leizhu* is the closest to the version here.[26] Xutang, Chinese patriarch of the Daitokuji line, was enlightened by this particular kōan. He assigned it to Daiō and so on down the line; thus it has always been an important kōan for the Daitokuji lineage.

Cold, hot, pain, pleasure, time to be ashamed: An allusion to the third of the "Three Reflections of Master Foyan Qingyuan" (1067–1120). See poem 209:

> Pain and pleasure, adversity and prosperity, the Way lies in the middle. Agitated or calm, cold or hot, I am ashamed of myself, remorseful.[27]

Hirano notes that the two questions forming the introductory kōan above can be understood as situations of prosperity, literally, "going with," and adversity, literally, "going against." "When the old sail has not been hoisted" is a situation of "going against," the wind blows in a contrary direction.

"After it is hoisted" is a situation of "going with," the wind blows fair from behind.[28] That interpretation, part of an oral tradition about the kōan, is the key to the reference to Foyan's three reflections.

Ears from the beginning are two pieces of skin: "Ears are two pieces of skin" in company with the phrase "tusks and teeth, one set of bone" occurs sporadically in Zen literature as a response to conundrums. More importantly, however, within the tradition of the Daitokuji lineage, "Ears are two pieces of skin" has been handed down as a capping phrase to the first answer in this kōan, "small fish swallows the big fish." "Tusks and teeth, one set of bones" caps "In the back garden, the donkey eats grass." According to Hirano, Ikkyū is alluding to this oral tradition of kōan response.[29]

One, two, three, ah! three, two, one: Again within the same tradition, "Five, four, three, two, one" is another appropriate capping to "small fish swallows the big fish" and "one, two, three, four, five" then caps "In the back garden the donkey eats grass."[30] This may be another allusion then, although the figures work well enough as a mirror-image representation of duality.

Nanquan with a flick of the wrist killed the cat: an allusion to the *Blue Cliff Record*, kōan no. 63:

> At Nanquan's one day, the monks of the East and West were fighting over a cat. When Nanquan saw them, he raised up the cat and said, "If someone can speak, I will not kill it." No one in the assembly answered. Nanquan cut the cat in two.[31]

The taking of life is, of course, one of the cardinal prohibitions of Buddhism. The resolution to this kōan may be found in the notes to poem 52.

Poem 46

Pleasure in Pain

苦中樂 *kuchū no raku*

酒喫三盃未濕唇	shū sanbai o kitsushite imada kuchibiru o uruosazu
曹山老漢慰孤貧	Sōzan rōkan kohin o isu

直横身火宅中看　　jiki ni mi o katakuchū ni yokotaete miyo
一刹那間萬劫辛　　issetsuna no kan bangō no shin

"You drank three cups of wine and still your lips are dry."
Thus, that old fellow Caoshan comforted the poor orphan.
Just lay your body down in a burning house and see
In the space of a moment, ten thousand eons of pain.

Notes:

Pleasure in Pain: The title for this poem and the succeeding one are taken from the appreciatory verse to the *Blue Cliff Record*, kōan no. 83:

> Pleasure in pain, pain in pleasure;
> who says gold is like dung.[32]

For a citation of the whole verse, see notes to poem 71.

"You drank three cups … the poor orphan: An allusion to kōan no. 10 from the *Wumen Guan*. Caoshan (840–901) was one of the founders of the Sōtō school:

> A monk … said to Caoshan, "I am a poor destitute monk. I beg you to bestow upon me the alms of salvation."
> Caoshan said, "Ācārya (teacher)."
> "Yes, Sir?" replied the monk.
> Caoshan said, "Someone has drunk three bowls of good wine but asserts that he had not yet moistened his lips."[33]

… a burning house: A metaphor for this world of passion which originates with the parable of the burning house in the *Lotus Sūtra*.[34]

This same theme is included in a sermon by Ikkyū that introduces poem 655 [not translated in the present selection]. The relevant passage is:

> When your whole body falls into a fiery pit, you see in fine detail the pleasure in pain. If you are able to see it, you will not be blind and ignore the realm of Karma. If you cannot see it, it will take a long time to become a Buddha.[35]

Poem 47

Pain in Pleasure

樂中苦 *rakuchū no ku*

此是瞿曇曾所經	kore wa kore Kudon no katsute heshi tokoro
麻衣草坐六年情	ma'e sōza rokunen no jō
一朝點檢將來看	itchō tenkenshi mochikitari miba
寂寞靈山身後名	sekibakutari Ryōzan shingo no na

This is what Gautama experienced,
Hemp garments, sitting on the grass, his condition for six years.
One morning, observing carefully, he came to see
The desolate loneliness of his name
    after the passing of his body at Vulture Peak.

Notes:
Pain in Pleasure: See notes to poem 46.
Gautama: Another name for Śākyamuni, the historical Buddha, derived from his clan name, Gotama.
Hemp garments, … six years: When he could no longer take pleasure in his life of ease as the prince of a wealthy kingdom, Śākyamuni left his home and went into the forest to practice rigorous ascetic disciplines for six years. He abandoned those practices shortly before experiencing enlightenment.
One morning, observing carefully, he came to see: An oblique reference perhaps to his enlightenment upon seeing the morning star as he meditated under the Bodhi tree. The enjambment here, however, presses us forward to take "the desolate loneliness of his name" as the object of the verb "to see."
Vulture Peak: A mountain in India where the Buddha is reputed to have preached several important sutras. In the Zen school, it is renowned as the site of the Flower Sermon in which the Buddha simply raised a flower and Kāśyapa, the only one who understood, smiled back. This wordless sermon and its silent understanding traditionally mark the beginning of the Zen school.

Prose Introduction to Poem 52

大隨庵邊有一龜。僧問、一切衆生皮裹骨。這箇衆生、爲甚骨裹皮。大隨以草鞋蓋於背上。

There was a tortoise around Dasui's hermitage. A monk asked, "All beings have skin around their bones; why does this creature have bone around his skin?" Dasui took his sandals and put them on the tortoise's back.

Poem 52

衆生顛倒幾時休	shujō tendō iku toki ka kyūsu
打著前頭又後頭	zentō o tachaku shite mata kōtō
信手救猫趙州老	te ni makasete neko o sukuu Jōshū rō
草鞋載去也風流	sōai nose saru mo mata fūryū

Human confusion, when will it end?
Strike before and again behind.
Without ado he saved the cat, old Zhaozhou,
Leaving with his sandals on his head was also fūryū.

Notes:

There was a tortoise ... : This kōan appears in the *Chuan Deng Lu*.[36]
Without ado, he saved the cat, old Zhaozhou: Here is the resolution (if the term applies) to the kōan about Nanquan killing the cat already quoted in the commentary to poem 44. It is presented as a separate kōan, no. 64, in the *Blue Cliff Record*:

> Nanquan brought up the preceding story and asked Zhaozhou what he would have done. Zhaozhou took off his straw sandals, put them on his head and walked away.
> Nanquan said, "If you had been there, the cat would have been saved."[37]

fūryū: Here the meaning is something like "far-out," that is, something marvelously appropriate in an inexplicable way. (See notes to poem 6.)

Poem 54

Rinzai Burned the Meditation Plank and Desk

臨濟燒机案・禪板 *Rinzai kian zenban o yaku*

此漢宗門第一禪	*kono kan shūmon dai'ichi no zen*
奪人奪境體中玄	*datsujin datsukyō taichūgen*
安身立命在那處	*anshin ryūmō izure no tokoro ni ka aru*
劫火洞然燒大千	*gōka tōnen toshite daisen o yaku*

This fellow is the number one Zen master in the school.
  "Take away subject, take away object,"
    "The mystery within form."
  A safe, secure life, where can it be found?
  A cataclysmic fire will utterly consume the Great Chiliocosm.

Notes:
Rinzai Burned the Meditation Plank and Desk: Rinzai (Ch. Linji) is the founder of the school of Zen to which Ikkyū belonged. Rinzai's master, Huangbo, had received as a symbol of the transmission from his teacher Baizhang a small desk and meditation plank. ("Meditation plank" is a literal translation, exactly what the object was is unclear.) Huangbo in turn wished to pass these objects on to Rinzai. Rinzai, however, apparently burned them to show his disdain for any worldly accreditation of his spiritual attainment. This event is related in the *Record of Rinzai* as follows:

> One day, Rinzai was taking leave of Huangbo. Huangbo asked him, "Where are you going?" Rinzai said, "If I'm not going south of the river, then I'll be returning north of the river." Huangbo, thereupon, tried to strike him. Rinzai firmly restrained him and gave him a slap instead. Huangbo gave a great laugh and called to his servant, "Bring me my former master's meditation plank and desk." Rinzai said, "Servant, bring fire." "Say what you will, only take them with you. Later, they may stay the tongues of the world."[38]

As can be seen above, this account leaves one in doubt as to whether Rinzai actually burned these heirlooms or merely threatened to. In the tradition of

the Rinzai school, at least so far as Ikkyū may be considered a spokesman for it, it is assumed he went ahead and burned them. The stories about Ikkyū burning his own certificate of enlightenment are of the same order.
Take away subject, take away object: The third of Rinzai's "Four Propositions." See poems 13–16. The third proposition represents the realization that both the subjective and objective realms are "empty" or void, which makes it fitting here because Ikkyū wants to emphasize the essential "emptiness" of the enlightenment experience itself and external recognition of it.
The mystery within form: One of Rinzai's "Three Mysteries." Rinzai himself did not specify what the "Three Mysteries" were; later commentators interpreted them as the "mystery within form," "the mystery within words," and "the mystery within mystery." They appear that way for example in the appreciatory words to *Blue Cliff Record*, kōan no. 15.[39] Hirano suggests Ikkyū understands "mystery within form" as a restatement of "take away man, take away object."[40] The two phrases, at any rate, stand *pars pro toto* for the teaching of Rinzai. They may also prepare us for the end of the poem, where the whole universe is taken away in flame. Certainly, that is the mystery in physical form; it seems so palpable and "real," and yet it can be absolutely "taken away."
A cataclysmic fire will lay waste to, and burn, … : An allusion to the *Blue Cliff Record*, kōan no. 29.

> A monk asked Dasui, "In the cataclysmic fire at the end of an eon, when the Great Chiliocosm is altogether destroyed, will 'this one' be destroyed or not?"
> Dasui said, "It will be destroyed."[41]

What "this one" represents is unclear. The commentator to the Iwanami edition of the *Blue Cliff Record* suggests "Innate Buddha-nature."[42] Yuanwu, the original commentator, teases his audience with this remark, "What sort of thing is 'this one?' The monks of the world will grope for this phrase and never get it. Scratch away and expect to itch."[43]
Great Chiliocosm: An abbreviation for the Great Three Thousand Millionfold World Sphere (*sanzen daisen sekai*), a term in Buddhist cosmology for the universe in the infinite sense.

Poem 66

The Great Master Yuanwu Strikes a Harmony with the Cosmic Organ

圓悟大師投機 *Engo Daishi tōki*

沈吟小艷一章詩
發動乾坤投大機
擊竹見桃若相比
須彌脚下石烏龜

> Quietly humming a line from the "little love song,"
> Launching heaven and earth into motion,
>   he harmonizes with the magnum organum.
> If he is compared to him who heard bamboo struck
>   or him who saw a peach blossom,
> He is the stone raven tortoise at the foot of Mount Sumeru.

Notes:
The Great Master Yuanwu: Yuanwu (1063–1135), a student of Wuzu (?–1104), is most famous for editing and appending the introductions, comments, and criticisms to the *Blue Cliff Record*. A sample of his style of comment was presented at the end of the notes to poem 54.

humming a line from a "little love song": Allusion to Yuanwu's enlightenment, *Wu Deng Hui Yuan*, roll 19:

> A prefect visited Wuzu and asked about the Path. Wuzu said, "When you were young, was there not a little love song you used to recite? There are two lines in it that are very close to Zen:
>   'She often called her maid for no reason at all,
>   Just so that her lover would recognize her voice.'"
> The prefect responded, "Yes, yes." Wuzu said, "Let us work on that a little more." Yuanwu happened to return to the monastery and asked the Master about his presentation of the little love poem. "Did the prefect understand or not?" Wuzu said, "He only recognized my voice." Yuanwu said, "But she just wanted her lover to recognize her voice. He recognized your voice, why was that incorrect?" Wuzu said,

"What was the meaning of Bodhidharma coming from the West? The oak tree in the garden." Yuanwu was suddenly enlightened.[44]

him who heard bamboo struck: Xiangyan was enlightened while sweeping the garden, when he heard a pebble strike a stalk of bamboo. (See p. 45.)
him who saw a peach blossom: Lingyun (c. 820), a student of Weishan, was enlightened by seeing a peach blossom.
He is the stone raven tortoise at the foot of Mount Sumeru: Hirano remarks that the source of this expression is obscure. He speculates that Ikkyū is referring to the tortoise in Chinese mythology who is thought to bear the mountains of the immortals on his back, but has instead put on his back Mount Sumeru, the center of the universe according to Buddhist cosmology. Hirano also cites a phrase from the *Chuan deng lu* where a raven tortoise holding Mount Sumeru up with his neck is a metaphor for a person of great strength and capacity.[45]

Poem 68

Praising the Fish-Basket Kannon

贊魚籃觀音 *gyoran Kannon o sansu*

丹臉青鬟慈愛深	*tanken seikan jiai fukashi*
自疑雲雨夢中心	*mizukara utagau un'u muchū no shin*
千眼大悲看不見	*zengen no taihi miredomo mizu*
漁妻江海一生吟	*gyosai kōkai isshō no gin*

Red cheeks, blue-black hair, compassion, and love deep;
Wondering at her feelings in the midst of a dream of cloud-rain.
One thousand eyes of Great Compassion
    are looked at but not seen.
A fisherman's wife by the river and sea, one whole life of song.

Notes:
Fish-Basket Kannon: one of the thirty-three transformation bodies of Kannon (Avalokiteśvara), coming under the general category of "wife of a layman." The name Fish-Basket Kannon has no source in the sutras but appears to be of

Chinese folklore origin.⁴⁶ She is often depicted as a beautiful woman holding a fish basket or riding on a fish. In the *Shishi Jigu Lüe* version of the legend about her, Kannon is transformed into a beautiful woman and many suitors vie for her hand. She puts them in competition reciting the sutras until only one man with the surname Ma is left. She marries him but dies the night of the wedding.⁴⁷ Whether this is the version of the legend that Ikkyū knew is difficult to say. The poem seems to imply that she subsequently lived a happily married life.

cloud-rain: See pp. 48–50 and notes to poem 6.

One thousand eyes of Great Compassion: Kannon is often described as having a thousand eyes and a thousand hands to indicate the Bodhisattva's great capacity for compassion and active help.

are looked at but not seen: This line could also be read "look out but are not seen," however, Hirano defends the reading followed here by inferring an allusion to the words of Yunmen in kōan no. 86 of the *Blue Cliff Record*:

> "Absolutely everyone has radiance within them, but when you look at it, you see it not, for it is dark and dim."⁴⁸

There are very few important female figures in Buddhist iconography; however, the Bodhisattva Kannon, who is often portrayed as a woman, may count as one. It is of interest that Ikkyū does not emphasize the miraculous aspects of the Bodhisattva but rather imagines Kannon simply as a fisherman's wife. This blurs the distinction between the miraculous and the ordinary.

The Scriptures Wipe Away Filth—three poems

經卷拭不淨　三首 *kyōkan fujō o nuguu—sanshu*

Poem 69

經卷元除不淨㦮　*kyōkan wa moto fujō o nozoku kami*
龍宮海藏弄言詮　*Ryūgū Kaizō gonsen o rōsu*
看看百則碧巖集　*miyo miyo hyakusoku Hekiganshū*
狼藉乳峰風月前　*rōzekitari Nyūhō fūgetsu no mae*

The scriptures from the start have been toilet paper,
The Dragon Palace Sea Treasury toys with words and phrases.
Have a look at the *Blue Cliff Record* with its hundred cases
Scattered wildly over Breast Peak before wind and moon.

Poem 70

弓影客盃多斷腸	kyūei no kyakuhai ooku danchō
夜來新病入膏肓	yarai shinbyō kōkō ni iru
愧慚我不及禽獸	gizansu ware kinjū ni oyobazaru o
狗尿栴檀古佛堂	inu wa nyōsu sendan no kobutsudō

The bow's reflection in the guest's cup, much rending of the guts.
Night comes and a new sickness enters the vital region.
Ashamed am I not to equal a beast;
The dog pisses on the sandalwood old Buddha Hall.

Poem 71

信手拈來除不淨	te ni makasete fujō o nozoku
作家面目露堂堂	sakke no menmoku ro dōdō
南山雲起北山雨	nanzan ni kumo okori hokuzan ni ame
一夜落花流水香	ichiya rakka ryūsui kanbashi

Without ado, he flicks his hand round and wipes himself.
The master's countenance is exposed and clear.
On the south side of the mountain, clouds arise,
    on the north side it rains,
A whole night of falling flowers and flowing water is fragrant.

Notes:
The Scriptures Wipe Away Filth: An allusion to Rinzai's statement, "The Twelve Fold Teachings of the Three Vehicles are all old paper for wiping filth."[49]

[69]

The Dragon Palace Sea Treasury: A conventional appellation for the Tripitaka, the great treasury of sutras. The *Hai Long Wang Jing*, the Sea Dragon King Sūtra, records the legendary visit of the Buddha to the Dragon King's palace below the sea in order to expound Buddhist Law and scriptures.[50] The sutra became well known very early in China and Japan because the chanting of it was thought efficacious for encouraging rainfall.

the Blue Cliff Record with its hundred cases: The *Blue Cliff Record* has already been mentioned several times as a source of allusion. This collection of kōans was a central work for the kōan Zen of the Rinzai school in Japan. It was compiled during the Song period by Xuedou (980–1052) and later added to by Yuanwu. (See notes to poem 66.)

Scattered wildly over Breast Peak: Breast Peak is where Xuedou compiled the *Blue Cliff Record*. This phrase alludes to a poem from the *Jianghu Fengyue Ji*, an anthology of Zen poetry, on the subject of Xuedou's tomb:

> The Three Sovereigns and Five Emperors, what about them?
> His suffering lasted twenty years.
> It did not get collected in the Great Storehouse of Sutras.
> Up to now, it is scattered wildly over Breast Peak.[51]

This laments the neglect of the *Blue Cliff Record*. Three Sovereigns and Five Emperors never saw its worth, so it had not been included in the canon, at least at that poet's time. By Ikkyū's time, the *Blue Cliff Record* had become a firmly entrenched part of the Zen canon, hence the irony.

The opening of this set of poems invokes a popular theme in Zen literature, that the orthodox scriptures must be abandoned if one would avoid getting caught in the net of duality. The allusion to the *Jianghu Fengyue Ji* poem recalling the time when the *Blue Cliff Record* was not appreciated seems to suggest it should not be counted among the scriptures to be rejected. Yet, the addition of the wind and moon to the image of its pages being wildly scattered imbues the scene with such a feeling of freedom and beauty that the poet seems to be saying it is right to cast the *Blue Cliff Record* away too. The two senses are poised in equilibrium.

[70]

bow's reflection: See notes to poem 26.

The dog pisses ... old Buddha Hall: An allusion to the *Blue Cliff Record*, kōan no. 96:

> On Wutai mountain, clouds steam rice.
> Before the old Buddha Hall, the dog pisses at the sky.[52]

The title of the series suggests that the poems will attack the conventional notion of the distinction between sacred and profane by resorting to the scatological. The last line of this second poem fulfills that expectation. However, the scatological image is borrowed from the same scripture we have been encouraged to scatter to the wind in the previous poem. At the recognition of the allusion one moves from the edge of scatological license back to the authority of the scriptures. Thus, in the act of reading the line, we experience the entrapment of the scriptures.

[71]
On the south side of the mountain, clouds arise ... : An allusion to Yunmen's kōan in the *Blue Cliff Record* about categorizing the situation where clouds on the south side of the mountain cause rain on the north side. More particularly, the allusion is to the appreciatory verse of that kōan:

> On the south side, cloud; on the north side, rain,
> The forty-seven Saints and six Patriarchs
>   look one another in the eye.
> In the land of the barbarians, a monk mounts the lectern.
> In the land of great Tang, they have not yet struck the drum.
> Pleasure in pain, pain in pleasure.
> Who says gold is like dung?[53]

The scatological connection has been made again, and in the appreciatory verse the leap has been made from the topic of the interrelation of all phenomena to the topic of the identity of opposites. "On the south mountain, clouds arise, on the north mountain it rains," calls up the union of opposites, because particularly in Ikkyū's poetry, rain following close upon cloud always suggests the classical euphemism for physical love, "cloud-rain." In the section on allusion, we have already analyzed poem 45 where Ikkyū elaborates his own erotic interpretation of Yunmen's kōan. Any reader of Ikkyū would immediately sense the hint of erotic allusion here.

A whole night of ... fragrant: This phrase originated from a statement of Master Xuedou, compiler of the *Blue Cliff Record*.

> "The Buddha had some secret words that Kāśyapa did not hide, 'One night of falling flowers rain fills the city with fragrant flowing water.'"[54]

In the first line of this poem, it is no longer necessary to say with what the master is wiping himself nor why it is significant that it be done "without ado." The reader has been cued by all that precedes to understand that it is "the scriptures." It is as if the pages of the *Blue Cliff Record* that materialized at the end of the last line in the preceding poem have finally been subdued and put in their proper place. The second line teases with an ambiguity. A "countenance exposed and clear" can refer either to intellectual clarity (the doors of perception cleansed, everything is obvious) or to the exposure of the master's anatomy. There is a tone of resolution and certainty to the opening lines of this poem. One wonders how the poet will be able to close the poem and the whole series when he has already run through so much of his iconoclastic ammunition. One anticipates perhaps a triumphant finale, one last thrust. Instead, we meet two lines dazzlingly multifaceted with associations and meaning.

The third line is a full-fledged quotation from the *Blue Cliff Record*, and as much commands the reader to face it as a kōan, The whole kōan as it appears in the *Blue Cliff Record* flashes through the mind, leaving the parting shot of the appreciatory verse, "Who says gold is like dung?" Being familiar with Ikkyū's predilection s leads one to sense an erotic overtone in the "cloud" and "rain" of Yunmen's kōan.

"A night of falling flowers and flowing water is fragrant" is also a quotation of a poetic tag used by Xuedou, compiler of the *Blue Cliff Record*. The phrase may be looked upon as a poetic touchstone for the philosophical view that all phenomena are interrelated. One might even think of it as a possible answer to Yunmen's kōan. In response to a situation where the connection between phenomena is obscure ("cloud on the south side causing rain on the north side"), the poet presents a situation where the connection is obvious and natural, the falling petals giving their fragrance to the water. If these two lines were being looked at in isolation, the discussion might end here; but their context in the set charges them with multiple meanings. Picking up the scatological thread again, "A whole night of falling flowers" in Chinese poetic diction conjures up a scene of drinking and feasting beneath the blossoms. Then the fragrant flowing water could be taken as a euphemism for the sorry intestinal consequences after an evening of intemperance. But the same scene conjures up another picture as well. "Fallen flower" is often a metaphor in Chinese poetry for a courtesan. Thinking of fallen flowers in that vein would suggest another interpretation for the "flowing fragrant water"; it becomes the "lascivious fluids" of a bacchanalia.

On the surface, the diction is so subdued and decorous; clouds and rain, blossoms fluttering onto rushing streams. Both lines are quotations from the scriptures, as though the poet has finally given up the struggle to break free from enshrined words. But he has not surrendered; instead, through the force of context, he has bent the words of the scriptures to suggest profane things. These two lines leave the reader with the philosophical, the scatological, and the erotic, the most contradictory of images and ideas juxtaposed and intermingled, impossible to separate.

Poem 74

Frogs

蛙 *kaeru*

慣釣鯨鯢笑一場	*keigei o tsuru ni narete warai ichijō*
泥沙碾步太忙忙	*deisha ni hiite hanahada bōbō*
可憐井底稱尊大	*awaremubeshi seitei ni sondai to shōsu*
天下衲僧皆子陽	*tenka no nōsō mina Shiyō*

Accustomed to fishing for whales, I had to laugh
At the frogs, thrashing through the mud so busily.
They are pitiable, those at the bottom of wells,
    calling themselves great;
All the patch-cloth monks under heaven are just like Ziyang.

Notes:
Frogs: The frog at the bottom of the well is well-known in China and Japan as a metaphor for narrow-minded people who consider themselves important simply because they are blind to the rest of the world.

patch-cloth monks: "Patch-cloth" became an epithet for monks because the Buddhist monastic codes enjoined monks to live in poverty, wearing robes that were patched over and over again. However, this instruction was observed more often in letter rather than spirit. For example, it became common for monk's robes to be made of a patch-work of gorgeous brocades, thus displaying opulence rather than poverty.

Ziyang: Gongsun Shu of the Han dynasty. He became the king of Sichuan and called himself Son of Heaven. His reign was cut short by assassination. In *History of the Later Han Dynasty*, roll 54, the general Ma Yuan says of him, "Ziyang was just a frog at the bottom of the well."[55]

Poem 75

Shakuhachi

尺八 shakuhachi

一枝尺八恨難任　　isshi no shakuhachi urami ni taegatashi
吹入胡笳塞上吟　　fuite koka saijō no gin ni iru
十字街頭誰氏曲　　jūji gaitō ta ga shi no kyoku zo
少林門下絶知音　　Shōrin monka chi'in o zetsusu

A single shakuhachi intones sorrow difficult to bear;
Blowing it, one enters into the song
    of a barbarian flute at the frontier.
In the city, at the crossroad, whose tune is it?
Among the students of Shaolin, I have no friends.

Notes:
Shakuhachi: A bamboo flute played vertically, capable of producing a broad range of sound from a low, throaty whisper to a shrill, piercing tremulo. Ikkyū is reputed to have played the shakuhachi himself.[56]

song of a barbarian flute at the frontier: China's long ever-beleaguered border demanded a constant supply of troops and administrators to maintain it. Most officials at some point in their career had to take a turn of duty on the bleak frontier, which is why the frontier lament has been from early times a

standard theme in Chinese poetry. The lonely sound of the barbarian flute bringing home to the poet the alien nature of his surroundings recurs often in frontier poems.
Shaolin: The dwelling place of Bodhidharma, the First Patriarch of Zen, hence here a reference to the Zen school.

Overtly simple, this poem draws its effect from a complex ambiguity. Blowing into the shakuhachi, the poet enters the song of the barbarian flute on the frontier. This can mean he enters the feelings of loneliness aroused by hearing the flute and realizing the strangeness of the land. At the same time, it can imply that the poet's tune on the shakuhachi is like a barbarian song, foreign, alien to his listeners. It is natural to feel isolated at the frontier but the poet feels alone in the middle of the city. He is both a solitary man of culture in the midst of barbarians and the lone barbarian stalking the streets of an alien city.

Poem 78

Chrysanthemums: An Arhat and Yang Guifei in the Same Vase

菊：羅漢楊妃同瓶 *kiku: rakan to Yōhi to dōbin*

楊妃爛醉一籬秋	*Yōhi ransui ichiri no aki*
茶褐相交爲好仇	*chakatsu ai majiwatte kōkyū to nasu*
失却神通居下界	*shintsū o shikkyakushite gekai ni kyosu*
應身天寶辟陽侯	*ōjin wa tenbō no Hekiyōkō*

Yang Guifei flushed in drunkenness, a hedgeful of autumn.
The tea-colored Arhat, mingled with her,
    makes a good companion.
He has lost his magic power, come down to live on earth,
For a Transformation Body, Marquis Biyang of the Tianbao era.

Notes:
Arhat: Within the Mahayana School of Buddhism, the term denotes an adept of the Hinayana "lesser vehicle" path. The Arhat is one who seeks

enlightenment for himself alone, not aspiring to the Bodhisattva path of awakening all the beings. This poem forms a pair with poem 77, which was analysed in the introduction (pp. 43-44). In that poem, Ikkyū satirized the Arhat for pursuing miraculous powers through self-centered religious practice. In this poem, Ikkyū makes fun of the Arhat ideal by imagining an Arhat losing all his powers because he has come under the influence of a beautiful woman. What appears to have inspired both poems, however, is the sight of chrysanthemums, one variety with a golden tea colour evoking the saffron robes of monks and another, presumably crimson red.

Yang Guifei: A famous "femme fatale," the favorite of the Tang emperor Xuanzong.

Transformation Body: Form taken by the Buddha in response to the needs of sentient beings.

Marquis Biyang: The marquis, whose name was Shen Yiji, is recorded in the *Shiji* as a man wielding great influence because of a special relationship with the empress. He is, then, the classic sycophant.[57]

Tianbao era: The era during the Tang dynasty when Yang Guifei flourished.

Poem 79

Snowball

雪團 *setsudan*

乾坤埋却没門關	kenkon maikyakushite monseki o botsusu
收取即今爲雪山	shūshū shite sokkon setsuzan to nasu
狂客時來百雜碎	kyōkyaku toki ni kitte hyaku zassui
大千起滅刹那間	daisen kimetsusu setsuna no kan

Heaven and earth buried, the gates and barriers gone.
Pile the snow up and now it is the Himalayas.
When the crazy vagabond comes; it turns to powder.
The Great Chiliocosm arises and disappears
    in the space of a moment.

Notes:

Snowball: an allusion to the *Blue Cliff Record*, kōan no. 42:

> Lay brother Pang was taking his leave of Yaoshan. Yaoshan ordered ten disciples to accompany Pang as far as the gate. Pang pointed to the snow falling in the sky and said, "Lovely snow, flake by flake, it falls yet does not land in separate places." A disciple named Quan asked, "Where does it fall?" Pang slapped him once. Quan said, "Lay brother, don't be so rough." Pang said, "How can you call yourself a disciple of Zen, the old King of Hell hasn't let you go yet." Quan said, "And what about yourself, lay brother?" Pang slapped him again and said, "You see as if blind, talk as if dumb." At this point, Xuedou interjects, "At the first question, he should just have rolled up a snowball and hit him with it."[58]

Great Chiliocosm: Buddhist term for the universe. (See notes to poem 54.)

Living in the Mountains—two poems

山居　二首 *sankyo—nishu*

Poem 89

淫坊十載興難窮　　*inbō jussai kyō kiwamari gatashi*
強住空山幽谷中　　*shiite kūzan yūkoku no naka ni sumu*
好境雲遮三萬里　　*kōkyō saegiru sanmanri*
長松逆耳屋頭風　　*chōshō mimi ni sakarau okutō no kaze*

Ten years spent in brothels, elation difficult to exhaust.
Now, forced to live amid empty mountains and gloomy valleys,
Thirty thousand miles of cloud spread
　　between here and those delightful places;
The wind in the tall pines around the house grates upon my ears.

Poem 90

狂雲眞是大燈孫	Kyōun makoto ni kore Daitō no son
鬼窟黑山何稱尊	kikutsu kokuzan nanzo son to shōsen
憶昔簫歌雲雨夕	omou mukashi shōka un'u no yūbe
風流年少倒金樽	fūryū nenshō kinson o shōseshi koto o

Crazy Cloud is truly the descendant of Daitō.
Demon caves and black mountains, what is there to revere here?
I remember old songs on the panpipes, evening of cloud-rain,
Fūryū youth tipping back the golden goblet.

Notes:

[90]
Daitō: Founder of Daitokuji. (See pp. 13–14 and notes to poem 6.)
Cloud-rain: See pp. 48–50 and notes to poem 6.
Fūryū youth tipping back the golden goblet: (See notes to poem 6 for explanation of *fūryū*). This line has been lifted whole from a poem by the Song dynasty monk, Fojian (1177–1249) in the *Ren Tian Yanmu*, a compilation of teachings and Buddhist verse from the five schools of Chan Buddhism active in China at the time. The poem is one of a series of verses collected as responses to "Rinzai Four Propositions." (See poems 13, 14, 15 and 16.) The borrowed line is the third line in Fojian's poem intended as a response to the fourth of Rinzai's propositions.[59] In *Having Once Paused*, Messer and Smith suggest that Fojian's line also references a Song story about verse composition in which four family members are composing poetry as a drinking game and the challenge is to come up with a line that uses both "moon" and "golden goblet."[60] What is particularly significant in Ikkyū's poem, however, is that this concluding statement of unabashed attachment to life's fleeting pleasures is actually a citation of Zen scripture.

These poems occur within a group of poems about life in the mountains: poem 88 "Mountain Road" (not translated here), these two poems, poem 91 "Instructing the Cook in the Mountains" (see next poem), and poem 92, "In the Mountains, Receiving a Letter from Nankō" (not translated). The poem "Mountain Road" has as a subtitle the place name Yuzuriha. It is likely that all the poems of this group date from Ikkyū's period of retreat at Yuzuriha (located between present-day Takatsuki and Kameoka) which is recorded in the *Nempu* as follows:

> The master's forty-ninth year [1442]. Ikkyū came for the first time to Yuzuriha mountain and rented a farm house there. There are poems about his life in the mountains. Later he established the Shida-dera and moved into it. Those disciples who missed him and came to him there were all the sort who could forget their own comfort for the sake of the Dharma. Therefore, they gathered firewood and dipped water from the torrents. The mountain road was twisted and full of pitfalls. They worked diligently, never tiring.[61]

Poem 91

Instructing the Cook in the Mountains

山中示典座 *sanchū tenzo ni shimesu*

歸宗一味日興餘	Kisū no ichimi nikkyō no amari
典座山中功不虛	tenzo sanchū kō munashikarazu
休覓淨名香積飯	Jōmyō kōshaku no han o motomuru koto o yameyo
何時饍有美雙魚	izure no toki ka zen ni bisōgyo aran

Guizong's one flavor could be enjoyed day after day
    and still have more to give.
Cook, here in the mountains, your skill is not in vain.
Stop seeking for Vimalakīrti's Feast of Massed Fragrances.
Whenever there are two tasty fish, it is a banquet.

Notes:
Guizong's one flavor: An allusion to the *Wu Deng Hui Yuan*:

> A monk was taking his leave. Guizong asked, "Where are you going?" The monk said, "I'm going here and there to study the Zen of Five flavors." Guizong said, "Other places may teach the Zen of Five flavors; here I have only the Zen of one flavor." "And what is the

Zen of one flavor?" said the monk. Guizong hit him. "I understand, I understand." "Then tell me, tell me." Just as the monk opened his mouth, Guizong hit him again.[62]

Vimalakīrti's Feast of Massed Fragrances: In the chapter entitled "The Buddha of Massed Fragrances" of the *Vimalakīrti Sūtra*, Śāriputra is worried about what to feed the assembled Bodhisattvas. Vimalakīrti tells him, "The Buddha taught release from all material things. How can one desire both to eat and to hear the Dharma? However, if there are those who want to eat, just wait a moment." Vimalakīrti conjures up an illusory Bodhisattva and sends him to the land of the Buddha of Massed Fragrances. He returns with a vase of the ambrosia of that land, the fragrance of which astonishes them all. As they are about to eat, Vimalakīrti invites them, saying, "Come and partake of the Tathāgata's sweet nectar and ambrosia that is perfumed with great compassion.[63]

two tasty fish: An allusion to two lines in a poem of Du Fu's called "Li Jian's House":

> About to eat the two tasty fish,
> Who would look for the heaviness of other flavors?[64]

Poem 93

From the Mountains, Returning to the City

自山中歸市中 *sanchū yori shichū ni kaeru*

狂雲誰識屬狂風	*Kyōun tare ka shiran kyōfū ni zoku sure koto o*
朝在山中暮市中	*asa ni sanchū ni ari kure ni wa shichū*
我若當機行棒喝	*ware moshi ki ni atatte bōkatsu o gyōseba*
德山臨濟面通紅	*Tokusan Rinzai omote kurenai o tsūzen*

Crazy Cloud, who knows to what wild wind he belongs?
Morning, in the mountains, evening, in the city,
If I, at the right occasion, were to wield the stick or shout "Katsu,"
Deshan and Rinzai would blush.

Notes:

wild wind: this phrase can also be interpreted as crazy style.
Deshan: See notes to poem 17.
Rinzai: Founder of the Rinzai school, noted for his use of the shout "Katsu." (See poem 512.)

Prose Introduction to Poem 94

昔有一婆子、供養一庵主。經二十年、常令一二八女子送飯給侍。一日令女子抱定云、正恁麼時如何。菴主云, 枯木倚寒岩、三冬無暖氣。女子歸舉似。婆子云、我二十年、只供養得箇俗漢。追出燒却庵。

Long ago, there was an old woman who for twenty years had supported the head of a hermitage. She always sent a sixteen-year-old girl to bring meals and serve him. One day she told the girl to embrace him and ask, "Right at that moment, what is it like!" The girl did so and the monk said, "I feel like an old withered tree leaning against a cold cliff during the third month of winter when there is no warm weather." The girl returned and described what had happened. The old woman said, "For twenty years I have been supporting a charlatan." Then she chased him out and burned the hermitage down.

Poem 94

老婆心爲賊過梯	*rōbashin zoku no tame kakehashi o watashi*
清淨沙門與女妻	*jōjō no shamon ni nyosai o atau*
今夜美人若約我	*konya bijin moshi ware o yakuseba*
枯楊春老更生梯	*koyō haru oite sara ni hikobae o shōzen*

The old woman's kindness was like lending a ladder to a thief;
So, to the pure monk she gave a girl as wife.
Tonight, if a beautiful woman were to entwine with me
The withered willow, though old this spring,
    would put forth new shoots.

Notes:

Long ago, there was an old woman ... : Although the ultimate source of the story is not known, it appears as a kōan in many Zen texts, twice in the *Xutang Lu*, for example. Yanagida says: "Among the various kōans in Zen, this one, 'the old woman burned the hermitage,' is one of the most difficult. It presents us with a great problem that we must continue to deal with right till the end, as long as we have life. Even Zen provides no set answer to the problem of relations between men and women."[65]

Prose Introduction to Poems 100–108

文安丁卯秋、大德精舍有一僧、無故而自殺矣。好事之徒遂譖之官。繫其餘殃而居囚禁者七五輩、足爲吾門之大亂。時人喧傳焉。豫聞之、即日晦迹山中。其意蓋出於不忍耳。適學者自京城來、說本寺件件之事、愈弗勝嘅歎、作偈言懷。時値重陽、故成九篇云。

In the autumn of the Fourth Year of Bun'an [1447], there was a monk at Daitokuji who for whatever reason committed suicide. Scandal-loving monks made slanderous reports to the officials. So, in connection with this calamity, five or seven of my fellow monks were imprisoned. This was sufficient to cause great trouble within my school. At that time, people were noisily spreading rumors about it. I listened to them and then, the last day of the month, disappeared into the mountains. The reason for my leaving was that I simply could not bear it. It chanced that a monk came by here, himself just from Kyoto. He informed me of the various things going on at the temple which are all the more unendurable and lamentable. As this happened to occur on the ninth day of the ninth month, I have made nine poems.

Poem 101

慚我聲名猶未韜　　hazu ware seimei nao imada kakusazu
參禪學道長塵勞　　sanzen gakudō jinrō o nagazeshi koto o
靈山正法掃地滅　　Ryōzen no shōhō shi o haratte messu
不意魔王十丈高　　omowazariki Maō jūjō takaran to su

I am ashamed my name and fame are not yet obscured;
Practicing Zen, studying the Way, dusty troubles grow;
The true doctrine of Ryōzen is swept from the earth and destroyed;
Unexpectedly, the King of Hell has grown a hundred feet high.

Poem 108

風外松杉亂入雲　　fūgai shōsan midarete kumo ni iru
諸方動衆又驚群　　shohō wa shū o ugokashi mata
　　　　　　　　　　　　gun o odorokasu
人境機關吾不會　　jinkyō no kikan ware esezu
濁醪一盞醉醺醺　　dakurō issan yotte kunkun

The wind outside, pines and cedars in disorder enter clouds.
Everywhere, the multitudes are moved, the masses astonished.
The kōan of subject and object, I do not understand.
One cup of cloudy *sake* and I am stinking drunk.

Notes:
Ninth day of the ninth month: Since in the cosmology of the *Yijing*, nine is the most *yang* of numbers, the ninth day of the ninth month (actually closer to middle October in the lunar calendar) was celebrated as the festival of double-*yang*. Festivities included outings to the mountains where one composed poetry in the open air and drank wine that had been steeped with chrysanthemum petals. The festival day that year found Ikkyū in the mountains but not in a mood to celebrate. The *Nempu* entry about this event states that Ikkyū had actually retreated to the mountains with the intention of starving himself to death in protest over the political problems at Daitokuji.[66]
nine poems: Only two of the nine poems are translated here, a third one (poem 107) appears in the section on allusion (p. 39)

[101]
doctrine of Ryōzen: Ryōzen's style of Zen. (See notes to poem 33.)

[108]
The wind outside ... : The first line is a reworking of a line from a poem by Chu Sizong in the *San Ti Shi*:

Pines, cedars in the wind outside, disordered mountains are green.
At a desk, burning incense, facing a stone screen,
I remember last year, after spring rain,
Swallow mud sometimes soiled *The Great Mystery* as I read.[67]

The Great Mystery was a Han philosophical work that was never fully appreciated. This book soiled with swallow mud represents the poet's own misunderstood and belittled talents. He has withdrawn from this humiliation to a mountain retreat. By alluding to this poem, Ikkyū amplifies the sense of his own isolation.

multitudes are moved, the masses astonished: The introduction to kōan 11 in the *Blue Cliff Record* praises a Zen master by saying "A casual word or phrase (from this master) and the multitudes are moved; the masses astonished."[68] In the context of this poem, it is not wisdom but rather ignorance and mischief that is stirring the masses.

kōan of subject and object: A reference to Rinzai's "Four Propositions." (See notes to poems 13–16.) The word used for kōan here is *kikan*, literally "juncture of opportunity." The line could also be interpreted to mean, "the meeting or juncture of subjective consciousness and the external world, I do not understand."

Wind Bell—two poems

風鈴　二首 *fūrin—nishu*

Poem 110

靜時無響動時鳴　*seiji ni kyō naku dōji ni naru*
鈴有聲耶風有聲　*suzu ni koe aru ka kaze ni koe aru ka*
驚起老僧白晝睡　*kyōkisu rōsō ga hakuchū no sui*
何須日午打三更　*nanzo nichigo ni sankō o mochiin*

In stillness it echoes not, in movement it rings;
Is it the wind or the bell that has a voice?
Waking up this old monk from his daytime nap,
What need is there to sound the midnight watch at noon?

Poem 111

見聞境界太無端	kenmon no kyōkai hanahada hashi nashi
好是清聲隱隱寒	yoshi kore seimei inin toshite samuki koto o
普化老漢活手段	Fuke rōkan no kasshudan
和風搭在玉欄干	kaze ni washite tōzai su kyokuranka

The realm of the senses is outrageous.
Beautiful this clear sound, faintly in the cold.
Old Rascal Puhua had lively tricks.
Harmonizing with the wind,
    it hangs above the polished balustrade.

Notes:
[110]
Is it the wind or the bell that has a voice?: An allusion to the *Chuan Deng Lu* chapter on the Sixth Patriarch, Huineng (638–713):

> Two monks were arguing over a banner fluttering in the evening wind. One said, "The banner moves." The other said, "The wind moves." Huineng said, "Truly neither the wind nor the banner moves; the movement is in the mind."[69]

sound the midnight watch at noon: Phrase originating in the *Guzunsu Yulu*, where it is used in a poem apropos Rinzai's teachings:

> "To be able to understand the meaning therein, sound the midnight watch at noon."[70]

[111]
faintly in the cold ... Old Rascal Puhua: Most of the Tang masters were quite eccentric in their conduct, but the most extravagantly unconventional of them all was Puhua. His antics are recorded in the *Record of Rinzai*. Puhua apparently lived at Rinzai's monastery but did not treat Rinzai as his teacher. This poem alludes to the miraculous circumstances surrounding his death:

> One day Puhua went about the streets asking people he met for a one-piece gown. They all offered him one, but Puhua declined them all.

Rinzai had the steward of the temple buy a coffin, and when Puhua came back the Master said: "I've fixed up a one-piece gown for you."

Puhua put the coffin on his shoulders and went around the streets calling out: "Rinzai fixed me up a one-piece gown. I'm going to the East Gate to depart this life." All the townspeople scrambled after him to watch.

"No, not today," said Puhua, "but tomorrow I'll go to the South Gate to depart this life."

After he had done the same thing for three days, no one believed him any more. On the fourth day not a single person followed him to watch. He went outside the town walls all by himself, got into the coffin, and asked a passer-by to nail it up. The news immediately spread. The townspeople all came running; on opening the coffin, they saw he had vanished, body and all. Only the sound of his bell could be heard in the sky, faintly receding into the distance.[71]

Harmonizing with the wind, it hangs above the polished balustrade: This line is taken whole from a sermon by Xutang:

> Rising in the hall to lecture, he said, "In the valley forest leaves fall, the voices of the frontier geese are cold. Seeing through the kōan is very difficult, very difficult. A hundred iron balls scatter. Harmonizing with the wind, it hangs above the polished balustrade.[72]

However, Xutang had borrowed this line from a poem by the Five Dynasties poet, Xu Zhongya:

> She rises at dawn, fearful of the spring cold,
> Lightly raising the vermilion blinds, gazes at the camellia.
> Not a handful of willow fluff to gather.
> Harmonizing with the wind,
>   it hangs above the polished balustrade.[73]

Xutang had already changed the meaning of the line by putting it in a totally different context. Ikkyū shifts the context again, a good illustration how the meaning of words and images, being provisional, is utterly dependent on context. Note that the original source of the allusion is another "boudoir lament."

Poem 113

Half a Cloud

半雲 *han'un*

膚寸無根點碧空	*fusun mukon hekikū ni tensu*
安身立命在其中	*anjin ryūmei sono naka ni ari*
夢魂昨夜巫山雨	*mukon sakuya fuzan no ame*
吟斷朝來一片蹤	*gin dansu chōrai ippen no ato*

One wisp, rootless, shifting, a spot in the blue sky—
Any safe, secure life is just therein.
Dream spirit, last night in the rain at Wushan;
The singing stops, morning comes, one fragment remains.

Notes:
Half a Cloud: This title is followed with a note indicating that it is the name for study. Presumably, someone asked Ikkyū to give their study a name and he offered "Half a Cloud" along with a commemorative verse.
Any safe, secure life: See poem 54 for the same expression.
Dream spirit, last night in the rain at Wushan: Reference to the story of the Goddess of Wushan visiting the King, the source of the expression "cloud-rain." (See pp. 48–50 and notes to poem 6.)

Prose Introduction to Poem 115

紹鴲藏主規地卜居。家徒四壁立。扁曰土庵。作偈以爲證云。

Monastic librarian Shōen is measuring up the ground and siting his dwelling, "just a little house, four plain walls." The plaque on the front will say "Earth House," I have composed a poem to commemorate it.

Poem 115

夏巢冬穴一身康　　kasō tōketsu isshin yasushi
帶水拖泥萬念忙　　taisui dadei man'nen isogawashi
稼穡艱難若領略　　kashoku kan'nan moshi ryōryakuseba
栴檀佛寺利名場　　sendan no butsuji rimyō no ba

As cool as a tree nest in summer, as warm as a cave in winter,
    comfortable for a body.
Up to one's waist in water, thrashing through the mud,
    mind ever busy,
If you understand the toil of farming,
Then you know that sandalwood monasteries
    are merely places for gain and fame.

Notes:
Monastic librarian Shōen: An unidentifiable person.
"*just a little house, four plain walls*": The description of the hovel Sima Xiangru, a famous Han-dynasty poet and free spirit, lived in after eloping with Wenjun.[74]
As cool as a tree nest in summer ... : A description of a comfortable house originating in the *Wenxuan*.[75]

Poem 117

Straw Raincoat and Hat

蓑笠 *saryū*

樵客漁人受用全　　shokaku gyojin juyō mattashi
何須曲淥木床禪　　nanzo mochiin kyokuroku mokushō no zen
芒鞋竹杖三千界　　bōai chikujō sanzenkai
水宿風餐二十年　　suishuku fūsan nijūnen

Woodcutters and fishermen,
    their understanding and application is perfect;

What need have they of the Zen of ornately carved chairs?
Straw sandals and bamboo staff,
    roaming the Great Chiliocosm,
Water-dwelling, wind-eating, twenty years.

Notes:
Straw Raincoat and Hat: The rain gear of peasants, fishermen, and pilgrims; a sub-note to the title indicates that the term was used as name for a hermitage, whether for Ikkyū or someone else is not recorded.
Great Chiliocosm: See notes to poem 54.
Water-dwelling, wind-eating, twenty years: Ikkyū uses this same phrase to describe Daitō during his twenty years living in a small hermitage close to Gojō Bridge. (See notes to poem 8.)

Prose Introduction to Poems 120, 121

華叟老師掩光而後、既洎二十餘稔也。壬申秋、敕諡大機弘宗禪師。仍製禪師詩、呈寄大用養叟和尚。且陳賀忱云。

It is already more than twenty years since Master Kasō veiled his light. Now, in the autumn of 1452, imperial decree has conferred on him the posthumous title Daiki Kōjū Zenji, "Zen Master of Great Opportunity, Propagator of the Essential Message." So I have composed some "Zen Master" poems for the Reverend Daiyū Yōsō. These describe my feelings of congratulation.

Poem 120

曾謝塵寰五十年   *katsute jinkan wo shasu gojū nen*
芳聲美譽是何禪   *hōmei biyo kore nan no zen zo*
子胥日晚倒行去   *Shisho hi osōshite tōkōshi saru*
靦面辱屍三百鞭   *tekimen shikane o hazukashimu*
                                   sanbyakuben

For fifty years he shunned the dusty world.
Fragrant names, splendid fame, is what kind of Zen?

Zixu in the evening of his life resorted to revolting behavior,
Right before his eyes, he had the corpse lashed
 three hundred times.

Poem 121

懶瓚辭詔也何似	Ransan mikotonori o jisu mata izure zo
煨芋烟鎖竹爐裏	waiu en sasu chikuro no uchi
大用現前眞衲僧	daiyū genzen shin no nōsō
先師頭面潑惡水	senshi no zumen ni akusui o sosogu

How about Lancan turning down the imperial order
Sweet yams smoking in the bamboo stove?
His great activity manifesting itself, this true monk,
On the master's face, throws slop water.

Notes:
Master Kasō: Kasō Sōden (d. 1428), Ikkyū's master, a stern man of rigorous virtue who preferred to keep to a small monastery in Katada rather than have to observe the political intrigues that embroiled the large monasteries in the capital. (See pp. 13–14).
Daiyū Yōsō: As senior disciple of the same master Kasō, Yōsō (1376–1458) was Ikkyū's elder brother in a religious sense. It was through good offices and the temple's full treasury that the honorary posthumous title had been obtained for Kasō. (See pp. 19–23.)

[120]
Zixu in the evening … : An allusion to the *Shiji*, roll 66. Wu Zixu's father and elder brother had been killed by the King of Chu. Wu Zixu therefore went over to the enemy state of Wu to help bring about Chu's defeat. When the armies of Wu conquered Chu, Wu Zixu was disappointed to find that the king was already dead. In order to satisfy his desire for revenge, he had the corpse exhumed and lashed three hundred times. Wu Zixu's reply to critics of his behavior was, "I am in the evening of my life and still have far to go; therefore, I have overturned proper conduct and carried out my intention in a revolting way."[76]

[121]

How about Lancan ... : Lancan, a Tang monk whose biography is not well documented, is represented in the *Chuan Deng Lu* only by one song of his own composition. A colorful legend, however, grew up around him:

> When Lancan was living as a hermit, the Tang emperor Dezong heard of him and invited him to court. Lancan was roasting yams over a fire of cow dung and would not even turn around to look at the imperial messenger. His nose running from the cold, he took a yam from the fire and began to eat. The messenger said, "Can't you even wipe your nose for His Majesty's messenger?" Lancan replied, "I have no time to wipe my nose for the common likes of you."[77]

In his own poem, he alludes to this event in two terse lines:

> I did not pay court to the emperor.
> What is there to envy in kings and dukes?[78]

great activity: A pun on the name Daiyū which means "great activity" and implies great action and attainment in Zen.

Poem 126

Praising Puhua

贊普化 *fuke o sansu*

德山臨濟奈同行	*Tokuzan Rinzai dōan o ikansen*
街市風顛群衆驚	*gaishi no fūten gunshū o odoroku*
坐脱立亡多敗闕	*zadatsu ryūbō haiketsu ooshi*
和鳴隱隱寶鈴聲	*wamei inintari gyokurin no koe*

How about if Deshan and Rinzai traveled along with him?
His mad antics on the street and in the marketplace
    amazed everyone.
Of all the monks who died sitting or standing, he bested many,
Ringing in harmony, faintly, the sound of a jeweled bell.

Notes:

Puhua: An eccentric companion of Rinzai's who had himself nailed into a coffin and then disappeared leaving behind only the sound of a bell. (See notes to poems 110 and 111.)
Deshan and Rinzai: See notes to poem 17.
Of all the Zen monks who died … : The manner in which a Zen master died is an important part of his biography. To die in the full lotus position after making one's last pronouncements in verse was an ideal. Puhua's death, on the other hand, was certainly one of the most imaginative on record.

Poem 128

Under One's Feet, the Red Thread

脚下紅絲線 *kyakuka no kōshisen*

持戒爲驢破戒人	*jikai wa ro to nari hakai wa hito*
河沙異號弄精神	*Gasha no igō seishin o rōsu*
初生孩子婚姻線	*Shoshō no gaishi kon'in no sen*
開落紅花幾度春	*kairakusu kōka ikudo no haru*

Those who keep the rules are asses,
    those who break the rules are men.
With different names as many as the Ganges' sands,
    the ways of teasing the spirit.
The newborn infant is bound with the threads of marital alliance.
How many springs have the scarlet blossoms opened and fallen?

Notes:
Under One's Feet, the Red Thread is a partial quotation of the third of what is commonly known as the "Three Pivotal Phrases" of Songyuan (d. 1202), who was a patriarch in Ikkyū's lineage. (See notes to poems 130, 491, and 492 for more about Songyuan.) The full question is, "Why is it that under the feet of the bright-eyed monk the red thread is not yet severed?"[79] This phrase appears independently in the *Songyuan Yulu*; only later did it come to be considered one of the "Three Pivotal Phrases." Ikkyū took the "red thread" as a metaphor for passion and used it often in his writings.

Poem 130

Self-Appraisal

自贊 *jisan*

華叟子孫不知禪	*Kasō no shison zen o shirazu*
狂雲面前誰說禪	*Kyōun menzen tare ka zen o toku*
三十年來肩上重	*sanjūnen kenjō omoshi*
一人荷擔松源禪	*hitori katansu Shōgen no zen*

Kasō's descendant does not know Zen.
In front of Crazy Cloud, who would explain Zen?
For thirty years, heavy on my shoulders
I have carried the burden of Songyuan's Zen.

Notes:
Self-Appraisal: Poems of self-appraisal were called upon to accompany the portrait of a Master. In such a poem, the Master would try to summarize the essence of his Zen. This poem appears on two famous portraits of Ikkyū, the one by Bokusai in the Tokyo National Museum and one showing Ikkyū with a long sword in the Shinjuan subtemple of Daitokuji.
Kasō's descendant: This could refer either to Yōsō, the antagonist in Ikkyū's life, or to Ikkyū himself since they both shared the same teacher, Kasō. If it is the latter, his statement in the poem becomes paradoxical, "I know Zen best for not knowing Zen."
For thirty years ... the burden: Echoes the last words of Tettō, first abbot of Daitokuji, "There was no one upon whom to bestow the Treasury of the True Dharma Eye. I bear the burden myself until the coming of Maitreya, Buddha of the future."[80]
Songyuan: (1132–1202) Master to Xutang, therefore another important figure in the Daitokuji lineage. Ikkyū identified himself with Xutang so strongly that he also felt a special affinity for Xutang's teacher. (See poem 128 and poems 491–492.)

As duplicated in the translation, the three rhyming lines of this poem all end with the word "Zen." This is outrageous from the point of view of conventional prosody, for all repetition of vocabulary was avoided in the short four-line form.

Three Poems to Show the Monks of My Circle—three poems

示會裏徒　三首 *eri no to ni shimesu—sanshu*

Poem 134

樂中有苦一休門　　*rakuchū ni ku ari Ikkyū no mon*
箇箇蛙爭井底尊　　*koko a arasou sekitei no son*
晝夜在心元字脚　　*chūya kokoro ni oku genjikyaku*
是非人我一生喧　　*zehi ninga isshō kamabisushi*

In the midst of pleasure there is pain in Ikkyū's school.
Each frog fighting for veneration at the bottom of the well;
Day and night busy thinking about the words of the scriptures;
Right and wrong, self and other, fussing away a whole life.

Poem 135

公案參來明歷歷　　*kōan sanji kitatte mei rekireki*
胸襟勘破暗昏昏　　*kyōkin kanbasureba an konkon*
怨憎到死難忘却　　*onzōshite shi ni itaru made bōkyakushi gatashi*
道伴忠言逆耳根　　*dōhan no chūgen ninkon ni sakarau*

Delving into the kōan, it becomes distinct and clear.
Break into, examine the heart, blackness is dark, dark.
There are resentments that until death are difficult to forget.
The sincere reproofs of fellow monks grate on the ears.

Poem 136

徒學得祖師言句　　itazura ni soshi no gonku o gakutokushite
識情刀山牙劍樹　　shikijō wa Tōzan no kibakenju nari
看看頻頻拳他非　　miyo miyo hinbin toshite ta no hi o kosuru o
銜血噴人其口污　　chi o fukunde hito ni fukeba sono kuchi
　　　　　　　　　　　kegaru

In vain do you learn the words and phrases of the old masters.
Knowledge is like the razor sharp tusks of Tōzan.
See them, following one upon another,
    bringing up the faults of others.
Whoever holds blood in his mouth to spit at others,
    his mouth is polluted.

Notes:

[134]
In the midst of pleasure there is pain: See poem 46.
Each frog: See poem 74.

[136]
tusks of Tōzan: Tōzan "sword mountain" is a mountain in hell with razor sharp tusks upon which the bodies of the damned were heaved.
Whoever holds blood ... : Such a powerful line, but not original to Ikkyū. Slightly different versions of it appear in several Zen texts. Perhaps most important for Ikkyū, it is used in the *Xutang Lu*. The passage there is: "A monk asked, 'Lingyun saw a peach blossom and was enlightened. The student monk everyday sees one branch, two branches of blossoms; why is he not enlightened?' Master Xutang said, 'He who fills his mouth with blood to spit at others first pollutes his own mouth.'"[81]

On Tiger Mount, the Snow Falls on Three Grades of Monks—two poems

虎丘雪下三等僧　二首 *Kukyū setsuka santō no sō—nishu*

Poem 140

少林積雪置心頭　　*Shōrin no sekisetsu shintō ni oku*
公案圓成上等仇　　*kōan enjōsu jōtō no tagui*
僧社吟詩剃頭俗　　*sōsha ni shi o ginzu teitō no zoku*
飢腸脫食也風流　　*kichō jiki o toku mo mata fūryū*

The piled snow at Shaolin placed in the mind,
The kōan completes itself for the upper-rank fellow.
The one in the monk's quarters composing poems
    is a shave-pated layman.
The one who is hungry and talks of food is also fūryū.

Poem 141

禪者詩人皆癡鈍　　*zensha shijin mina chidon*
雪下三等多議論　　*setsuka no santō giron ooshi*
妙喜若是大慈心　　*Myōshi moshi kore daijishin naraba*
說食僧與香積飯　　*jiki o toku sō ni kōjakuhan o ateyo*

The meditator and the poet are both stupid.
The three grades of monks on a snowy day, so much controversy.
If Miaoxi had a heart of great compassion,
The monk who spoke of food would have gotten
    a Feast of Massed Fragrances.

Notes:

On Tiger Mount, the Snow Falls … : These two poems are based on an episode in the *Dahui Wuku* where Master Dahui (1089–1163) reflects on the apt remarks of a former master:

> Master Yuantong Xiu on a snowy day once wrote: "In snowy weather there are three types of monks. The highest-grade monk is in the meditation hall doing zazen. The middle-grade monk is making his ink, taking up his brush, and composing poems about snow. The lowest-grade monk is huddled round the fire pit talking about food." Now it is winter in the year 1127 on Tiger Mount, the snow is falling and the monks can all be divided into those three types. I laughed out loud and thought, "So the words of a former comrade are not mere fabrications."[82]

[140]
The piled snow at Shaolin …: An allusion to the kōan about the Second Patriarch's interview with Bodhidharma.

> Bodhidharma was facing the wall. The Second Patriarch was standing in the snow and cut off his own arm. "Master," he said, "I have no peace of mind, I beg you to pacify my mind." Bodhidharma said, "Well, show me your mind and I'll pacify it for you." The Second Patriarch said, "But when I look for my mind, I can't find it." "There," said Bodhidharma, "I have pacified your mind."[83]

[141]
Miaoxi: A sobriquet of Dahui, which may be translated as "Wondrous Joy."
great compassion … Feast of Massed Fragrances: An allusion to the "Feast of Massed Fragrances" of the *Vimalakīrti Sūtra*. Vimalakīrti describes the feast as "the Tathāgata's nectar and ambrosia perfumed with great compassion." (See notes to poem 91.)
fūryū: Here, the meaning is close to "charming" with connotations of "far-out." (See notes to poem 6.)

Poem 144

On a Brothel

題婬坊 *inbō o daisu*

美人雲雨愛河深	*bijin no un'u aiga fukashi*
樓子老禪樓上吟	*Rōshi Rōzen rōjō no gin*
我有抱持啑吻興	*ware ni hōji shōfun no kyō ari*
竟無火聚捨身心	*tsui ni kajū shashin no shin nashi*

A beautiful woman, cloud-rain, love as deep as a river,
Old Reverend Pavilion Master listens to the song
    up in the pavilion.
I find elation in embraces and kisses,
I have no sense of casting my body into flames.

Notes:
Old Reverend Pavilion Master listens to the song: The meaning of this line and of the rest of the poem is tied to its allusion source, the following anecdote in the *Wu Deng Hui Yuan*:

> Pavilion Master[Louzi]: It is unknown from whence he came, and his actual name has been lost, but one day when this man was wandering through a marketplace, he stopped to adjust his gaiters in front of a wine pavilion. From up in the pavilion, he heard someone singing: "Since you have no heart, I might as well give mine up too." Suddenly experiencing true enlightenment, that man therefore took the sobriquet "Pavilion Master."[84]

The word "pavilion" connotes an upscale drinking establishment providing "wine, women, and song." The women would have their living quarters upstairs. We are to imagine that it is daytime, and one of women is singing to practice or console herself. The charm in the story resides in the punning potential of "no heart" (無心) in her song, which can also mean "without (deluded) mind." The pivot inherent in this phrase apparently gave Pavilion Master the push he needed to achieve enlightenment.

casting my body into flames: According to Hirano, this phrase connotes an enlightened state of mind in which "one does not fear death." [85]

This poem introduces a new figure in Ikkyū's "community of the imagination," that is, Zen masters and poets of the past, usually in China, with whom Ikkyū identified in a personal way.[86] His identification with the patriarchs in his lineage such as Xutang and Songyuan is to be expected. Ikkyū's singling out an obscure monk like Pavilion Master (Louzi) for particular emulation is more idiosyncratic. On the basis of this anecdote about achieving enlightenment through hearing a sad love song, Pavilion Master became for Ikkyū a touchstone for enlightenment in connection with the pleasure quarters and sexual relationships. Later in his life, in two poems written during the period of his relationship with the blind singer Mori (see poem frontispiece and poem 531), Ikkyū adopts "Pavilion Master" as a sobriquet for himself.

Poem 145

Addressed to a Monk in the Hall of Long Life

示延壽堂僧 *enjūdō no sō ni shimesu*

無常殺鬼現前時	*mujō no sekki genzen no toki*
末後牢關說向誰	*matsugo no rōkan tare ni ka sekkō sen*
百事難休五欲鬧	*hyakuji kyūshi gatashi goyoku isogawashi*
六窓欲鎖八風吹	*rokusō tozan to hossureba happū fuku*

When the killing demons of impermanence are before you,
To whom can you speak about the final prison?
A hundred affairs are impossible to still, the five desires are noisy.
You want to bar the six windows of the senses,
    but the eight winds blow them open.

Notes:
Hall of Long Life: Like Nirvana Hall, a name for the monastic infirmary.
final prison: A metaphor for the final kōan, which in this case is death itself.
the five desires: The desires that arise from the five realms of perception: form, sound, fragrance, taste, and texture.
the six windows of the senses: the five senses plus thought.
the eight winds: eight things that agitate and delude the mind: gain and loss, disparagement and flattery, praise and slander, and pain and pleasure.[87]

Poem 153

Śākyamuni Practicing Ascetic Discipline

苦行釋迦 *kugyō no Shaka*

六年飢寒徹骨髓	rokunen no kikan kotsuzui ni tessu
苦行是佛祖玄旨	kugyō wa kore busso no genshi
信道無天然釋迦	iu koto o shinzu tennen no shaka wa nashi to
天下衲僧飯袋子	tenka no nosō hantaisu

For six years hunger and cold pierced his bones to the marrow.
Ascetic discipline is the mysterious teaching
　　of the Buddhas and Patriarchs.
I believe what is said, there is no natural Śākyamuni:
Now in the world, patch-cloth monks are just rice bags.

Note:
Śākyamuni Practicing Ascetic Discipline: Śākyamuni devoted himself to ascetic practices for six years. This poem was composed as an appreciatory verse for a scroll by the painter Jasoku depicting Śākyamuni as an ascetic. The work's inscription dates it as Kōshō 2 (1456).[88]

Poem 156

Self-Appraisal

自贊 *jisan*

風狂狂客起狂風	fūkyō no kyōkyaku kyōfū o okosu
來往婬坊酒肆中	raiōsu inbō shūshi no uchi
具眼衲僧誰一拶	gugan no nōsō tare ka issatsusen
畫南畫北畫西東	minami o kakushi kita o kakushi seitō o kakusu

Crazy madman stirring up a crazy style
Coming and going amid brothels and wineshops.
Which of you clear-eyed patch-cloth monks can assail me?
I mark out the south, I mark out the north, the west and east.

Note:
I mark out the south…: Hirano remarks that this line calls to mind two passages in Zen texts. One is kōan no. 9 in *Blue Cliff Record* where Zhaozhou responds to a monk who asks, "What is Zhaochou?": "East Gate, west gate, south gate, north gate." The other is the extended section in the *Linji Lu* (*Rinzai roku*) that records the crazy behavior of Puhua. In that section, Puhua's chant as he marches through the streets ringing his bell includes the line, "When they come at me from the four directions and eight points between, I strike as a whirlwind."[89] (See other poems on Puhua, 110, 111, and 126.)

Like poems 130 and 153, this poem was composed for an inscription on a painting, in this case, another portrait of Ikkyū. The inscription records that the portrait was presented to a lay disciple of Ikkyū, Sōrin, a merchant of Sakai, who, after the Ōnin war, was the chief donor for the rebuilding of Daitokuji.[90]

Poem 166

Praising the Dharma Master Ci'en Kuiji

贊慈恩窺基法師 *Jion Kiki Hōshi o sansu*

窺基三昧獨天眞	*Kiki zanmai hitori tenshin*
酒肉諸經又美人	*shu niku shokyō mata bijin*
座主眼睛猶若此	*zasu no ganzei nao kaku no gotoshi*
宗門唯有箇宗純	*shūmon tada kono Sōjun ari*

Kuiji's samādhi alone was natural and real.
Wine, meat, the scriptures, and beautiful women,
The eye of the abbot was just like this.
In our school, there is only this Sōjun.

Notes:

Dharma Master Ci'en Kuiji: Kuiji (632–681) is the official first Patriarch of the Faxiang, Yogācāra, school of Buddhism in China. He was the disciple of Xuanzang, the illustrious and intrepid pilgrim, who brought an enormous collection of sutras from India and with them the transmission of the Yogācāra teaching. It was for Kuiji to write the commentaries to these sutras and to formulate the theoretical writings of the school. A legend persists about his unconventional behavior, that, for example, he loved the sutras but could not give up wine and women. The legend probably reached Ikkyū through the *Conglin Shengshi*, a Song Zen text which has a biographical entry for Kuiji. The pertinent section thereof follows:

> Furthermore, when he saw the emperor, he would not make obeisance. He just went to and fro, followed by three carts filled with the sutras, wine, food, and women."[91]

Hence, he became known as the Three-Cart Monk. Stanley Weinstein, in a biographical study of Kuiji, virtually proves, by reference to the oldest, and often ignored, sources for Kuiji's biography, that the legend dates from the Song period, and has no basis in fact whatsoever. He suggests that Kuiji may well have been called disparagingly the Three-Cart Monk in Song times, not for incontinent behavior but for his unique interpretation of the *Lotus Sūtra*. He asserted that "the doctrine of the Three Vehicles represents the ultimate truth of Buddhism, whereas the doctrine of the all-embracing One Vehicle which transcends the separateness of the Three Vehicles is only a provisional teaching, designed to lead the unenlightened to the truth of the Three Vehicles." Such an interpretation invited fierce criticism from members of other schools, for whom the One-Vehicle teaching of the *Lotus* was a cherished doctrine. Weinstein remarks that failure of the official Song biographer to indicate this and "even worse, his inclusion of patently slanderous material ... has resulted in a manifestly unsympathetic attitude toward Ci'en on the part of many Buddhist historians, which has persisted in one form or another to the present day."[92] Ironically, the apocryphal legend that slurred Kuiji's character, so far as most schools of Buddhism were concerned, made him a kind of hero for the Zen school, which has always valued spirituality untainted by overserious religiosity.
samādhi: Concentration of mind in meditative state, here equivalent to enlightened perception.
Sōjun: Ikkyū

Poem 175

Congratulating Daiyūan's Monk Yōsō upon Receiving the Honorary Title Zen Master Sōe Daishō

賀大用庵養叟和尚賜宗惠大照禪師號 *Daiyūan Yōsō Oshō Sōe Daishō Zenji no gō o tamau o gasu*

紫衣師號奈家貧	*shie shigō ie no hin o ikansen*
綾紙青銅三百緡	*ryoshi seidō sanbyaku min*
大用現前贗長老	*daiyū genzen no gan chōrō*
看來眞箇普州人	*mikitareba shinko Fushū no hito*

Purple robes, honorary titles, how can the house be poor?
The Imperial Edict alone cost three hundred strings
    of copper coins.
The appearance of great activity, the old charlatan,
If you just look at him, you can tell he is really
    a man from Puzhou.

Notes:

Daiyūan's Monk Yōsō ... Receiving the Honorary Title Zen Master: Yōsō was the elder disciple of Kasō, Ikkyū's elder brother in terms of the lineage, but as far as Ikkyū was concerned, Yōsō was selling out the spirit of their tradition. This was a case in point.

Ostensibly Yōsō was honored with this title in recognition of his work in rebuilding Daitokuji after the fire of 1453, but there was more to it than that. The title of *Zenji*, Zen Master, was usually only awarded posthumously. In fact, Yōsō was the first abbot of Daitokuji to be so distinguished. Furthermore, as the first line of the poem mentions, Yōsō was also given the privilege of wearing purple robes, normally an honor allowed only to the abbots of Gozan temples.

The granting of such extraordinary privileges had been the monopoly of the Ashikaga shogunate. That the Imperial Court was allowed to grant these honors to Daitokuji, a monastery totally outside the Gozan system, meant that exclusive prerogatives had been pried away from the shogunate. Of course, there would have been compensation. The shogunate was more and more in need of funds. If a monastery outside the Gozan ranks was prepared to pay

Gozan-size fees for honorary titles, the relinquishment of the exclusivity of title-granting prerogatives must have seemed a small loss.

For Yōsō, it was an important gain. In terms of prestige, it put Daitokuji on an equal footing with the Gozan again. However, to Ikkyū, it was scrambling after name and empty honor.

great activity: This is the literal meaning of the Daiyū component of Yōsō's name, itself derived from the name of his hermitage within the Daitokuji temple complex. See notes to poem 121.

a man from Puzhou: Puzhou is a province in Sichuan renowned for producing robbers, thus the expression "man from Puzhou" was proverbial for thief.

Poem 176

Addressed to a Monk at Daitokuji

寄大德寺僧 *Daitokuji no sō ni kisu*

人多入得大燈門　　*hito ooku nittokusu Daitō no mon*
這裏誰捐師席尊　　*shari tare ka shiseki no son o sutsuru*
淡飯麁茶我無客　　*tanpan socha ware ni kyaku nashi*
醉歌獨倒濁醪樽　　*suika hitori taosu dakurō no son*

Many are the men who enter Daitō's gate.
Therein who rejects the veneration of the master role?
Thin rice gruel, coarse tea, I have few guests;
Singing drunkenly, all alone, I drain a goblet of muddy *sake*.

Poem 179

Inscription for Yōsō's Daiyūan Hermitage

題養叟大用庵　*Yōsō no Daiyūan o daisu*

山林富貴五山衰　　*sanrin wa fūki Gozan wa otorou*
唯有邪師無正師　　*tada jashi nomi atte shōshi nashi*

欲把一竿作漁客　　ikkan o totte gyokyaku to naran to hossu
江湖近代逆風吹　　gōko kindai gyakufū fuku

The temples are wealthy but the Gozan are declining;
There are only false masters, there are no true masters.
I would like to pick up a pole and become a fisherman,
But these days, on river and sea, a contrary wind blows.

Notes:
This is the second of two poems under the same title.

Gozan: The five upper ranks of the Rinzai monastic system. (See pp. 5–6.)

Poem 180

Baizhang Fasting

百丈絶食　*Hyakujō zesshoku*

大智禪師難行道　　*Daichi Zenji nan gyōdō*
末法爲人眞落草　　*mappō no i'nin makoto ni rakusō*
飽食痛飲熟銕丸　　*hōshoku tsū'in nettetsugan*
初懼泉下閻羅老　　*hajimete osoru senka no Enrarō*

The Zen master Dazhi trod a path difficult to follow,
For the sake of people of the final Dharma,
　　truly falling upon weeds.
Those who have glutted and soused shall get molten metal balls.
Then they will first learn to fear Yamarāja at the Yellow Springs.

Notes:
Baizhang Fasting: Legend credits Baizhang (749–814) with being the first monk to draw up a code of discipline particularly suited for Zen temples. His first and most celebrated rule was "a day of no work is a day of no eating." It is said that when Baizhang was very old, he still would not put his gardening tools aside. His disciples could not bear to see him toiling in the fields, and so

one day hid his tools, whereupon Baizhang stopped eating.[93]
Dazhi: An honorific name for Baizhang.
people of the final Dharma: That is, people with few resources for salvation. As the time between the life of the Buddha and the present lengthens, it was thought that enlightenment becomes more difficult to obtain.
molten metal balls: This is what they will be given to eat as punishment.
Yamarāja at the Yellow Springs: Originally the King of Twilight but then, by extension, the King of Hell (*Yellow Springs*).

Poem 184

Presented to a Gathering

示衆 *shū ni shimesu*

忍辱仙人常不輕	Ninniku Sennin Jōfukyō
菩提果滿已圓成	bodai no ka michite sude ni enjō
撥無因果任孤陋	inga o hatsumushite korō ni makasu
一箇盲人引衆盲	ikko no mōjin shumō o hiku

As for the Immortal of Forbearance
    and the Bodhisattva Never-Disparaging,
The fruit of their enlightenment was full and complete.
If one ignores karma and abandons oneself to narrowness
One becomes a blind man leading the blind.

Notes:
Immortal of Forbearance: A figure in the *Diamond Sūtra* who practiced forbearance, making no distinction between self and other.[94]
Bodhisattva Never-Disparaging: Bodhisattva in the *Lotus Sūtra*, whose attribute was a profound respect for all in the universe, "… when he saw the fourfold multitude from afar, he would make a special point of going to them, doing obeisance, and uttering praise, saying, 'I dare not hold you in contempt, since you are all to become Buddhas!' Within the fourfold multitude were some who gave way to anger, whose thoughts were impure, who reviled him with a foul mouth …, yet he did not give way to anger but constantly said, 'You shall all become Buddhas!'"[95]

Prose Introduction to Poem 187

松源和尚上堂云、舉、僧問巴陵、祖意教意是同是別。巴陵云、雞寒上樹、鴨寒下水。白雲師祖云、巴陵只道得一半、白雲則不然、掬水月在手、弄花香滿衣。師拈云、白雲盡力道、只道得八成。有問靈隱、只向他道、人我無明一串穿。

Master Songyuan rose to lecture and presented this case.
    A monk once asked Baling: "Is the meaning of the Zen Patriarchs and the teaching of the Buddha the same or different?"
    Baling said, "Chickens, when they are cold, roost in trees; geese when they are cold, settle in the water."
    Our ancestor Baiyun said: "Baling said only half of it.
    I would say it differently: Scoop up water, and the moon is in your hands. Play with flowers, and their fragrance fills your clothes."
    Our Master Songyuan, taking this further said: Baiyun, even though he put all he had into what he said, gets only eight points. If someone were to ask me, I would just say: the ignorance of distinguishing self and other is stuck on one stick.

Poem 187

祖意教意別與同	soi kyōi betsu to dō to
商量今古未曾窮	shōryō konko imada katsute kiwamarazu
松源老老婆心切	Sōgen Rō ga rōba shinsetsu
人我無明屬己躬	ninga mumyō kokyū ni zokusu

Is the meaning of the Patriarchs and the Teaching
    different or the same?
The measuring up, now and then, never ends,
Old Songyuan, kind as a grandmother, tells us
The ignorance of distinguishing self and other
    begins with ourselves.

Notes:
Master Songyuan rose to lecture: Master Songyuan was one of the patriarchs of Ikkyū's spiritual lineage. (See notes to poem 128.) This discourse from

the *Songyuan Yulu*[96] presents in chronological order some of the definitive views on the question of whether the meaning of Zen and Buddhism proper is different or the same, a question almost as old as the school of Zen itself. Songyuan first presents the opinion of a Tang dynasty monk, Baling, one of the numerous first-generation progeny of Yunmen, then the view of Baiyun (1025–1072), an early Song monk six generations before Songyuan himself in the same line. Altogether, then, counting Ikkyū's poem, we have four different generations of comment on this question. As this example demonstrates, by the Song dynasty it was virtually impossible to speak of any of the basic questions of the school without referring to some of the more famous pronouncements that had already been delivered on the subject. This is the tradition that informs Ikkyū's style of philosophical comment and one of the reasons why his poetry is so replete with allusions.

Poem 188

Nirvana Hall

涅槃堂 *nehandō*

眼光落地涅槃堂	*gankō chi ni otsu nehandō*
自悔自慚螃蟹湯	*mizukara kui mizukara hazu bōkai no tō*
七手八脚萬劫苦	*shichishu hakkyaku mangō no kurushimi*
無常刹鬼火車忙	*mujō no sekki kasha isogawashi*

The eyes' light fallen to the earth, Nirvana Hall
Remorse and shame, one is like a crab thrown into hot water.
Seven arms, eight legs suffer ten thousand eons of pain.
The killer demons of impermanence are busy
    with their burning chariots.

Notes:
Nirvana Hall: See notes to poem 33.
The eyes' light fallen to the earth ... like a crab thrown into hot water: This metaphor for illness originated with Yunmen:

One day when the eyes' light falls to the ground, what would you compare it to? There is nothing that resembles it so much as a crab thrown into the soup pot with its legs and arms flailing about.[97]

Prose Introduction to Poem 209

佛眼遠禪師三自省曰、報緣虛幻、不可彊爲。浮世幾何、隨家豐儉。苦樂逆順、道在其中。動靜寒溫、自愧自悔。

In the Three Reflections of Master Foyan Qingyuan, it is said: "Reward and retribution, cause and effect are empty hallucinations, you cannot force anything. What does the floating world amount to; one is rich or poor depending on one's household. Pain and pleasure; adversity and prosperity; the Way lies in the middle. Agitated or calm; cold or hot, I am ashamed of myself, remorseful."

Poem 209

自悔自慚溫與寒	*mizukara kui mizukara hazu on to kan to*
看看三界本無安	*miyo miyo sangai moto yasuki koto nashi*
愚迷正是衆生樂	*gumei wa masa ni kore shujō no raku*
嘗蜜猶忘井底難	*mitsu o namete nao seitei no wazawai o wasuru*

Ashamed, remorseful, one is hot then cold.
Just have a look, in the Triple Sphere, there is no safety.
Ignorance is truly the comfort of the masses;
A taste of honey and we forget the danger
    at the bottom of the well.

Notes:
Three Reflections of Master Foyan Qingyuan: The "Three Reflections" of Foyan (1067–1120) appear in the *Guzunsu Yulu*.[98] Ikkyū cites the third of the three.
Triple Sphere: The realm in which the myriad beings are caught in the endless transmigration of birth and death.

A taste of honey and we forget ... : Reference to a parable that appears in several sources. Hirano's paraphrase of it is as follows:

> On a wide plain, a man, encountering a great fire and chased by a mad elephant, took refuge in a dry well. Above the well, a vine was hanging on which he climbed into the well. However, at the bottom of the well were three poisonous dragons and four poisonous snakes. Moreover, two rats, one black and one white, were gnawing away at the vine. Just at that moment, a stinging bee let a little honey drop into the man's mouth. Craving more honey, the man forgot all his troubles. The wide plain is the Triple Sphere; the elephant is the demon of impermanence; the vine is life; the rats are the sun and moon; the well is hell; the three dragons are the poisons of covetousness, anger, and stupidity; the four snakes are the four great elements of earth, water, fire, and wind; the bee is the five desires. When we begin to crave the objects of desire, we forget the woes of birth and death.[99]

Poem 210

Composing a Poem and Trading It for Food

作偈博飯喫 *ge o tsukuri han ni kaete kissu*

來往東山昔若今	*higashiyama ni raiō su mukashi ima no gotoshi*
飢時一飯價千金	*kiji no ippan atai senkin*
荔支素老佛魔話	*reishi So Rō Butsuma no wa*
慚愧詩情風月吟	*zankisu shijō fūgetsu no gin*

As I go to and fro in Higashiyama, old times are as though now.
When you are starving, a bowl of rice is worth
    a thousand pieces of gold.
For the lichees, old Qingsu returned the Buddha-Devil kōan.
I am ashamed to sing of lyrical feeling, of wind and moon.

Notes:

Higashiyama: Here, loosely refers to Kenninji where Ikkyū first studied Chinese poetry at the age of thirteen.

For the lichees, old Qingsu ... : Qingsu, a Song-dynasty monk and disciple of Ciming was a symbol of uncompromising virtue in Ikkyū's personal mythology. He missed perfection by making the single mistake of instructing one pupil and becoming embroiled in the question of the certification of enlightenment. The kōan Qingsu put to this one student, however, is one greatly admired by Ikkyū. Here is the account in the *Xu Chuan Deng Lu*:

> There was one Qingsu who had studied a long time with Ciming. He dwelt in retirement and would not have anything to do with other people. One day, Doushuai was eating honey-preserved lichees. Qingsu happened to pass his door. Shuai called out, "These are fruit from my old village, please share them with me." Qingsu said, "Since my former master died, a long time ago, I have not had a chance to eat this fruit." Doushuai said, "And who was your former Master?" Qingsu said, "Ciming. I had the honor of serving him for only thirteen years." Doushuai was astonished. "If you were equal to serving him thirteen years, how could you fail to understand his Path?" Then, he gave him the remaining lichees and gradually came to know him.

There follows an interlude where Qingsu discusses the former masters in their line. Doushuai, more impressed than ever with Qingsu's understanding, begs for further instruction. Qingsu at first modestly declines but finally relents and says: "'You have a go at telling me all that you have understood about life.' Doushuai tells him everything he has experienced. Qingsu said: 'You can enter the realm of the Buddha but you are not able to enter the realm of the Devil.'"[100]

Ikkyū often refers to this encounter between Qingsu and Doushuai. He admired Qingsu for remaining without disciples and felt it was a shame that he finally relented and instructed Doushuai. Yet, the Buddha-Devil kōan that issued from their encounter was one of his favorites. The sense of the kōan seems to be that one must interact with evil in some way if one's enlightenment is to be complete.[101]

Poem 216

Fisherman

漁父 *gyofu*

學道參禪失本心	*gakudō sanzen honshin o shissu*
漁歌一曲價千金	*gyoka no ikkyoku atai senkin*
湘江暮雨楚雲月	*Shōkō no bo'u So un no tsuki*
無限風流夜夜吟	*mugen no fūryū yoyo no gin*

Learning the Way, studying Zen, you lose the Original Mind.
One tune from the fisherman is worth a thousand pieces of gold.
Rain at dusk on the Xiang river, the moon among
    the clouds of Chu,
Fūryū without end, night after night singing.

Notes:
Fisherman: Poems romanticizing the life of fishermen occur quite often in Zen literature of the Song period. Ikkyū inherited this tradition.
Xiang river ... the clouds of Chu: These place names call up Qu Yuan's encounter with the fisherman on the banks of the Xiang. (See pp. 41–42.)
fūryū: Refers to the natural grandeur of the fisherman's environment as well as the sublimity of such a vocation.

Poem 223

Addressed to a Monk Who Killed a Cat

示斬猫僧 *zanmyō no sō ni shimesu*

是吾會裏小南泉	*kore waga eri no shō Nansen*
信手斬猫公案圓	*te ni makasete neko o kiru kōan madoka nari*
錯來自悔行斯令	*ayamatte mizukara koyu kono oshie o gyōjite*
驚起牡丹花下眠	*botan kaka no nemuri kyōkiseshi koto o*

In my group, there is a little Nanquan;
Trusting his hand, he killed the cat, the kōan is complete.
Mistaken, he regretted that in practicing this teaching,
He disturbed its nap under the peony blossoms.

Notes:
Addressed to a Monk who Killed a Cat ... Little Nanquan: Reference to the kōan in which Nanquan killed a cat when no one in the assembly could proffer a word of Zen to end the argumentation over the cat's ownership. (See notes to poems 44 and 52.) One can only surmise the circumstances surrounding this poem. Perhaps, one monk striving to break through the Nanquan kōan actually killed a cat
... its nap under the peony blossoms: An allusion to a dialogue recorded in the *Wu Deng Hui Yuan*:

Daguan said, "What is it like, when halfway through the night, the true brightness of Heaven dawns without dew?"
Guyin said, "Under the peony blossoms, sleeps a cat."[102]

Poem 234

About Disturbances at Daitokuji

題大德寺動亂 *Daitokuji no dōran ni daisu*

禪者爭禪詩客詩	zensha wa zen o arasoi shikyaku wa shi
蝸牛角上現安危	kagyū no kakujō ni anki o genzu
殺人刀矣活人劍	satsujin no tō katsujin no ken
長信佳人獨自知	Chōshin no kajin hitori mizukara chisu

The practitioners of Zen fight over Zen, the poets over poetry;
On the horns of a snail appear safety and danger.
The knife that kills, the sword that makes men live—
Only the lovely lady of Changxin knows.

Notes:

On the horns of a snail: a proverb equivalent to "a storm in a tea pot" drawn from the *Zhuangzi*:

> There is a creature called the snail …. On top of its left horn is a kingdom called Buffet, and on top of its right horn is a kingdom called Maul. At times they quarrel over territory and go to war, strewing the field with corpses by the ten thousands, the victor pursuing the vanquished for half a month before returning home."[103]

The knife that kills, the sword that makes men live: This phrase originates in the appreciatory verse to kōan no. 11 in the *Wumen Guan*.[104] It was often applied metaphorically to Zen instruction in the sense that a Master's wise words are a sword that can destroy delusion and bring enlightened perception to life.
the lovely lady of Changxin: reference to Lady Ban of the Han dynasty, the favorite concubine of the emperor until she was displaced by the infamous Zhao sisters. She wrote a poem expressing her sorrow over loss of favor. (See notes to poem 293.) Afterward, she requested permission to retire and serve the dowager empress at Changxin Palace. Hirano suggests she is a symbol here of someone removed from conflict and therefore able to view it with a cool objective eye.[105] Lady Ban, the lovely lady of Changxin, is an important figure in the pantheon of Ikkyū's poetic imagination. Note her crucial appearance in Ikkyū's "enlightenment" poem (see pp. 14–16), and her mention in one of Ikkyū's first recorded poems. (See p. 10.)

Congratulating Elder Ki on the New Construction of Eagle Tail Monastery and Inquiring after His Leprosy (Two of a series of ten poems, nos. 238–247, under the same title)

賀燨長老鷲尾新造寺以訪癩病 *Ki Chōrō ga Shūbi no shinzō no tera o gashi motte raibyō o tou*

Poem 240

鷲峰建立大伽藍　　*Shūhō ni daigaran o kentatsusu*
普請崩山又碎岩　　*fushinshite yama o hōsu*

五臓敗壊成膿血　　gozō hai'eshite nōketsu o nasu
黄衣癩肉臭汗衫　　hōe no rainiku shū kansan

On Eagle Peak, he constructs a grand monastery.
By building, mountains are crumbled, cliffs are torn apart.
Your five organs rot, making pus and blood;
The yellow robe over your leprous flesh is a stinking sweat rag.

Poem 244

風流入室芯蒻尼　　fūryū shitsu ni iru bisshuni
因憶慈明狹路時　　yotte omou Jimyō kyōro no toki
腸斷纖纖呈露手　　harawata wa dansu senzen teiro no te
暗吟小艶一章詩　　hisoka ni ginzu shōen isshō no shi o

So fūryū, admitting nuns to his cell;
It makes one think of Ciming's narrow path.
One is rent by the graceful hand put forth,
Secretly humming the "little love song."

Notes:

[240]
Elder Ki: Sōki, a disciple of and spiritual heir to Yōsō (See pp. 19–22 and notes to poem 120.) He was also heir to the vehement disparagement Ikkyū had formerly heaped on Yōsō.
Eagle Tail Monastery: Where exactly this may have been and the circumstances surrounding its construction are not known.
Leprosy: Those who falsify the Dharma were thought to contract leprosy. In the *Jikaishū* (Self-Admonitions), Ikkyū graphically describes Yōsō dying of leprosy.[106] Here Ikkyū imagines Sōki contracting the same disease. It must have been only in Ikkyū's imagination because Sōki died in 1496 at the ripe old age of 88. This poem is the third in the series of ten, which revile Sōki principally for the building project but also for "selling" Zen teachings for monetary as well as sexual favors. [244]
fūryū: Elsewhere, this term has meant "rustic beauty" or something like "far out"; here, it has erotic connotations. (See notes to poem 6.)

Ciming's narrow path: In a kōan, Ciming chooses a "narrow path" which has been interpreted to mean a narrow alley in the brothel district. (See notes to poem 6.)

"little love song": A couplet from the "little love song" is used in a Zen dialogue to awaken a student to the conditionality of language. (See notes to poem 66.)

This poem is the seventh in the same series. Here Elder Ki is attacked for lechery. It is interesting that two allusions having very positive connotations elsewhere, the "little love song" and the Ciming reference, become quite negative and sarcastic because of the context. The same can be said of the term *fūryū*.

Poem 249

Thanking a Man for the Gift of Soy Sauce

謝人贈鹽醬 *hito no shoyu o okuru o shasu*

胡亂天然三十年	*uron nari tennen sanjū nen*
狂雲作略這般禪	*Kyōun ga saryaku shahan no zen*
百味飲食一楪裏	*hyakumi no hanshoku ichō no uchi*
淡飯麄茶屬正傳	*tanpan socha wa shōden ni zokusu*

Reckless, natural, for thirty years
Crazy Cloud has practiced this kind of Zen;
A hundred flavors of meat and drink in one cup,
Thin gruel, twig tea belong to the True Transmission.

Poem 251

Composed When Ill

病中 *byōchū*

美膳誰具一雙魚	*bizen tare ka sonaen issōgyo*
小艷工夫日用虛	*shōen no kufū nichiyū munashi*
婬色吟身頭上雪	*inshoku no ginshin tōjō no yuki*
目前荒草未曾鋤	*mokuzen no kōsō imada katsute sukazu*

Beautiful feast, who will prepare the two tasty fish?
The "love song" kōan, useless in daily practice.
A body singing lustful tunes, white snow on my head,
Before my eyes, weeds not yet plowed.

Notes:
This is one of two poems under the same title. The other is on p. 29.

two tasty fish: Phrase from a Du Fu poem connoting a simple meal in good company. (See notes to poem 91.)
The "love song" kōan: The kōan in which Wuzu used a couplet from a love song to awaken his student to the conditionality of language. (See notes to poem 66.)
weeds not yet plowed: An allusion to a pronouncement of Rinzai:

> A lecture master asked, "The Twelvefold Teachings of the Three Vehicles reveal the Buddha nature, do they not?" Rinzai said, "Your weeds are not yet plowed."[10]

Picture of an Arhat Reveling in a Brothel—two poems

羅漢遊婬坊圖　二首 *rakan inbō ni asobu—nishu*

Poem 254

羅漢出塵無識情　　*rakan shutsujin shikijō nashi*
婬坊遊戲也多情　　*inbō no yuge mata tajō*
那邊非矣那邊是　　*nahen hi ka nahen ze ka*
衲子工夫魔佛情　　*nōsu no kufū mabutsu no jō*

The Arhat has left the dust, no more desire.
Playful games at the brothel, so much desire.
This one is bad, this one is good.
The monk's skill, Devil-Buddha desire.

Poem 255

出塵羅漢遠佛地　　*shutsujin no rakan butsuchi o toozakaru*
一入婬坊發大智　　*hitotabi inbō ni ireba daichi o hassuru ni*
深咲文殊唱楞嚴　　*fukaku warau Monju Ryōgon to uchi ni tonauru koto o*
失却少年風流事　　*shikkyakusu shōnen fūryū no koto*

Emerging from the dust, the Arhat is still far from Buddha.
Enter a brothel once and great wisdom happens.
I laugh deeply at Mañjuśrī reciting spells in the Śūraṅgama Sūtra,
Lost and gone are the pleasures of Ānanda's youth.

Notes:
Arhat: See p. 15 and notes to poem 78.

[254]

desire: As this translation tries to indicate, the rhyme word in all three lines is the same, that is *qing/jō*. This word has, however, a wide range of meanings from "heart," "feeling," hence "passion," to the less subjective "circumstances" or "conditions." The meaning of *jō* in the last line is purposefully ambiguous. Taken as "condition," one could paraphrase the meaning of the last two lines as "Making distinctions between good and evil, the monk's skill lies in knowing the essential condition of the Buddha and the Devil." Yet, the philosophical language may be suggesting the lewd, since, given the context, the two lines could just as easily mean "That girl is no good, this girl will do; the monk's skill is having the appetite of a devilish Buddha."

[255]
Mañjuśri reciting spells ... Ānanda's youth: In the *Śūraṅgama Sūtra* the Buddha's disciple, Ānanda, while on his begging rounds, is enticed into a brothel by a spell-binding woman. The Bodhisattva Mañjuśri chants a spell that releases Ānanda from the lady's charms.

Poem 264

A Layman Reciting a Poem Before the Gate of a Brothel and Then Returning

俗人婬坊門前吟詩歸 *zokujin inbō no monmae ni shi o ginjite kaeru*

樓子無心彼有心	*Yōshi mushin kare ushin*
婬詩詩客色何婬	*shi ni insuru shikyaku shoku nanzo insen*
宿雨西晴小歌暮	*shuku'u nishi ni haru shōka no kure*
多情可愛倚門吟	*tabō aisubeshi mon ni yotte ginzu*

Pavilion Master had no mind but he has a mind.
A poet lusty for poems, how can his desire be lustful?
After the long rain, clear in the west, a little song at sunset;
So much feeling, lovable, the man leaning on the gate and singing.

Note:
Pavilion Master had no mind but he has a mind: Here is another poem referencing the obscure monk Pavilion Master (Louzi) who took his name from achieving enlightenment, that is, achieving "no mind," by hearing a

courtesan singing up in a pavilion. (See notes to poem 144.) Ikkyū imagines or perhaps actually saw a layman singing at the gate of a brothel without going in.

Reading Du Fu's Poetry—two poems

看杜詩　二首 *To Ho shi—nishu*

Poem 268

古今詩格舊精鬼　　kokin no shikaku kyū seiki
江海飄零又主恩　　kōkai ni hyōrei suru mo mata shūon
仰叫虞舜一生淚　　aoide Gu Shun o sakebu isshō no namida
淚痕濺洒裹乾坤　　ruikon o senshashite kenkon o uruosu

Whether in old or new style poetry, his soulfulness just as before,
Wandering the water ways, he still enjoyed his sovereign's favour.
Gazing aloft, he cried to Yu Shun, a life full of tears,
The stains of those tears sprinkling down drench the world.

Poem 269

淚愁春雨又秋風　　namida ureu shun'u mata shūpū
食頃難忘天子宮　　shokukei mo bōji gatashi
詩客名高天宝事　　shikyaku na takashi Tenbō no ji
寒儒忠義又英雄　　kanju no chūgi mata eiyū

Tears of grief whether in spring rain or autumn wind,
Not for a moment did he forget his service at the Imperial Palace.
His lofty fame as a poet rests in narrating the Tianbao era,
A poor scholar, loyal, upright and heroic.

Notes:
Reading Du Fu's poetry: Ikkyū alludes often to poems of the Tang poet Du Fu (712–770). Du Fu has long been placed in the top echelon of Tang poets,

with Tang poetry itself regarded as the summit of Chinese poetry. In this two-poem set, Ikkyū sums up the tenor of Du Fu's life and poetry focusing particularly on the chaotic years following the An Lushan rebellion (755–763). Du Fu did not have a particularly successful professional career and had just managed to secure a modest post a year before the rebellion broke out. He fled the capital Chang'an finding a place of refuge for his wife and family in Fuzhou. Then on his way to serve the emperor in exile in Chengdu, he was captured by the rebels and detained in Chang'an. He managed to escape a year later and rejoin the court still in exile. He was given a relatively high post as Reminder, but, too honest with his opinions to flourish in court life, he was soon demoted. Thereafter, except for a few years of reclusive life with his family in Chengdu, Du Fu spent the rest of his life on the road. Du Fu was prolific, and his poems cover an immense range of topics in a dazzling variety of styles. A humane compassion threads through his work. In these two poems, Ikkyū portrays Du Fu as the exemplary Confucian scholar and poet who never gave up his ideals even while political order collapsed around him.

[268]
old or new style poetry: This refers to the major division in Chinese poetry between "old" more free form poetry and the "new" style of regulated verse.
as before: Before the troubles of the An Lushan rebellion.
Yu Shun: One of the Five Sage Emperors of ancient history who were invoked as symbols of a golden age of wise government and simple virtues among the people.

[269]
Tianbao era: 742–755 Later part of the reign of Emperor Xuanzong (r. 712–756) which comprised both the golden age of the Tang dynasty and the beginning of its decline.

Poem 280

Remorse over Sins for which My Tongue Should Be Pulled Out

懺悔拔舌罪 *bazzetsu no zai o sangesu*

言鋒殺戮幾多人　　*genpō satsurikusu ikuta no hito*
述偈題詩筆罵人　　*ge o nobe shi o daishite fude hito o nonoshiru*
八裂七花舌頭罪　　*hachi retsu shichi ka settō no zai*
黄泉難免火車人　　*Kōsen manegare gatashi kasha no hito*

With spears of words, how many men have I killed?
Composing religious odes, putting forth poems,
    my brush has reviled men.
Seven flowers torn eight ways, sin on the tip of my tongue;
At the Yellow Springs, it will be difficult to escape
    the men in the fiery carts.

Notes:
Seven flowers torn eight ways: A metaphor for confusion and destruction which appears sporadically in Zen texts.
Yellow Springs: See note to poem 180.

Poem 284

With a Poem About a Brothel, Putting to Shame Those Brothers Who Obtain the Dharma

婬坊頌以辱得法知識 *inbō no ju o motte tokuhō no chikshiki o hazukashimu*

話頭古則長欺漫　　*watō no kosoku giman o chō zu*
日用折腰空對官　　*nichiyū koshi o otte munashiku kan ni taisu*
榮衒世上善知識　　*eigen sejō no zenchishiki*
婬坊兒女着金襴　　*inbō no jijo kinran o tsuku*

With kōans and old examples, arrogant deception grows;
Every day you bend your back to meet officials in vain.
Proud boasters are this world's Friends of Good Knowledge;
The young girl in the brothel wears gold brocade.

Notes:
Obtain the Dharma: This phrase was associated with the practice of buying answers to the kōans. Apparently, as the number of monks increased and the study of kōan was regularized, the notion that there were certain "acceptable" answers spread. Collections of suitable responses were compiled and, it appears, actually sold. The practice was called "to sell the obtaining of the Dharma."[108]
Friends of Good Knowledge: Conventional phrase for earnest students of the Buddhist teachings.
gold brocade: Monks' ceremonial vestments were made of gold brocade. The implication is that monks, just like the brothel girl, wore brocade to sell something.

Poem 287

Acts of Grace

徳政 *tokusei*

賊元來不打家貧	zoku wa ganrai ie no hinnaru o utazu
孤獨財非萬國珎	kodoku no zai wa mankoku no chin ni arazu
信道禍元福所復	shinzuraku wazawai wa moto fuku no fukusuru tokoro o
青銅十萬失靈神	seidō jūman reishin o shissu

Robbers never strike poor houses.
One man's wealth is not wealth for the whole country.
I believe that calamity has its origin in good fortune.
You lose your soul over 100,000 pieces of copper.

Notes:

Acts of Grace: Term for the Muromachi shogunate's proclamations of moratorium for debts. Throughout the period, when particularly hard-pressed, groups of farmers and sometimes townfolk as well would rise in revolt to demand cancellation of debts. (See p. 3.)

Poem 291

The Correct Skill for Great Peace

太平正工夫 *taihei no shōkufū*

天然胡亂正工夫	*tennen uron no shō kufū*
昨日聡明今日愚	*sakujitsu no sōmei kyō no gu*
宇宙陰晴任變化	*uchū no insei henka ni makasu*
一回斫額望天衢	*hito tabi shakugakushite tenku o nozomu*

Natural, reckless, correct skill;
Yesterday's clarity is today's foolishness,
The universe has dark and light, entrust oneself to change.
One time, shade the eyes and gaze afar at the Highway of Heaven.

Notes:

the Highway of Heaven: The word "highway" is written with an unusual character. Particularly in conjunction with the sense of the third line, it leads one to suspect an allusion to the *Yijing* (Book of Changes), one of the earliest places where the expression occurs. In Hexagram 26 "*Daxu*, Great Domestication," the final line, an auspicious prognostication, says, "What is the Highway of Heaven but prevalence!"[109]

Poem 292

The Correct Skill for a Disorderly Age

亂世正工夫 *ranse no shōkufū*

丈夫須具正見	*jōbu wa subekaraku shōken o gusubeshi*
諸妄想隨境現	*moromoro no ansō kyō ni shitagatte genzu*
馬問良馬麼無	*uma o tou ryoba nari ya ina ya*
人答此刀利劍	*hito ha tou kono katana wa riken nari to*

The strong one must equip himself with the right view;
Deluded notions in keeping with the object manifest themselves.
About a horse, one asks, "Do you have a good one or not?"
They reply, "This sword is sharp."

Notes:
If the sense of poem 291 was that in times of peace, one can drift with the flow, then, by contrast, this poem states that in times of disorder one must constantly be on one's guard as nothing will be what it seems.

Reduce Desires and Know Contentment—two poems

小欲知足　二首 *shōyoku chisoku—nishu*

Poem 293

千口不多富貴愁	*senku mo ookarazu fūki no urei*
家貧甚苦一身稠	*ie mazushushite hanahada kurushimu isshin mo ooshi to*
涓水鯉魚斗水望	*kenzui no rigyo tosui no nozomi*
明朝鰧扇廣河流	*myōchō rōsen kōga ni nagaru*

"A thousand mouths are not enough,"
　　so the rich family complains;
For the poor family in hardship, even one is too many.

The carp in the rivulet wished only for a ladle full of water.
Next morning, a winter fan floats on the wide river.

Poem 294

果滿羅漢有三毒	kaman no rakan mo sandoku ari
純一願少欲知足	junichi ni negau shōyoku chisoku
無衣貧病得相治	mue no hinbyō sōji suru o etari
山堂一夜聞促織	sandō ichiya sokushoku o kiku

An enlightened Arhat still has the Three Poisons,
Earnestly wishing to "reduce desires and know contentment,"
Surely, that would assuage the pain of thread-bare poverty.
In a hill temple, all night, listening to crickets hastening the looms.

Notes:
[293]
A thousand mouths are not enough ... : This appears to be a proverb that was appropriated by the Zen school. Hirano notes a place in the *Xu Chuan Deng Lu* where this expression is used as a capping phrase.[110] It also appears in the *Xutang Lu* in this form, "The rich complain a thousand mouths are too few, the poor lament that one body is too many."[111]
The carp in the rivulet: An allusion to the "External Things" chapter in the *Zhuangzi*:

> Zhuang Zhou's family was very poor and so he went to borrow some grain from the marquis of Jianhe. The marquis said, "Why, of course! I'll soon be getting the tribute money from my fief; when I do, I'll be glad to lend you three hundred pieces of gold. Will that be all right?"
>
> Zhuang Zhou flushed with anger and said, "As I was coming here yesterday, I heard someone calling me on the road. I turned around and saw that there was a perch in the carriage rut. I said to him, 'Come, perch—what are you doing here?' He replied, 'I am a Wave Official of the Eastern Sea. Couldn't you give me a dipperful of water so I can stay alive?' I said to him, 'Why, of course! I'm just about to start south to visit the kings of Wu and Yue. I'll change

the course of the West River and send it in your direction. Will that be all right?' The perch flushed with anger and said, 'I've lost my element! I have nowhere to go! If you can get me a dipperful of water, I'll be able to stay alive. But if you give me an answer like that, then you'd best look for me in a dried fish store.'"[112]

a winter fan floats on the wide river: An allusion to Lady Ban's poem, comparing a woman's loss of favor to a fan once autumn chills the air. (See also pp. 14–15.)

> To begin I cut fine silk of *qi*.
> White and pure as frost or snow,
> Shape it to make a paired-joy fan,
> round, round as the luminous moon,
> to go in and out of my lord's breast,
> when lifted to stir him a gentle breeze.
> But always I dread the coming of autumn,
> cold winds that scatter the burning heart,
> when it will be laid away in a hamper,
> love and favor cut off midway.[113]

While the moral of the title is simple and understandable, the poem itself points out the complexity of desire and sufficiency in the world. In reality, the desire of the rich grows with their ability to afford it. Also, their very desire, no matter how selfish, leads to the feeding of many mouths. On the other hand, at certain levels poverty, when the desire has been reduced to the wish for survival, there is no room for further reduction. The carp was in that situation. In the case of Lady Ban, symbolized by the winter fan, her lord's reduced desire led to her being cast out. The final image of the fan thrown away flowing down the river is rich in symbolic connotation but defies fixed interpretation.

[294]
Three Poisons: Buddhist term for the three basic afflictions of craving, hatred, and foolishness.
In a hill temple, all night, listening to crickets hastening the looms: Hirano suggests that a poem by Tang poet Liying (?–832) entitled "Lodging at Xubaitang (Void-Pure Hall)" provides the background for this line.

Autumn moonlight slants suffusing Void-Pure Hall with light,
While the chirp chirping of cold crickets fills thick swaths of trees.
River wind lasting til dawn makes it impossible to sleep as,
Sounding twenty-five times,
    the night watches of autumn drag on.[114]

Both poems in this set end with evocative natural imagery that is enriched by allusive connections with secular Chinese verse. The term that Ikkyū uses for "cricket" in poem 294 literally means "hastens the looms." It became a metaphorical way of referring to crickets because when the crickets cry in autumn, people felt urged to weave fabric for winter clothes. It is particularly fitting in this poem because it links well with the mention of "thread-bare poverty" (literally, "no clothes") in the third line.

Poem 308

No One Sees It the Same

各見不同 *kakuken fudō*

水流四念不同心	*suiryū shinen fudō no shin*
佛界魔宮亙古今	*bukkai to makyū kokin ni wataru*
寒窓風雪梅花月	*kansō no fūsetsu baika no tsuki*
酒客弄盃詩客吟	*shūkyaku hai o rōsu shikyaku wa ginzu*

The mind flows like water through the four mindfulnesses
    never the same.
The Buddha realm, Māra's fortress, bestride past and present.
Cold window, wind-blown snow,
    moon among the plum blossoms;
The drinker toys with his cup, the poet hums a poem.

Notes:

the four mindfulnesses: This is a discipline of meditating on the "body" to realize its impurity, on "sensation" to realize that the perception of things pleasant and unpleasant is the root of pain, on "thought" to realize its

impermanence, and on "objects" to realize their absence of self.[115]
Māra's fortress: The Devil's realm.

Poem 315

The Gentleman's Wealth

君子財 *kunshi no zai*

詩人財寶是文章　　　*shijin no zaihō wa kore bunshō*
儒雅乾坤日月長　　　*juga no kenkon jitsugetsu nagashi*
窓外梅花吟興樂　　　*sōgai no baika ginkyō no tanoshimi*
腸寒雪月曉天霜　　　*chō wa samushi setsugetsu gyōten no shimo*

The poet's wealth is elegant phrases:
In the world of scholarly elegance, days and months are long.
Plum blossoms outside the window, the exaltation of poetic chant;
The belly chills: snow, moon, dawn sky, frost.

Poem 332

The Last Chrysanthemum in the South Garden

南園殘菊 *nan'en no zangiku*

晚菊東籬衰色秋　　　*bangiku tōri suishoku no aki*
南山且對意悠悠　　　*nanzan ni shibaraku taishite omoi yūyū*
三要三玄都不識　　　*sanyō sangen subete shirazu*
渕明吟興我風流　　　*Enmei ga ginkyō waga fūryū*

Late chrysanthemums by the east hedge, fading color in autumn;
As I face the southern hills for a while, my thoughts are far away.
The "Three Essentials," the "Three Mysteries,"
　　I do not understand at all;
The joy in Tao Yuanming's song is my kind of *fūryū*.

Notes:

chrysanthemums by the east hedge ... southern hills: allusion to a poem by Tao Yuanming:

> I built my hut beside a traveled road
> Yet hear no noise of passing carts and horses.
> You would like to know how it is done?
> With the mind detached, one's place becomes remote.
> Picking chrysanthemums by the Eastern hedge,
> I catch sight of the distant southern hills:
> The mountain air is lovely as the sun sets
> And flocks of flying birds return together.
> In these things is a fundamental truth
> I would like to tell but lack the words.[116]

The "Three Essentials," the "Three Mysteries": Rinzai's teachings.

> The Master further said: "Each statement must comprise the Gates of the Three Mysteries, and the gate of each Mystery must comprise the Three Essentials. There are temporary expedients and there is functioning. How do all of you understand this?"[117]

fūryū: Here, fūryū means something like enlightenment. (See notes to poem 6.)

Poem 344

兩片皮復一具骨	ryō henbi mata ichigu no hone
鳥蟲馬牛更魔佛	chōchū bagyū sara ni mabutsu
混沌未分暗昏昏	konton mibun an konkon
雲月知爲誰風物	ungetsu wa shiru ta ga tame no fūbutsu ka o

Two pieces of skin and one set of bone.
Birds, bugs, horses, and cows, furthermore Māra and Buddha.
When the primordial chaos was not yet separated,
    the darkness was pitch black,
The clouds and moon knew for whom they were beautiful.

Notes:

Two pieces of skin and one set of bones: Abbreviated form of "Ears are two pieces of skin; tusks and teeth, one set of bone," a phrase used for capping kōans. (See notes to poem 44.)

Poem 352

Taking a Metaphor for Reality

認喩作實 *tatoe o mitomete jitsu to nasu*

野老却來日用今	*yarō gōrai nichiyū ima*
私車公案誤晴陰	*shisha no kōan sei'in o ayamaru*
昨夜打窓零落葉	*sakuya mado o utsu reiraku no ha*
蕭蕭聽作雨聲吟	*shōshō toshite usei no gin o nasu*

For this old coot, a daily practice since ages past, and now,
The kōan "privately carriages pass" confuses clear and cloudy.
Last night, to the falling leaves striking against the window,
Forlorn, I listened and composed a poem about the sound of rain.

Notes:
daily practice: The use of metaphor for instruction.
privately carriages pass: This kōan is cited by Rinzai as follows:

> Weishan said: "No words have actual significance."
> "Not so," disagreed Yangshan.
> "Then what do you think?" asked Weishan.
> "Officially a needle is not permitted to enter; privately carriages can get through."[118]

In principle, Zen denies that words can ascertain the truth, yet as expedient means they are resorted to constantly.

For the poet, the sound of the dry leaves falling becomes an auditory metaphor for rain.

Poem 362

Praising Saint Hōnen

贊法然上人 *Hōnen Shōnen o sansu*

法然傳聞活如來	*Hōnen tsutae kiku iki nyorai to*
安坐蓮華上品臺	*anzasu renge jōbon dai*
教智者如尼入道	*chisha o oshiete ama nyūdō nite*
一枚起請最奇哉	*ichimai kishō mottomo kinaru kana*

Hōnen, I have heard, was a living Buddha,
Peacefully sitting on the highest rank of the lotus dais,
Teaching learned men as though they were novice nuns;
Hōnen's One-Sheet Document, how marvelous!

Notes:
Hōnen: (1133–1212) Founder of the Jōdoshū, or Pure Land School, which focused its attention on Amida Buddha.
as though they were novice nuns: As though they were simple-hearted and illiterate.
Hōnen's One-Sheet Document: Contains the essence of his doctrine:

> The method of final salvation that I have propounded is neither a sort of meditation such as has been practiced by many scholars in China and Japan, nor is it a repetition of the Buddha's name by those who have studied and understood the deep meaning of it. It is nothing but the mere repetition of "*Namu Amida Butsu*" without a doubt in his mercy, whereby one may be born into the Land of Perfect Bliss …. Those who believe this, though they clearly understood all the teachings Shakya taught throughout his whole life, should behave themselves like simple-minded folk, who know not a single letter, or like ignorant nuns or monks whose faith is implicitly simple. Thus without pedantic airs, they should fervently practice the repetition of the name of Amida, and that alone.[119]

Although considered to be doctrinally opposed to each other, the Pure Land School and Zen both reject the scholastic or intellectual approach to

Buddhism. Zen is always emphasizing the inadequacy of words to convey the truth, while the Pure Land School considers intellectual knowledge a hindrance to salvation.

Poem 367

Ridiculing Literature

嘲文章 *bunshō o azakeru*

人具畜生牛馬愚	hito wa sonau chishō bagyū no gu o
詩文元地獄工夫	shubun ha moto jigoku e no kufū
我慢邪慢情識苦	gaman jaman jōshiki no ku
可歎波旬親得途	tansubeshi hajun shitashiku michi o eru koto o

Men embody the stupidity of horses and cows.
Poetry and literature are originally devices of Hell.
Self-pride, false pride, suffering from the passions;
We must sigh that thus intimately the devil has his way with us.

Note:
devil: translation of *hajun*, a transcription of the Sanskrit *pāpīyān*, "the more evil one," meaning demon or devil in general or used specifically as an epithet for Māra, the Devil in Buddhism. Here, the meaning is between the general and the specific.

Poem 376

室內閑吟一盞燈	shitsunai no kangin issan no tō
自然無道箇詩僧	jinen ni iwazu kono shisō
愁人春興猶寒夜	shūjin no shunkyō nao kanya
袖裏花賤梅萼氷	shūri no kasen baigaku kooru

Within a hut, quietly singing beside the lamp;
Naturally with nothing to say, this poet-monk.

For a melancholy man inspired by spring, nights are still too cold;
On figured slips of paper in my sleeve, the plum buds are frozen.

Notes:

figured slips: Slips of decorated paper used for writing poetry. Often the motif would be floral. Plum blossoms are a flower of the early spring when it is still very cold. Here, it is plum buds rather than blossoms and it is so cold that Ikkyū imagines even the painted buds are frozen. This leaves him, as a man inspired by spring, without words for a poem, except that the poem itself belies his statement.

Poem 381

Recollecting the Past

懐古 *kaiko*

愛念愛思苦胸次　　*ainen aishi kyōji o kurushimu*
詩文忘却無一字　　*shibun o bōkyakushite ichiji mo nashi*
唯有悟道無道心　　*tada godō dōshin nashi*
今日猶愁沈生死　　*kyō nao ureu shōji ni shizuman koto o*

Dwelling on love, longing for love pains my breast,
Poetry and literature all forgotten, not a single word remains.
There is only awakening to the path,
    not the mind to follow the path.
Today, all the more, I grieve over sinking into birth and death.

Poem 383

The Stick

警策 *keisaku*

苦哉色愛太深時	*ku naru kana shokuai hanahada fukaki toki*
忽忘却文章與詩	*tachimachi bōkyakusu bunshō to shi o*
不前知是自然福	*zenchisezu kore jinen no fuku nari to*
猶喜風音慰所思	*nao yorokobu fūin no shoshi o isuru o*

How painful, when physical attachment is very deep;
Suddenly everything is forgotten, prose and verse;
I never knew before this natural happiness;
Still delightful, the sound of the wind soothing my thoughts.

Note:
The Stick: The Zen master's stick used to rap students into awakening.

Poem 384

夢熟巫山夜夜心	*yume wa jukusu fuzan yaya no shin*
蘇黄李杜好詩吟	*So Kō Ri To kōshi ginzu*
若將淫欲換風雅	*moshi inyoku o motte fuga ni kaureba*
價是無量萬兩金	*atai wa kore muryō no man ryōgin*

Utterly absorbed in the dream of Wushan, night after night;
Su, Huang, Li, and Du composed good poems.
If I could transform lust into elegance,
It would be worth untold myriad pieces of gold.

Notes:
dream of Wushan: See pp. 49–50.
Su, Huang, Li, and Tu: Su Dongpo (1037–1101), Huang Shan'gu (1045–1105), Li Bai (701–726), and Du Mu (803–852), several of the great Tang and Song poets.

Poem 385

Deluded Enlightenment

迷悟 *meigo*

無始無終我一心	mushi mujū wa ga isshin
不成佛性本來心	bujō busshō honrai shin
本來成佛佛妄語	honrai jōbutsu wa butsu no mōgo
衆生本來迷道心	shujō honrai meidō no shin

No beginning, no end, this mind of ours;
It does not achieve Buddhahood, the innate mind.
Innate Buddhahood was the Buddha's wild talk.
The beings' innate mind is the path to delusion.

Notes:
Buddhahood: That all sentient creatures have the Buddha-nature and are capable of achieving Buddhahood is an article of faith in Mahayana Buddhism, hence the twisting of the mind in Zhaozhou's kōan: "Does the dog have the Buddha-nature?" "No!" This poem is both prosodically and philosophically like the Zhaozhou kōan in that it overturns accepted conventions.

As in poem 254, the rhyme words are all one word, in this case "mind." Such a practice would look quite inept from a conventional aesthetic standpoint. Also, within this very short poem, Ikkyū has managed to repeat other vocabulary items not only twice but three times, again a highly unorthodox thing to do. It was usually thought to demonstrate paucity of imagination that, given the wealth of Chinese vocabulary, one should have to use the same word twice in a short poem. Yet, paradoxically, the poem's weakness is its strength. The repetition of the blocks of Buddhist terminology set up a staccato rhythm that pounds home the unorthodox and unsettling message.

Addressed to a Monk Who Burned Books—three poems

示焚書籍僧　三首 *shoseki o yaku sō ni shimesu—sanshu*

Poem 388

始皇自然辯邪正　　*Shikō jinen ni jashō o benzu*
波旬餘殃如看掌　　*hajun no yoō tanagokoro o miru gotoshi*
看看劫火洞然時　　*miyo miyo gōka tōnen no toki*
書籍金剛不壞性　　*shoseki kongō fue no shō*

Shihuang all by himself distinguished false and true;
His demon curse plain as the palm of your hand.
Have a look when the cataclysmic fire lays waste the universe,
Books have an indestructible diamond nature.

Poem 389

樹下石上茅廬　　*juka sekijō bōro*
詩文疏鈔同居　　*shibun shoshō dōkyosu*
欲焚囊中遺藁　　*nōchū no ikō o yakan to hosseba*
先須忘腹中書　　*mazu subekaraku fukuchū no sho o bōsubeshi*

Even under a tree on a rock in a rush hut,
Poetry, prose, the commentaries, and digests all dwell together.
If you want to burn the old manuscripts in your bag,
You must first forget the books in your belly.

Poem 390

腹中地獄成　　*fukuchū ni jigoku naru*
無量劫識情　　*muryōgō no shikijō*
野火燒不盡　　*yaka yakedomo tsukizu*
春風草又生　　*shunpū kusa mata shōzu*

In the belly, hell takes shape;
Immeasurable eons of passion.
Wild fire burns but never destroys it;
The spring breeze blows and the grass grows again.

Notes:
[388]
Shihuang: The Qin Emperor who was the first ruler to unite China. Because he wished to have history begin with his own reign, he attempted to burn all history and literature written previously. His reign was brief.
His demon's curse: Presumably, the Qin Emperor's fate to die without successors. The word translated as "demon" is once again *hajun*, originally a Sanskrit term for demon. See note to poem 367.
cataclysmic fire: See the notes to poem 54.
indestructible diamond nature: An allusion perhaps to the story of Deshan burning his scriptural commentaries in the first flush of enlightenment.[120] Since the *Diamond Sūtra* was very important in Deshan's early spiritual development, popular legend had Deshan burn the *Diamond Sūtra*.

[390]
Wild fire burns ... : The last two lines paraphrase three lines of a poem by Bai Juyi, "Taking as a Subject, the Ancient Plains Grass, I Send Someone Off."

Luxuriant, the grass on the plain,
In one year, withers and flourishes.
The wild fire burns but cannot destroy it.
When the spring wind blows,
The fragrant grass encroaches on the ancient path;
It meets the azure sky and rough wall,
As I sent you off again, old friend,
My heart overflows with the feeling of parting.[121]

These three poems become progressively shorter; first a seven-word line, then a six-word line, and finally a five-word line. It is almost as though the flames were licking away at them. They admonish a monk simple-minded enough to think that by burning the books in his bag, he could extinguish the words in his mind.

Poem 394

Mourning Soldiers Dead in the War

吊戰死兵 *senshihei o chōsu*

赤面修羅血氣繁	sekimen no shura kekki shigeshi
惡聲震動破乾坤	akusei shindō shitei kenkon o yaburu
鬪諍負時頭腦裂	tōsō makuru toki tōnō saku
無量億劫舊精魂	muryō okugō kyū seikon

Red-faced asuras, rank with the spirit of blood,
Screaming insults, in wild movement, demolish heaven and earth.
When they lose a battle, their skulls are split.
Immeasurable millions of eons their ancient spirits shall roam.

Note:

asuras: Titans forever at war who are placed below human beings in the Buddhist hierarchy of the six courses. (See notes to poem 33.)

Poem 441

Hell

地獄 *jigoku*

三界無安	sangai yasurakanaru koto nashi
猶如火宅	nao kataku no gotoshi
箇主人公	kono shujinkō
瑞巖應喏	Zuigan ōtakusu

In the Triple Sphere, there is no stability,
It's just like a house on fire.
"Here, Master?"
Ruiyan answered, "Yes."

Notes:

Triple Sphere: See notes to poem 209.
like a house on fire: See notes to poem 46.
"Here, Master?": An allusion to *Wumen Guan*, kōan no. 12. Ruiyan is supposed to have talked to himself as follows:

"Hello, Master."
"Yes."
"Better sober up."
"Yes."
"Don't be fooled by others."
"Yes, yes."[122]

Poem 454

I Hate Incense

嫌抹香 *makkō o kirau*

作家手段孰商量	sakke no shudan tare ka shōryōsen
說道談禪舌更長	setsu dō dan zen shita sara ni nagashi
純老天然惡殊勝	junrō wa tennen shushō o nikumu
暗顰鼻孔佛前香	an ni bikū shikamu butsuzen no kō

Who can measure a master's means?
Explaining the Way, discussing Zen,
    their tongues just grow longer.
Old Jun has instinctively disliked sanctimony,
    In the darkness, my nose wrinkles, incense before the Buddha.

Note:
Old Jun: Abbreviation of Ikkyū's name Sōjun.

Reverend Songyuan—two poems

松源和尚　二首 *Shōgen Oshō—nishu*

Poem 491

松源靈隠老師禪　　*Shōgen Rin'nin Rōshi no zen*
破法攀條省數錢　　*hō o yaburi jō o yōzu shōsūsen*
囊中我没半文蓄　　*nōchū ni ware hanmon no takuwae nashi*
狂客江山三十年　　*kyōkyaku kōzan sanjūnen*

The Zen of Master Songyuan Lingyin
By breaking the rules held to principle, saved a few coins.
In my purse, not even a half penny saved—
This madman, rambling river to mountain, thirty years.

Poem 492

巡堂合掌又燒香　　*jundō gasshō mata shōkō*
竪拂拈槌座木床　　*juhotsu nentsui mokushō ni zasu*
臨濟正傳也何處　　*Rinzai no shōden mata izuko zo*
一休東海斷愁腸　　*Ikkyū Tōkai ni shūchō o dansu*

Circumambulate, bow, burn incense,
Raise the whisk, sound the block, sit on the carved chair…
Where in all this is Rinzai's true transmission?
Ikkyū on the Eastern Sea rends his grieving guts.

Notes:
Songyuan: Important patriarch in Ikkyū's lineage. See notes to poems 128 and 130. These two poems are inscribed on a portrait of Songyuan done by Soga Bokkei (?–1473) in 1469,[123] the second year of the Ōnin War when Ikkyū was residing at Shūon'an in Takigi.

[491]
Lingyin: Name of one of Songyuan's temples incorporated into his name.

By breaking the rules held to principle: Allusion to the opening statement in kōan no. 10 in the *Blue Cliff Record*, "If there is a principle, go by the principle; if there is no principle, go by the example."[124] Hirano glosses the meaning of this instruction as follows, "In Zen, there are no binding conventional forms; one follows actual examples and makes them one's own."[125] Ikkyū seems to be making a paradoxical statement here: breaking the rules (in other words, making his own actions an example for future generations, is how Songyuan adhered to principle.

saved a few coins: Although there is no historical evidence that Songyuan lived in poverty, Ikkyū clearly identified with him as a master who followed an independent path and lived in modest circumstances.

[492]

Circumambulate...: The act of walking around a sacred object or space, a common practice in both Hindu and Buddhist ritual that found its way into Zen. The first two lines list many of the ritual activities in Zen temples. A master raises the fly whisk when he is about to speak. A wooden block is sounded with a mallet to assemble the monks. The master seats in a carved wooden chair when he addresses the monks.

Eastern Sea: Ikkyū often refers to himself as "of the Eastern Sea," and it is interesting that with this expression, he situates himself geographically as though he were looking from China toward Japan.

Poem 494

Gathering Horse Dung to Cultivate the Mottled Bamboo

拾馬糞修斑竹 *bafun o hiroi banchiku o shūsu*

看看我養鳳凰心	*miyo miyo ware hōōshin o yashinau*
燕雀鳩鴉山野禽	*en jaku kyū a wa sanya no kin*
臨濟栽松一休竹	*Rinzai wa matsu o ue Ikkyū wa take*
三門境致後人吟	*sanmon no kyōchi gōnin no gin*

Have a look, I nourish the phoenix mind,
Swallows, sparrows, pigeons, and crows are just wild fowl.
Rinzai planted pine, Ikkyū plants bamboo;
Of the monastery's pleasant ambience, later people will sing.

Notes:
This poem is a companion to poem 493 discussed on pp. 46–48.
Mottled Bamboo: A variety of bamboo dappled with dark splotches. Popular legend explains the origin of the mottling: It is said that when Lord Shun died on a tour of inspection to the south, his wives came as far as the Xiang river and wept for him. Their tears fell on the bamboo, staining it for evermore. Thus, another common name for mottled bamboo is Xiang-Wife Bamboo.
Rinzai planted pine ... : In the *Record of Rinzai*, Huangbo comes across Rinzai one day planting pines,

> When Rinzai was planting pine trees, Huangbo asked: "What is the good of planting so many trees in the deep mountains?"
>
> "First, I want to make a natural setting for the main gate. Second, I want to make a landmark for later generations," said Rinzai, and thumped the ground with his mattock three times.
>
> "Be that as it may, you've already tasted thirty blows of my stick," replied Huangbo.
>
> Again Rinzai thumped the ground with his mattock three times and breathed out a great breath.
>
> "Under you, my line will flourish throughout the world," said Huangbo.[126]

Ikkyū plants bamboo: Ikkyū's fondness for bamboo is recorded in the *Nempu* as well.

> South of the vegetable bed, Ikkyū had planted bamboo, which had grown into a grove that was good for keeping cool. He suffered from the heat every summer, so he had a small pavilion built among the bamboo. They cut rushes for a roof and wove bamboo for a floor mat. Ikkyū would go there in a sedan chair and spend half the day taking his ease.[127]

Poem 512

Praising Master Rinzai

贊臨濟和尚 *Rinzai Oshō o sansu*

喝喝喝喝喝	*katsu katsu katsu katsu katsu*
當機得殺活	*tōki setsukatsu o etari*
惡魔鬼眼睛	*akuma no kiganzei*
明明如日月	*myōmyōtaru koto nichigetsu no gotoshi*

Kyaa, kyaa, kyaa, kyaa, kyaaaaa!
Meeting the occasion, he either kills or gives life.
Devil demon eyes,
Bright, bright as sun and moon.

Notes:
This poem appears as an inscription in Ikkyū's own calligraphy on a portrait of Rinzai with furrowed brow and bulging eyes.[128]
kyaa: Renders the onomatopoeic graph *katsu* that represents the sound of Rinzai's shout. Rinzai was famous for his use of shouting to awaken his students to enlightenment. In the *Record of Rinzai* he talks about the functioning of the shout:

> The Master asked a monk: "Sometimes a shout is like the jeweled sword of the Vajra King; sometimes a shout is like the golden-haired lion crouching on the ground; sometimes a shout is like a weed-tipped fishing pole; sometimes a shout doesn't function as a shout. How do you understand this?"
> The monk hesitated. The Master gave a shout.[129]

Bright, bright as the sun and moon: There is a powerful visual simplicity to this last line, since the two components making up the character for "bright" are the characters for "sun" and "moon."

Prose Introduction to Poems 531 and 532

盲女森侍者、情愛甚厚。將絶食殞命。愁苦之餘,作偈言之。

My blind attendant Mori has strong feelings of love; she has refused to eat and may die. Out of an excess of pain and sorrow about it, I have made some poems.

Poem 531

百丈鋤頭信施消　　　Hyakujō no tō shinse kie
飯錢閻老不曾饒　　　hansen Enrō katsute yurusazu
盲女艷歌咲樓子　　　mōjo no enka Rōshi o warau
楚臺暮雨滴蕭蕭　　　Sōdai no bo'u teki shō shō

Baizhang's hoe extinguished the need for alms,
With rice money, the Old King of Hell has never been liberal.
The blind girl's love songs shame Pavilion Master,
On Chu's Terrace, rain at sunset drip drop drop.

Poem 532

看看涅槃堂裡禪　　　miyo miyo Nehandōri no zen o
昔年百丈钁頭邊　　　sekinen Hyakujō no kakutō no hen
夜遊爛醉畫屏底　　　yayū ransuisu gahei no tei
閻老面前奈飯錢　　　Enrō no menzen hansen o ikansen

Look, look, at Zen within Nirvana Hall!
Long ago, where Baizhang plied his hoe,
There were nights of drunken revelry beneath painted screens,
Now, facing the Old King of Hell,
　　how to come up with rice money?

Notes:

she has refused to eat: The implication is that food is short so she refuses to eat to save food for Ikkyū.

[531]

Baizhang's hoe extinguished the need for alms: Baizhang was the Zen master who established the monastic rule, "A day of no work is a day of no eating." When, in his old age, his disciples hid his tools to spare him farm labour, he refused to eat. He is famous then for being someone willing to starve himself for principle. See also notes to poems 33 and 180. In the context of their situation, Mori is willing to starve herself for love of another. This implied comparison is freighted with irony and the underlying realization that when food is completely gone, farming is not a solution.

Old King of Hell: Translates *Enrō*, an abbreviation for Yamarāja, the King of Hell. This line and line four in poem 532 allude to the commentary in kōan no. 66 in the *Blue Cliff Record* where a monk is berated for coming up short on wisdom with the challenge: "The Old King of Hell demands of you, 'You seek food, where's your money?'"[130]

The blind girl's love songs shame Pavilion Master: Pavilion Master was the name taken by the eccentric monk who was enlightened to "no mind" by a courtesan up in a wine pavilion singing of her lover having "no heart." See notes to poem 144. Here, Ikkyū uses the name to refer to himself. Mori's love songs make him ashamed because his Zen wisdom seems useless in these dire straits, and she shows the greater fortitude by refusing to eat. It is not that her love songs intend to mock him; it is how he perceives it.

Chu's Terrace: The name of the place where the King of Chu was visited by the Goddess of Wushan, which calls up all the connotations of "cloud-rain," here invoked in a minor key.

[532]

Nirvana Hall: Infirmary in a monastery, here a metaphor for a life and death situation.

These are the first poems in the *Crazy Cloud Anthology* to mention Mori, the paramour of Ikkyū's later years, about whom little is known. Judging from Ikkyū's poems, she seems to have been a professional singer, which was a traditional occupation for the blind. For all that her existence in the realm of objective fact is shadowy, her presence in the love poems to or about her is very real. (See pp. 23–24.)

The poems concerning Mori are grouped together but the chronology of them appears confused. For example, poem 542 toward the end of the series seems to be talking about the beginning of their serious relationship. It is likely that these two poems were written during the first part of the Ōnin War (1467–1477) when the fierce fighting in the capital area resulted in food shortages. The *Nempu* records several times when Ikkyū was forced to flee the conflict. Perhaps Mori accompanied him on one of these flights. He usually ended up finding refuge in Sumiyoshi or Sakai. A portrait that can be dated to the early 1470s depicts Ikkyū and Mori together. In the poem inscribed on the portrait, Ikkyū repeats the line, "The blind woman's love songs shame Pavilion Master." This painting is dedicated to Tamagaki, a lay disciple of Ikkyū, who was a merchant in Sakai, someone who would have provided Ikkyū with support during these difficult years.[131] See frontispiece.

Poem 533

Lady Mori Rides in a Cart

森公乘輿 *Shinkō koshi ni noru*

鸞輿盲女屢春遊	*ranyo no mojo shibashiba shunyūsu*
欝欝胸襟好慰愁	*utsu'utsutaru kyōkin shū o nagusamuru ni yoshi*
遮莫衆生之輕賤	*sa mo araba are shujō no keisen*
愛看森也美風流	*aishi miru Shin mo mata bi fūryū*

In a phoenix cart, the blind girl often goes on spring outings.
When my heart is oppressed,
　　she is good to comfort my melancholy.
So let everyone disparage us,
I love to see Mori, so fair a beauty is she.

Notes:
phoenix cart: Cart decorated with the phoenix emblem, therefore a vehicle of the aristocracy. Perhaps Ikkyū just imagines her in circumstances of splendor. The title "Lady Mori" has aristocratic over tones too.

Poem 535

A Beautiful Woman's Dark Place Has the Fragrance of a Narcissus

美人陰有水仙花香 *bijin no in ni suisen no ka ari*

楚臺應望更應攀	Sōdai wa masa ni nozomubeki sara ni yozubeshi
半夜玉床愁夢顏	hanya no gyokushō shūmu no kao
花綻一莖梅樹下	hana wa hokorobu ikkei baiju no shita
凌波仙子遶腰間	ryōha no senshi yōkan o meguru

Chu's Terrace, one must regard from afar and moreover climb.
The middle of the night, on the jeweled bed,
    a bittersweet dream's face,
The flower opens under a branch of the plum tree,
Delicately the narcissus revolves between thighs.

Note:
Chu's Terrace: See note to poem 531.

Poem 536

Calling My Hand Mori's Hand

喚我手作森手 *waga te o motte Shin no te o nasu*

我手何似森手	waga te wa Shin no te ni izure zo
自信公風流主	mizukara shinzu kō wa fūryū no shu nari
發病治玉莖萠	hatsubyō sureba gyokukei no moyuru o naosu
且喜我會裏衆	shakisu waga eri no shū

My hand, how does it resemble Mori's hand?
I believe the lady is the master of fūryū,
When ills arise, she cures the jeweled stem and it sprouts,
Then they rejoice, the monks of my assembly.

Notes:
My hand, how does it resemble Mori's hand?: This line reworks the second of the Song dynasty Master Huanglong's "Three Gates." These are questions designed to pivot the mind toward enlightened consciousness. The second question was: "My hand, how does it resemble the Buddha's hand?"[132] Ikkyū has elevated Mori by invoking a juxtaposition once again with a Zen master and, through the allusion, even with the Buddha.
fūryū: See notes to poem 6.
the jeweled stem: A metaphor for the phallus.

This is one of very few poems in the *Crazy Cloud Anthology* in the six-character line form, itself a relatively rare form in Chinese poetry. Choosing Huanglong's six-character phrase as the foundation for the first line seems to have determined the form.

Poem 537

Promise to Be Born in the Time of Maitreya

約彌勒下生 *miroku no ashō o yakusu*

盲森夜夜伴吟身　　mō Shin yaya ginshin ni tomonai
被底鴛鴦私語新　　hitei no enō shigo arata nari
新約慈尊三會曉　　arata ni yakusu Jison san'e no akatsuki
本居古佛萬般春　　hongo no kobutsu banban no haru

Blind Mori every night accompanies my singing;
Under the covers, mandarin ducks, intimate talk always new;
Promise anew to meet in the dawn of Maitreya.
Here at the home of the old Buddha, all things are in spring.

Notes:

Maitreya: The Buddha of the future who is supposed to appear 5,670,000,000 years after Śākyamuni's death.
mandarin ducks: A common symbol for fidelity in East Asia because they take only one mate for life.
intimate talk: Allusion to the scene in the famous Bai Juyi poem, "Everlasting Sorrow," where the Emperor Xuanzong and his concubine Yang Guifei wish for their love to last through future reincarnations:

> In the middle of the night, when no one was around, intimate talk:
> If in the sky, then let us be the two wings of a single bird;
> If on land, let us be the connected branches of a single trunk.[133]

the dawn of Maitreya: Literally, the "dawn of Maitreya's Three Assemblies." When Maitreya appears in the future, it is believed he will lecture three times to the multitudes.

Prose Introduction to Poem 539

九月朔、森侍者、借紙衣村僧、禦寒。瀟洒可愛。作偈言之。

On the first day of the ninth month, my attendant Mori borrowed a paper cloak from a village monk to protect herself from the cold. How fresh and lovable!

Poem 539

良宵鳳月亂心頭　　*ryōshō no fūgetsu shintō o ranshi*
何奈相思身上秋　　*shinjō o ai'omou aki o ikansen*
秋霧朝雲獨蕭洒　　*shūmu cho'un hitori shōsha*
野僧紙袖也風流　　*yasō no shishū mo mata fūryū*

Fine evening, wind and moon, in my heart confusion.
How will we fare as autumn overcomes us?
Autumn mist, morning cloud, alone so delicate and fresh;
In the paper sleeves of a country monk, fūryū.

Notes:

paper cloak: Handmade paper clothing was, in Ikkyū's day, a garment of the very poor.[134]

fūryū: Charming or beautiful in a rustic way. (See notes to poem 6.)

Prose Introduction to Poem 541

文明二年仲冬十四日、遊藥師堂、聽盲女艷歌。因作偈記之。

On the fourteenth day of the eleventh month, the second year of Bunmei [1470], I traveled to Yakushidō and heard the blind girl's love songs. Accordingly, I made a poem recording the occasion.

Poem 541

優遊且喜藥師堂   *yūyū shakisu yakushidō*
毒氣便便是我腸   *dokuke benbentaru wa kore waga chō*
愧慚不管雪霜鬢   *gizansu sessō no bin ni kansezu*
吟盡嚴寒愁點長   *gin tsuki genkan shūten nagashi*

I traveled leisurely to Yakushidō and rejoiced there.
A poisonous spirit swells in my belly;
I blush, not to be concerned about my hoary head.
Singing her heart out in the bitter cold,
    sad beats lengthen the night.

Notes:
Yakushidō: A temple in the Sumiyoshi area. The *Nempu* entries indicate that Ikkyū lived around the Sumiyoshi area for about three or four years, avoiding the Ōnin War.

A poisonous spirit: Perhaps referring to the unseemly stirrings of desire in the aged monk but more importantly keying an allusion to a story of love between two monks that was well known at the time. The legend originated in Tang-period China. An older monk, Liyuan, and a younger monk, Yuanze, were deeply devoted to one another but were fated to be separated by Yuanze's early death. Just before he died, he predicted his rebirth and promised to meet Liyuan again thirteen years later at the Stone of Three Births. Liyuan kept the tryst and found at the appointed place a young cowherd. The cowherd cautioned Liyuan not to come near for "there is a poisonous spirit in me; I am not a human being." But to console his friend he sang a song of which the last two lines were:

> I blush that you have come so far to meet me;
> Although my body is different, love lasts forever.[135]

Weaving an allusion to the star-crossed monks into the poem allows Ikkyū to express both ambivalence and receptiveness at once.

Poem 542

憶昔薪園居住時　　omeba mukashi shin'en ni kyojū no toki
王孫美譽聽想思　　ōson biyō sōshi o kiku
多年舊約卽忘後　　tanen no yakusoku sunawachi bōzeshi gō
更愛玉堦新月姿　　nao aisu gyokukai shingetsu no Sugata

> I recall the old times living at Takigi,
> You heard of the renown of the king's descendant and loved him.
> For many years, old promises were forgotten, but now
> All the more I love the form of the new moon on the jeweled stairs.

右、餘寓薪園小舍有年。森侍者聞餘風彩、已有嚮慕之志、餘亦知焉。然因循至今。辛卯之春、邂逅于墨吉、問以素志、則諾而應。因作小詩述之。

Concerning the above, I lodged for some years in a small dwelling in Takigi. The attendant Mori, having heard of my appearance and manner, already held feelings of affection toward me. I, too, knew of it but remained undecided until now, the spring of Shinbo [1471], by chance in Sumiyoshi I asked her about her feelings. She replied in the affirmative.

Notes:
the king's descendant: Often taken as a reference to Ikkyū's royal birth.
new moon on the jeweled stairs: An illusion to Li Bai's poem "The Jeweled

Stairs Repine" in which the autumn moon represents a woman's face. In Ikkyū's poem, the new moon in spring refers to Mori.

This poem and its afterword suggest that Ikkyū had known Mori before while he was residing in Takigi, and that their chance encounter in Sumiyoshi rekindled a relationship. Perhaps Mori too had taken refuge in the Sumiyoshi area because of the war. Moreover, the headnote of the previous poem and the afterword to this one provide the only definite dates for his relationship with Mori: winter of 1470 and spring of 1471. Also noteworthy is that 1471 is the one year in this timeframe when the Nempu remains silent on Ikkyū's activities. Perhaps in the chaos of wartime, Ikkyū and Mori actually co-habited as the poems seem to imply. Yet, we cannot be sure. Yanagida warns that even though the presence of the name "Attendant Mori" in the Shinjuan documents recording the ceremonies held on the 13th and 33rd anniversaries of Ikkyū's death indicate that a person of that name had a significant relationship with Ikkyū, it is not certain that the "blind girl Mori" of the poems was not the creation of Ikkyū's literary imagination. Yanagida's close reading of these two poems demonstrate how they fulfill a "contract" with the Chinese literary tradition that may supersede factual truth.[136]

Poem 543

A Vow Taken to Repay My Deep Debt to Lady Mori

謝森公深恩之願書 *Shinkō no shin'on ni shasuru no gansho*

木稠葉落更回春　*ki shibomi ha ochi sara ni haru ni kaeri*
長緑生花舊約新　*en o chōji hana o shoji kyūyaku arata nari*
森也深恩若忘却　*Shin ya shin'on moshi bōkyakuseba*
無量億劫畜生身　*muryō okugō chikushō no mi naran.*

The tree budded leaves that fell,
　　but once more round comes spring;
Green grows, flowers bloom, old promises are renewed.
Mori, if I ever forget my deep bond with you,
Hundreds of thousands of eons without measure,
　　may I be reborn a beast.

Poem 544

Lady Mori's Afternoon Nap

森公午睡 *Shinkō no gosui*

客散曲終無一聲	*kyaku sanji kyoku owarite issei naku*
不知極睡幾時驚	*gokusui ikuji ni odoroku ka o shirazu*
覿面當機胡蝶戲	*tekimen tōki kochō no tawamure*
誰聞日午打三更	*tare ka kikan nichigo ni sankō o tasu o*

The guests have scattered, the piece is over, not a sound;
No one knows when she will awake from this deep sleep.
Face to face, now a butterfly plays.
Who hears the striking of the midnight watch at noon?

Notes:
a butterfly plays: Any mention of a butterfly in connection with sleeping immediately calls up the butterfly parable in the *Zhuangzi*. "Once Zhuang Zhou dreamed he was a butterfly flitting and fluttering around, happy with himself and doing as he pleased. He did not know he was Zhuang Zhou. Suddenly he woke up and there he was, solid and unmistakable Zhuang Zhou. But he did not know if he was Zhuang Zhou who had dreamt he was a butterfly, or a butterfly dreaming he was Zhuang Zhou."[137]
the striking of the midnight watch at noon: See the notes to poem 110. Here, however, it seems to be a playful way of saying, "She's sleeping as deeply as though it were the middle of the night."

Poem 545

Night Conversation in the Dream Chamber

夢閨夜話 *mukei no yawa*

有時江海有時山	*aru toki wa kōkai aru toki wa yama*
世外道人名利間	*segai no dōjin myōri no kan*

夜夜鴛鴦禪榻被　　yaya no enō zentō no hi
風流私語一身閑　　fūryū no shigo isshin shizuka nari

Sometimes by river and sea, sometimes in the mountains;
Even outside the world, the monk is in the midst of fame and gain.
Night upon night, mandarin ducks snuggling
    on the meditation platform,
Fūryū, intimate talk, the whole body at ease.

Notes:
Dream Chamber: Another of Ikkyū's sobriquets. (See the introduction to poems 819, 820, 821, and 822.)
mandarin ducks: See note to poem 537.
Fūryū: Hints of the erotic. (See notes to poem 6.)
intimate talk: See note to poem 537.

Poem 555

Fisherman

漁父 *gyofu*

江頭日暮水悠悠　　kōtō ni hi kure mizu yūyū
絲線斜垂江漢秋　　shizen naname ni taru Kōhan no aki
江海風流誰共說　　kōkai no fūryū tare to tomo ni tokan
乾坤ノヘ一漁舟　　kenkon henfutsu hito gyoshū

On the river the sun sets, the water flows gently,
The line hangs obliquely, autumn on the Jiang and Han.
Fūryū by the river or the sea, with whom does he speak?
Between heaven and earth, rocking to and fro, a fishing boat.

Notes:
on the Jiang and Han: The Chang Jiang (Yangzi River) and the Han River. The Han River joins the Yangzi at Wuhan. Here, the two river names stand as icons for all rivers.

fūryū: Connotes the free, untrammeled spirit of the fisherman. (See notes to poem 6.)

Poem 569

Humorous Composition on Becoming Abbot of Daitokuji

大德寺住持愚作 *Daitokuji Jūji no gusaku*

紫衣長老面通紅	*shi'e no chōrō men beni o tsūzu*
五欲現前生八風	*genyoku genzenshi happū o shōzu*
先祖面門澆惡水	*senzo no menmon ni akusui o sosogi*
絕交順藏主家風	*zekkōsu kun zōsu no kafū*

A purple-robed elder, my face flushes crimson,
The five desires before my eyes arouse the eight winds,
I throw slop water on the faces of my predecessors,
Abandon my own "Librarian Jun" style.

Notes:
Abbot of Daitokuji: As mentioned in the introduction, Ikkyū was invited to become the abbot of Daitokuji in 1474 when the monastery had been completely destroyed in the fighting of the Ōnin War. See pp. 26–27 for the official poem he wrote for that occasion. He followed it with this "humorous composition" in which he castigates himself in the same language he had used to criticize Yōsō. See poem 121.

five desires, eight winds: The five desires arising from the senses and the eight things that agitate the mind. See notes to poem 145.

predecessors: Presumably, his own master Kasō and the founding patriarchs of Daitokuji, Daitō and Tettō.

Librarian Jun: A version of Ikkyū's own name. It uses a different character 順 for the Jun element in Sōjun, usually written 宗純. Ikkyū often signed his calligraphy works with 順. No explanation has been advanced by *Kyōunshū* commentors as to why he signed himself as "Librarian" here, but I surmise that it was for humorous effect since "librarian" might be one of the lowly offices in a temple.

Poem 573

Bai Letian

白樂天 *Hakurakuten*

留得詞華百億春	todome etari shika hyakuoku no haru
千言萬句與居新	sengen manku kyo to tomo ni arata nari
古今獨證之無老	kokin hitori shōsu kore wa murō
世許出頭天外人	yo wa yurusu tengai ni shuttō suru hito nari to

Elegant words that will last a hundred million springs,
A thousand words, ten thousand phrases,
    new with every dwelling place,
Long ago and now, he alone proves writing does not age,
The world grants he is one who soared beyond heaven.

Notes:
Bai Letian: A sobriquet of the Tang poet, Bai Juyi. (See pp. 31–34.)
new with every dwelling place: Bai Juyi's career included many different posts and also periods of exile.

Poem 594

Cause and Effect for a Lustful Monk

邪淫僧因果 *jain sō no inga*

因果果因何日窮	inga ga'in izure no hi ka kiwamaru
輪廻三界獄囚中	rin'ne no sankai gokushū no naka
夜來八億四千思	yarai hyakuoku yonsen no shi
雲雨巫山枕上風	un'u Fuzan chinjō no kaze

Cause to effect, effect to cause, on what day will it end
For the inmates of the prison of transmigration
    in the Triple Sphere?

Night comes with eight hundred million four thousand thoughts;
The cloud-rain of Wushan blows over the pillow.

Notes:
Triple Sphere: See note to poem 209.
eight hundred million four thousand thoughts: an expression occurring sporadically in Buddhist texts. It conveys the irrepressibility and limitlessness of thoughts.
cloud-rain of Wushan: See pp. 49–50 and notes to poem 6.

Poem 605

Retreating from Mikanohara and Going to Nara

退瓶原赴奈良 *Mikanohara o shirizoku Nara ni omomuku*

行路難難知其幾	*kōro nan sono ikubaku naru ka shirigataku*
山是大寂水是謂	*yama wa kore daijaku mizu wa kore iu*
萬里路兮萬卷書	*banri no ro bankan no sho*
初知杜陵詩情味	*hajimete shirinu Toryō no shijō no aji*

Such a hard going, hard to know how far I've come,
Mountains are a vast quietude, so the waters say.
Ten thousand miles, ten thousand scrolls of writing,
for the first time I taste Du Ling's poetic spirit.

Notes:
Retreating from Mikanohara and Going to Nara: The *Nempu* entry records this:

> Ikkyū's 76th year, 1469. In the seventh month, the troops of the West army [the Yamana faction in the Ōnin War] entered Takigi. Ikkyū fled to the Jisaian in Mikanohara. On the second day of the eighth month he left Mikanohara and went to the southern capital [Nara], where he only stayed one night. On the third, he went to Izumi and stayed overnight. On the fifth, he left Izumi again and took up temporary residence in the Sōseian in Sumiyoshi. This place had been built by the monk Takunen, and was much loved by Ikkyū

as a place rich in memories of that monk. Furthermore, both Settsu and Izumi were in a barbaric state and not livable."[138]

Mountains are a vast quietude, so the waters say: A contrast is drawn in this line between the silence of the mountains and the voice of the rivers running down and through them. Kageki glosses this line in modern Japanese as: "Mountains are a realm of silent Nirvana, rivers babble as they flow."[139]

Du Ling: Du Fu. Even in this present limited selection of poems, there are six mentions of the Tang poet Du Fu: poems 91, 268, 269, 605, 606, and 823. Du Fu lived through the An Lushan rebellion (755–763) both as a prisoner in the rebel occupied capital and as a refugee. It is Du Fu's writings of this period that Ikkyū can now fully understand.

Poem 606

或神仙境或天宮　　arui wa shinsankyō arui wa tenkyū
家國凶徒路未通　　kakoku no kyōto ni michi imada tōsezu
因憶杜陵洒花淚　　yotte omou Toryō no hana ni sosogishi
　　　　　　　　　　namida o
秋香黃菊地腥風　　shūka no kōgiku chi no seifū

Whether in a mountain spirit realm or celestial palace,
our nation is in the hands of villains, the roads impassable.
So I recalled Du Ling sprinkling flowers with tears,
autumn's scent, golden chrysanthemum, on earth an acrid wind.

Notes:
mountain spirit realm: Phrase taken from kōan 61 in *Blue Cliff Record* to refer both to actual mountains through which Ikkyū is fleeing and also metaphorically to the enlightened state of a mountain ascetic. I suggest Ikkyū uses the phrase ironically here to imply that, in his condition as a refugee, even an enlightened state of mind is no help. What does help is recalling Du Fu's transformation of similar suffering into poetry.[140]

Du Ling's sprinkling flowers with tears: Alludes to Du Fu's poem "Spring View," which was written while Chang'an was occupied by rebel troops:

The state crumbles, mountains and rivers remain.
The city in spring, grass and shrubs grow rankly.
Feeling the times, flowers sprinkle tears.
Lamenting separation, birds startle the heart.
The signal fires have burned continuously for three months;
A letter from home would be worth a myriad pieces of gold.
I scratch my white head, thinning the hair even more;
Soon there will not be enough to stand up to a comb.[141]

The Second Year of Kanshō—Starvation—three poems

寛正二年餓死　三首　*Kanshō ninen gashi—sanshu*

Poem 640

寛正年無數死人　　*Kanshō no nen musū no shinin*
輪廻萬劫舊精神　　*rin'esu bangō kyū seishin*
涅槃堂裏無懺悔　　*nehandō ri sange naku*
猶祝長生不老春　　*nao chōsei furō no haru o iwaeri*

In the years of Kanshō, countless people dead,
Ancient spirits caught on the Wheel of Transmigration,
    ten thousand eons.
In the Nirvana Hall, there is no repentance,
One still prays for long life and endless spring.

Poem 641

極苦飢寒迫一身　　*gokku no kikan ishin ni semari*
目前餓鬼目前人　　*mokuzen no gaki mokuzen no hito*
三界火宅五尺躰　　*sankai no kataku goshaku no tai*
是百億須彌苦辛　　*kore hyakuoku no Shumi no kushin nari*

Extreme pain of hunger and cold oppressing one body,
Before my eyes—a hungry ghost, before my eyes—a man,

Within the burning house of the Triple Sphere, a five-foot frame:
This is ten billion Mount Sumerus of suffering.

Poem 642

盡十方乾坤衆生　　jin jippō kenkon no shujō
嬌慢情識劫空情　　kyōman jōshiki gōkū no jō
佛魔人畜總混雜　　butsuma jinchiku subete konzatsu shi
天然業果始須驚　　tennen no gōka subekaraku odorokubeshi

Exhausted, the beings in all directions between heaven and earth,
Arrogant and judgmental, the condition of mind
　　at the end of the eons,
Buddha and devil, man and beast, all mixed up,
For the first time, I must take fright at the natural effects of karma.

Notes:
The Second Year of Kanshō: 1461. The years preceding the Ōnin War were blighted by poor harvests and natural calamities. While there is a rough chronological order to the *Crazy Cloud Anthology*, it may be noticed that the order is not always adhered to, as here poems related to the period before the war come after poems 605 and 606, which were written during the war.

[640]
In the Nirvana Hall: Monastery infirmary. The *Nempu* entry for roughly the same period records that Ikkyū was suffering from an illness, so that he may be referring to himself in these last two lines.

[641]
hungry ghosts: See notes to poem 33.
the burning house of the Triple Sphere: "Burning house" is a metaphor originating in the *Lotus Sūtra* for the instability of existence in the world. "Triple Sphere" is the realm of transmigration.
Mount Sumerus: In Buddhist cosmology, Mount Sumeru is the huge mountain at the center of the world.

[642]

judgmental: "judgmental" translates the term 情識 *qingshi* J. *jōshiki*, which can mean simply mental discrimination but has a negative connotation in Zen texts. Kageki cites a key example of its usage in kōan no. 9 of the *Blue Cliff Record*, "Everywhere they go up into the hall or enter the room to teach. What do they expound? It is all just calculated judgments based on mental discrimination."[142]

effects of karma: This translation follows the text of the *Kyōunshū* in *Chūsei zenke no shisō* (1972). In the *Ikkyū Oshō Zenshū Kyōunshū* (1997), the base text for this translation, the character for "karma" 業 is emended to "leaf" 葉 to strictly accord with the Okumura manuscript. However, the running script forms of these two characters are so close as to be easily confounded, and "leaf" does not make sense in the context, although Kageki makes a valiant attempt, ending up with the gloss, "Only natural [food stuffs such as] leaves and fruits are shocked [when really it should be government officials.]"[143] I record this just to show how much depends on a single word.

Prose Introduction to Poem 648

文正元年八月十三日、諸國軍兵充滿京洛。餘門客不知平與不平。可謂是無心道人。因作偈示之云、

The thirteenth day of the eighth month of the first year of Bunshō, soldiers from the various provinces fill the capital. The members of my school do not know if it is peace or war. They might be called "mindless" clerics. Therefore, I composed a poem and instructed them with it, saying:

Poem 648

亂世普天普地爭　　ransei ni wa futen fuchi arasoi
太平普天普地平　　taihei ni wa futen fuchi taira nari
禍事事事劍刃上　　kaji kaji kenjin no jō
山林道人道難成　　sanrin no dōjin michi narigatashi

The world at war, all heaven, all earth, battle.
The time of Great Peace, all heaven, all earth, are calm.

Misfortune, misfortune, on the edge of a sword.
The Path followers of the monasteries find the Path
    difficult to attain.

Notes:
first year of Bunshō: 1466, the year before the outbreak of the Ōnin War.
"mindless": literally "no mind." The term usually has a positive meaning in Zen. Take for example the statement of Deshan, "Only when you have no thing in your mind and no mind in things are you vacant and spiritual, empty and marvelous." But here Ikkyū is poking fun at his followers; they cannot make up their minds whether it is peace or war; they have "no mind" about it.
Misfortune ... a sword: Calls up a statement of Rinzai's: "A monk asked Rinzai, 'What is it like on the edge of a sword?' Rinzai said, 'Misfortune, misfortune.'"[144]
Path followers: This term was translated as "clerics" in the prose introduction because it does simply mean men of the cloth. It is translated literally here to try to catch the pun on "Path."

There is an entry in the *Nempu* which may refer to this poem:

> Ikkyū's 74th year, first year of Ōnin, 1467.
> In the sixth month there was an uprising. Both factions paraded to the Prime Minister's residence. No one could tell whether Liu or Xiang would win.
> In the eighth month Ikkyū left the Katsuroan and fled to Kokyūan in the Eastern foothills. At that time there was a great deal of action in the capital, and the Katsuroan was destroyed by the flames of war.
> In the ninth month Ikkyū left Kokyūan and went to the Shūon'an at Takigi. All the village elders received him with happiness and joy.
> Ten years before, he had warned his disciples, "There are omens of war. I see the streets of the capital flooded with soldiers. You should quickly take precautions and put your affairs in order before it is too late." He put his warning into a poem. Because he had predicted things accurately, every one had great respect for his foresight.[145]

If this entry does indeed refer to poem 647, it demonstrates that the chronology of the *Nempu* sometimes does not accord with the dates that occur in the prefaces to Ikkyū's own poems. The *Nempu* entry, for example, says that the warning poem was written ten years before the Ōnin War, but the preface to Ikkyū's poem states it was written only the previous year.

Poem 691

Sea Cloud

海雲 *kaiun*

昨夜無風波浪洪　　sakuya mufū naredo harō ookiku
卷舒有路爲誰通　　kenjo michi ari ta ga tame ni tsūzu
百川歸處若知足　　hyakusen kisuru tokoro moshi taru o shiraba
膚寸横空滅却空　　fusun sora ni yokotawarite sora o mekyakusen

Last night, there was no wind, the waves were huge;
Rolling in, rolling out, there is a road, for whom does it pass?
If the place to which a hundred rivers return knows contentment,
A little piece of cloud athwart the sky wipes out empty space.

Note:
Sea Cloud: This poem is from the *gō* "sobriquets" section of the *Crazy Cloud Anthology*. That is, they are names bestowed by Ikkyū upon his pupils. Most of the people who received these names are unidentifiable now. As might be expected, many of the poems that commemorate the names are obscure because the context must have been quite a personal one.

Poem 716

Sonrin, Forest of Venerability

尊林 Sonrin

餘飼雀兒愛甚。一日忽然自斃、哀慟倍恆。是以瘞葬祭奠如人。
初呼之曰雀侍者、後以雀代釋、又字曰尊林。因以一偈證焉云、

I nurtured a little sparrow and loved it very much. One day it suddenly died. My grief being extraordinary, I buried it with a funeral ceremony just as if it had been a person. At first I had called it Jakujisha, Sparrow Attendant, and later changed the character Jaku [Sparrow] to Shaku [Śākyamuni]. I also gave it the formal name, Sonrin, Forest of Venerability. Hence, I commemorated this with a poem.

丈六紫磨金色身
娑羅雙樹涅槃辰
脱出外道死活手
千山萬木百花春

Sixteen-foot burnished golden body,
When he entered Nirvana in the grove of paired śāla trees,
He escaped life and death in the outsider's hand,
A thousand mountains, ten thousand trees,
    a hundred flowers in spring.

Notes:
Sonrin: This is another poem in the section of poems commemorating the giving of a name. It fortunately has a prose introduction to explain on whom the name was bestowed, as well as the circumstances that occasioned the poem. A scroll of this piece in Ikkyū's own hand is still extant.[146]
Sixteen-foot burnished golden body ... : a description of the Buddha's body.
When he entered Nirvana ... : These two lines evoke the scene of the Buddha's deathbed. With gentle humor, Ikkyū compares the death of his pet sparrow with the Nirvana of the Buddha.
escaped life and death in the outsider's hand: Outsider means someone not

committed to the Buddhist faith. The line as a whole alludes to an episode cited in the commentary to kōan no. 9 in the *Blue Cliff Record*:

> There was an outsider who came to question the World Honored One holding a sparrow in his hand. He said, "Tell me, is this sparrow in my hand dead or alive?" The World Honored One then went and straddled the threshold and said, "you tell me, am I going out or coming in?" … The outsider was speechless, then he bowed in homage.[147]

Poem 772

On a Spring Outing to the Mausoleum of Retired Emperor Go Komatsu in Unryūin at Sennyūji

泉涌寺雲龍院後小松院古廟春遊 *Sennyūji Unryūin Go Komatsu kobyō no shūyū*

對僧清話忘清遊	*sō ni taishi seiwa shite seiyū o wasure*
花落鳥啼山更幽	*hana ochi tori naki yama sara ni yū nari*
新草古苔廟前雨	*shinsō kotai byōzen no ame*
幾回春色幾回秋	*ikukai no shunshoku ikukai no aki*

In pure talk with another monk,
    I forget having come on a pure outing,
Blossoms falling, birds singing,
    the mountain ever more dark and quiet,
New grass, old moss, rain before the mausoleum,
How many times has spring come round,
    how many times autumn?

Notes:
This poem is one of a group of four poems under the same title.
Emperor Go Komatsu: If the *Nempu* is correct, the Emperor Go Komatsu was Ikkyū's father.
Unryūin at Sennyūji: Unryūin was a private retreat established by Emperor Go Komatsu within the Sennyūji monastery.

Prose Introduction to Poems 820, 821, 822, 823

渴焉夢水、寒焉夢裘、夢閨房乃餘之性也。近古世有三夢之稱。所謂夢窓夢嵩無夢和尚也。餘頃以夢閨扁吾齋焉。厥名雖踐三夢之躅、而實不同三夢之事。盖彼三師、隆德盛望、爲人所推。餘則老狂薄倖、漂吾所奸而已。因題四詩、以爲夢閨記云、

If one is thirsty, one will dream of water. If one is cold, one will dream of a fur robe; to dream of the bed chamber, that is my nature. In old times and recently, there have been three named "Dream"; that is, the reverends Musō "Dream Window," Musū "Dream High," and Mumu "No Dream." I recently took the name "Dream Chamber" and set it on a plaque over my study. Although that name treads in the footsteps of the other three "Dreams," it really does not match their affairs at all. Whereas those three masters were men of a vigorous virtue and flourishing aspiration singled out by people, I am just an old madman down on my luck advertising what I like. So I composed four poems, entitling them "Chronicle of the Dream Chamber."

Poem 820

茅廬話到壽陽宮	bōro hanashi wa ataru Juyōkyū
胡蝶優遊興未窮	kochō yūyū shite kyō imada kiwamarazu
枕上梅花窓外月	chinjō no baika sōgai no tsuki
吟魂夜夜約春風	ginkon yaya shunpū ni yakusu

Talk in the thatched hut reaches the Palace of Shouyang;
The butterfly elegantly sports, excitement never exhausted.
On the pillow, a plum blossom, outside the window, the moon,
A singing soul, night after night, entwined with the spring breeze.

Poem 821

寒哦秀句在三冬	kanga suku wa santō ni ari
醉後樽前盃酒重	suigo mo sonzen haishū o kasanu

枕上十年無夜雨　　chinjō jūnen ya'u naku
月沈長樂五更鐘　　tsuki wa shizumu Chōraku gokō no kane

Chilly, singing elegant phrases in the winter months,
Drunk, the wine cups still pile up before the cask,
For ten years, on the pillow no night rain,
The moon sinks at Changle as the fifth watch bell rings.

Poem 822

洞房深處幾詩情　　dōbō fukaki tokoro ikubaku no shijō zo
歌吹花前芳宴清　　kasui no kazen bōen kiyoshi
雲雨枕頭江海意　　un'u no chintō kōkai no i
鴛鴦水宿送殘生　　en'ō no suishuku zanshō o okuran

Deep in the bed chamber, how much inspiration!
Song and flute before the blossoms, the fragrant feast is pure,
Cloud-rain on the pillow, I would wander free on river and sea,
Spend my remaining life as one with mandarin ducks
    lodging on water.

Poem 823

巫山雨滴入新吟　　*Fuzan no uteki shingin ni iri*
婬色風流詩亦婬　　*inshoku fūryū shi mo mata insu*
江海乾坤杜陵涙　　*kōkai no kenkon Toryō no namida*
鄜州今夜月沈沈　　*Fushū no konya tsuki chinchin*

The rain drops of Wushan fall into a new song;
I am smitten with lust, fūryū, and poetry too.
River and sea, the whole world and Du Ling's tears,
At Fuzhou tonight the moon keeps sinking.

Notes:
Musō "Dream Window": Musō Soseki (1275–1351), the founder of Tenryūji, an extremely influential and politically involved Zen prelate.

Musū "Dream High": Musū Ryōshin (d. 1281) of Tōfukuji.
Mumu "No Dream": Mumu Issei (d. 1368), also of Tōfukuji.

[820]
Palace of Shouyang: Refers to Lady Shouyang, a concubine of the Southern Song Emperor Wu, who dreamed that plum blossoms scattered over her face while she was sleeping and could not be removed. This was said to be the origin of a kind of cosmetic known as "Plum Blossom Powder." The link here is with the topic dreams and the erotic connotation of cosmetics.[148]
The butterfly elegantly sports ... : Reference to Zhuang Zhou's butterfly dream. See notes to poem 544.

[821]
night rain: Metaphor for tears but perhaps also alluding to cloud-rain as well.
fifth-watch bell: The night was divided into five watches. The fifth watch was from 3:00 A.M. to 5:00 A.M.
Changle: A palace in Chang'an, the name of which may be translated as "Extended Pleasure." The line calls up a couplet from the *Wakan Rōei Shū*:

> The sound of the bell of Changle ends fades out
>   beyond the blossoms,
> The color of the willows by Dragon Pond deepen in the rain.[149]

[822]
Cloud-rain: See pp. 49–50 and notes to poem 6.
Mandarin ducks: See notes to poem 537.

[823]
rain drops of Wushan: Another reference to the story of the Wushan Goddess, hence imparting an erotic atmosphere. (See notes to poem 6)
fūryū: In all its senses, from rustic elegance and romance to having a free spirit. See notes to poem 6.
Du Ling's tears; / At Fuzhou tonight, the moon sinks: An allusion to the poem Du Fu wrote while a prisoner at Chang'an after the An Lushan rebellion. He had sheltered his family at Fuzhou, a town removed from the path of the marching armies. On the way back from Fuzhou, he was captured and detained at Chang'an. Gazing at the moon in Chang'an, he imagined his wife must be watching the same moon in Fuzhou.

Moonlight Night

Tonight, at Fuzhou, the moon,
From the bedchamber, my wife gazes alone.
I long for my far-away little ones,
Who are too young to understand the worry of Chang'an.
Scented mist moistens her cloud hair.
Clear light chills her jade white arms,
When will we two lean out of the open casement again
And let the double glistening tracks of our tears
    dry in the moonlight?[150]

Prose Introduction to Poem 839

一休老頃、染氣痢之患、愈而又發者兩三次、皆曰危矣。蓋事忤於心、則氣爲之泄焉。昨偶失所蓄之墨、百計搜索而不獲矣。果氣不快、痢亦欲下、左右皆失其色。遂述失墨之詩一篇、以爲顧命之訓。寫詩未滿紙、墨忽見焉。其喜不在言也。吁、今舉世珎貨奇寶是嗜。一笏之墨不啻弊屣而一失及死。彼多欲之人、如或聞此詩、以少愧于其心乎哉。左右因命、即作敘冠詩書、寘于座右云。詩曰、

When I, Ikkyū, got old, I contracted the illness of diarrhea. I would recover and then contract it again, two or three times in succession. Everyone said, "It is dangerous." But when affairs went against my heart, my vital essence would leak. Yesterday, as chance would have it, I lost a stick of ink that I had been saving. I looked for it a hundred ways but could not find it. As a result, my spirit was not happy, and the diarrhea threatened to start again. All my attendants turned pale. So, I composed a poem about the lost ink as a lesson about life. I was just copying out the poem and had not yet finished filling the paper when the ink suddenly appeared. My joy could not be contained in words. Aah, these days everyone is fond of precious goods and rare treasures. One stick of ink is not worth a broken sandal, and yet, this one loss might have caused my death. As for someone with many desires, if he perhaps were to hear this poem, I wonder if he might feel a little shame. At the request of my attendants, I composed a preface for the poem to let it serve as a kind of maxim. The poem said:

Poem 840

暗世今無翰墨風	ansei ima kanboku no fū naku
風流情思又何空	fūryū no jōsō mata nanzo munashiki
三生此地吟魂苦	kono chi ni sanshō shite kinkon kurushimi
萬杵霜華華頂東	banjo no sōka kachō no higashi

A dark world now, there is no style with the ink and brush;
Thoughts of fūryū too, how futile!
For three lives on this earth the singing spirit suffers,
Ten thousand times pounded, the frost flowers east of Hua Ding.

Notes:
fūryū: See notes to poem 6.
The ten-thousand-times pounded frost flowers on the east slope of Hua Ding: The best ink is supposed to be made with the charcoal of the orchid tree that grows on Hua Ding, the highest of the five peaks that comprise Tiantai mountain. Another ingredient is finely powdered cuttlefish shell, which, because it is white, is elegantly referred to as the "ten-thousand-times pounded frost flowers." Here, for example, is a couplet from a poem in the *Jianghu Fengyue Ji*, entitled "Sending Ink to a Friend":

> Moon bright Hua Ding, windy pure night,
> The ten-thousand-times pounded frost flowers fall
>   on a wool coat.[151]

The sense in Ikkyū's poem seems to be that the spirit suffers ordeals on the Wheel of Transmigration just as the finest ink is made through many poundings. His loss of an ink stick was just one more pounding on the mortar that purges desire.

Afterword

Reflections, Realizations, Suggestions for Research Possibilities

More than thirty-five years separates the first edition of this book from the present one. It feels fitting to end with some reflections on both the continuity and change in my perception of Ikkyū, a few realizations gained from the process of doing new work for this volume, and suggestions for future research that other scholars might be inspired to explore. I will do this in a "cursive" rather than discursive manner, weaving in some records of experiences that stand out from my fifty-five years of engaging with Ikkyū and his poetry.

Ikkyū and the Red Thread

As mentioned in the introduction, Ikkyū is unique among Zen masters of the past for raising up the red thread of sexual desire over and over again as a kōan. When I was working intensively on the *Kyōunshū* "Crazy Cloud Anthology" in my twenties and thirties, I thought that Ikkyū's engagement with the theme of sex made his poetry "contemporary" and relevant, for ours has been an age much taken up with sex. Nonetheless, my focus was on understanding the Zen philosophy underpinning all his poetry. I was attracted to Yanagida Seizan's thesis that Ikkyū's poetry should be read as an "I-novel," a fictionalized account of a person's life replete with metaphorical meanings and not raw autobiography. I still think Yanagida's position acts as a corrective for an overly literal reading of Ikkyū's work. On the other hand, this time through the anthology, I was struck forcefully by the ecstasy and the ache that radiates from so many of Ikkyū's poems with sexual desire at their core. In my seventies myself now, the same age when Ikkyū was writing his ardent poems for the blind singer Mori, realizing how life-long this preoccupation was for Ikkyū, I am left with a feeling of wonderment verging on bewilderment.

Katō Shūichi, in his foreword to the first edition of this work, drew an analogy between Ikkyū and the poet John Donne, declaring that their "metaphysics of eros" did not have to wait for Freud. While working on these revisions, I kept feeling that Ikkyū has a kindred spirit in the singer/songwriter Leonard Cohen, and not only because Cohen spent twenty years of his life meditating at the Zen monastery on Mount Baldy. Cohen's posthumously released album, *Thanks for the Dance*, sums up the two passions of his life: a thirst for spiritual enlightenment and an enchantment with love in all its forms but most of all in its physical expression. I felt the same sense of wonderment that I mentioned feeling about Ikkyū, when I saw that, for one of his posthumous messages to the world, Cohen should choose to give an account of a sexual encounter long ago in Santiago with a woman who seems to be a moonlighting streetwalker. His last verse in that song directly addresses judgemental listeners and ironically apologizes for his own inability to make such judgements. In that song, it seems to me that Cohen stands side by side with the Ikkyū who toward the end of his life takes the sobriquet "Dream Chamber" as "an old madman down on my luck advertising what I like." (See poems 820–823.)

Literature and Religion

Even though the majority of Ikkyū's poems are explorations of Zen philosophy and textual traditions, my approach to his poetry has been and remains primarily literary. One of the questions I was asked at my

MA oral exam was, "What's the difference between literature and religion?" On the bus on my way to the exam, I had been reading Dōgen's poetry. With that experience fresh in my mind, I answered that for medieval monks like Dōgen and Ikkyū, I did not think there was any difference. Poetry was an integral part of their religious practice. I still think that is true even while recognizing that for Zen monks, there was a fine line between employing poetry to express spiritual truth and becoming so absorbed in literary aspirations that, in Ikkyū's words, "thus intimately the devil has his way with us." (See poem 367.)

This time through Ikkyū's poetry, another thing that particularly caught my attention was the strong role played by citations of secular Chinese poetry. Of course, the bond between Zen discourse and secular poetry was already forged in China. It starts with the Tang period Chan masters and expands greatly in the Song period. This synergy between secular poetry and Zen is a fertile field for study. The chapters, "Literary Study in Kōan Practice" and "The Kōan and the Chinese Literary Game" in Victor Hori's *Zen Sand: The Book of Capping Phrases for Kōan Practice* provide an excellent start and demonstrate that the study of secular Chinese poetry is still a living practice in Rinzai Zen training. The recent work of Tom Mazanec on the development of Buddhist poetry from the Tang to the early Song lays a good foundation for understanding the Chinese context. Also recently, Jason Protass has shed light on Song monastic literary culture and its interaction with the founding members of Ikkyū's spiritual lineage. Thus, there is much to do and a growing community of young scholars to do it.

Allusion, New Digital Resources, and Other Lines of Approach to Poetic Composition

I still consider the understanding of allusions as key to the appreciation of Ikkyū's poetry. Indeed, most of the revisions to the translations in this edition were the result of discovering the right allusion, usually with the help of commentaries produced by contemporary Japanese scholars since the first edition of this book was published. The search for possible allusions in Ikkyū's poetry has been aided immensely by the advent of digitally searchable files and the internet. From the *Taisho Tripitaka* to the *Complete Poems of the Tang*, massive libraries of digital texts are available online. It was possible to complete the revisions of this book during the pandemic lockdown precisely because of this remarkable revolution in the availability of resources. Sarah Messer and Kidder Smith, in their recent book of translations of Ikkyū's poetry, *Once Having Paused*, dispense entirely with traditional bibliographical references on the grounds that any reader of Chinese and Japanese can locate the texts digitally. However, these same aids make it easy to find many possible allusions for the same expression, and many allusions to Zen anecdotes appear in different sources. There is often an embarrassment of choice, and, I think just listing the possible sources shortchanges the necessary work of interpretation, even though one may never be sure which one is exactly right.

Didier Davin, in a recent article, has suggested another possible avenue of inquiry to narrow down the right allusion. This is to consider the process of composition of Chinese poetry by a Japanese writer like Ikkyū. The principle form that Ikkyū wrote was the quatrain (to keep things simple, this discussion ignores differences between old and new style quatrains). The quatrain requires rhymes at the end of the first, second, and fourth lines. Many, but not all of the words in a rhyming category are apparent in Japanese pronunciation. Actually, because Japanese has so many fewer sounds than Chinese, the greater problem is that many words rhyme in Japanese pronunciation but do not rhyme according to proper Chinese rubrics. Chinese poets faced a version of this same problem. The rhyme categories were established in the Tang dynasty, but because of pronunciation changes in the language, later Chinese poets also needed an aid to make correct choices. Rhyme dictionaries were created to fulfill this need and also functioned as regular dictionaries by providing definitions of words in the form of examples of usage. Davin suggests that Ikkyū would likely come up with one line for his poem and then troll rhyme dictionaries to find an appropriate set of rhymes for the other lines. Davin's approach clarified an allusion brilliantly in the third of Ikkyū's poems on Rinzai's Four Propositions. (See notes to poem 15.) The Chinese rhyming dictionaries available in Ikkyū's time are, of course, very rare texts now. But their accessibility is only an OCR scan away. There are other resources too that can throw light on other aspects of how Japanese writers composed Chinese verse. Brian Steininger has translated large excerpts of a Heian period manual for Chinese verse composition in his *Chinese Literary Forms in Heian Japan*. The book illuminates by shifting one's perception of Chinese poetry written by Japanese authors from the finished work to the actual process of how the poetry was composed. This is fertile ground for other scholars to plough in the context of the medieval period.

Insights Gained from Preparing the Romanized Texts for the Poetry

It was Quirin Press editor Olivier Burckhardt's suggestion that I add Romanized texts to this edition to give readers some idea of how these poems might sound read aloud. This actually raises a complicated issue, which I would like to explain by detailing how my understanding of this issue evolved over the years. In 1976, before going to Japan for two years' research, I gave a lecture with readings of draft translations of Ikkyū's poetry at The Western Front, an artist's cooperative in Vancouver. A poet friend, Roy Kiyooka, at the end asked me how Ikkyū would have sounded out his Chinese poems. I found the question difficult to answer. Ikkyū had no knowledge of spoken Chinese and would certainly not have read his poems aloud in Chinese. Poems in literary Chinese, whether by Chinese or Japanese authors, when read aloud in Japanese, have been rendered for more than a millennium using a system known as *kundoku* "reading in the native way," which involves transposition into Japanese word order employing specialized forms of classical Japanese grammar. *Kundoku* readings can vary according to individual interpretation and readerships, for example, whether the readers are Buddhist monks or Confucian scholars. There is a wide degree of latitude in the choice of which words to fully naturalize into Japanese (*kun*) and which to leave in Sino-Japanese pronunciation (*on*). If all words are in *kun*, it reads like a Japanese translation; If almost all words are left in *on*, the effect is more like Chinese. An example will make this clearer. Here is a single line from a Bai Juyi couplet included in the 11th century *Wakan Rōei Shū*, "Anthology of Poems to Chant Aloud." It will illustrate the most naturalized style and is provided in Chinese glyphs, Romanized pinyin of modern standard Chinese, *kundoku* rendering in Japanese script, Romanization, and English translation:

> 霞光曙後殷於火
> *xiaguang shuhou yinyu huo*
> 霞の光は曙けてのち火よりも殷し
> *kasumi no hikari wa akete nochi hi yori akashi*
> The skyglow just after dawn is redder than fire.

Here for contrast is a single line from poem 385 in this collection:

> 無始無終我一心
> *wushi wuzhong wo yixin*
> 無始無終我が一心
> *mushi mujū waga isshin*
> No beginning, no end, this mind of ours.

This line exemplifies a *kundoku* reading style closest to *bōyomi* "reading straight as a stick," which was the preferred style for reading sutras aloud. It particularly suits this poem, which reads like a parody of a sutra. All Chinese glyphs are read in Sino-Japanese pronunciation and only one Japanese grammatical particle has been added.

Not only is there this wide a range of possibilities for creating *kundoku* readings, but styles have changed over time. In the first stages of my research, I had used *kundoku* readings by modern scholars as interpretive tools, but I did not think they represented how the poems were read aloud in Ikkyū's time. So, my answer to Kiyooka that night was, "We do not and cannot know how Ikkyū sounded out his own poems, whether aloud or in his own head." I did not find the answer satisfying.

Soon after, in Japan, Reverend Hirano Sōjō gave me a photocopy of the Okumura manuscript, the oldest of the *Kyōunshū* manuscripts that bears Ikkyū's signature in two places, indicating that he had seen it and presumably approved it. It contains *kunten*, the marks that indicate how the poem should be read in *kundoku*: what the word order should be, which Japanese inflections and grammatical particles to add and so on. *Kunten* were not added to all poems in the manuscript but to enough that one gets a reasonably accurate idea of how Ikkyū's poems were read aloud in his own time. The chanting of Chinese poetry aloud, *shigin*, is still practiced today. To get an inkling of that art, I studied *shigin* for a year in Kyoto with a teacher who had been recommended because he was trying to revive the *kundoku* reading style of the medieval Zen monks. There was so much else, however, that I still needed to learn in order to complete my translations that, even having seen the door opening to answer Kiyooka's question, I did not go through it.

Preparing the Romanized texts for this edition, however, produced revelations I was not expecting. I noticed first that Hirano and Kageki's *kundoku* readings followed as much as possible the style suggested by the *kunten* in the Okmura manuscript. Transcribing their *kundoku* readings and reading them aloud was a pleasurable and moving experience. In my head, I could hear my *shigin* teacher's voice from all those years ago blended with Reverend Hirano's voice, because he always read the poems aloud several times as we studied them together. What surprised me most of all was that occasionally reading the *kundoku* readings aloud, an improvement to the translation leapt into view. Here is one small example, the last line from poem 108 in the original Chinese, *kundoku* reading in Romanization, and literal translation of how I first understood the line.

> 濁醪一盞醉醺醺
> *dakurō issan yotte kunkun*
> muddy *sake* one cup am drunk, drunk, drunk

My original translation for this line ignored the repeated characters at the end of the line that mean "to be drunk" or "to smell of drink," because they seemed redundant. I just rendered the line simply and bluntly as:

> One cup of cloudy *sake* and I am drunk.

This time through, however, when sounding the *kundoku* aloud as I transcribed it, *kunkun* suddenly brought to mind the Japanese colloquial expressions *punpun*, "to stink, usually of drink" and *kunkun* "sniff, sniff," and the line became:

> One cup of cloudy *sake* and I am stinking drunk.

It is these small insights or inspirations that lead to changing a word here and there that bring delight to the translator's work.

In conclusion, I would say that even if we can never know *exactly* how Ikkyū read his poems aloud, we can get close enough to make the effort of trying worthwhile. There is more research that could be done on this topic. A systematic study of the *kunten* in the Okumura manuscript would lay a foundation. Comparisons could be made with how citations of Chinese poetry are rendered in other texts of the medieval period, such as Noh plays or compilations of poetic tags for Zen monks like the *Zenrin kushū* "Capping Phrases for Zen Monasteries."

Imagining the *Kyōunshū/Crazy Cloud Anthology* for the Brave New Digital World

Quirin Press has given this version of the *Kyōunshū* a new lease on life in print format, for which I am very grateful. Personally, I will never be able to derive the same pleasure from reading a digital text as I get from holding a book in my hands. Nonetheless, I can imagine the possibility for a more audacious form of publication.

The world is hurtling more and more toward digital forms of literacy that favour a dispersed reading and the inclusion of visual and mixed media material. Due to all the background material and embedded allusions that a reader needs to appreciate the poems, the *Kyōunshū* encourages a kind of dispersed reading, back and forth from the notes to the poem before the meaning emerges fully. In *Once Having Paused*, Messer and Smith experimented with a different format in order to circumvent this problem by placing all the allusions ahead of the poem translation and composing them in a narrative form rather than as explanatory notes. This gives the readers the requisite background knowledge ahead of the poem so that they can encounter it almost like an intended reader. Their format is effective and engaging while still remaining within the print medium, but hypertexts are also an interesting option.

Many years ago, a poet friend and early adopter of computer technology, Lionel Kearns, had encouraged me to think about publishing a digital version of the *Kyōunshū* using hypertexts for all the background material. Instead of moving the eyes back and forth up and down the page, with a click of the mouse, one could move quickly to another screen where a wealth of information could be provided. Now, of course, one can easily include visual images, such as photos of places mentioned and reproductions of art works of the period. Even recordings of someone trained in *shigin* chanting the *kundoku* readings of the poems could be included. The possibilities are tantalizing.

I was approached about ten years ago by "pioneer blogger" Justin Hall, who had spent some years in Japan reporting on video game developments for online publications. In the early 2000s, he had borrowed *Ikkyū and the Crazy Cloud Anthology* from the Foreign Press Library in Tokyo and became so enthralled with Ikkyū's poetry that he kept the book out for four years. He considered taking it away with him when he returned to the United States. He had noticed that the book had been taken out very few times since it had been deposited there in 1986 and surmised it would not be missed. He did the right thing in the end, however, and returned it, determined to search out a second-hand copy of the book on the internet. He did find one at a shockingly high price, which provided him with material for a blog entitled, "The most expensive book I ever bought." He contacted me to suggest a collaboration on a digital version of the *Crazy Cloud Anthology* that would somehow incorporate a video game aspect. It was an intriguing idea that I did not fully understand, and we got as far as creating an imperfect OCR of the original book. Then, his mercurial interests took him elsewhere and other projects carried me off too. I relate this episode not to regret an opportunity missed, but to circle back to the enduring value of having books in print form. Had that book not been in the Foreign Press Library, both Justin and I would have missed a mutually enriching experience.

A book in print form, carefully produced to be free of errors and on acid-free paper, can wait quietly for even centuries in libraries until just the right reader comes along and discovers something vital they needed to understand. By contrast, the digital mode of publication is so much more ephemeral and now distressingly subject to the commercial exploitation of the basest of human fears and desires. I am under no illusion that Ikkyū's poetry will ever find a large audience, but it is a repository of insight and experience well worth keeping in print. Long may there be books in print and libraries to shelter them.

Abbreviations

IZ   *Ikkyū Oshō Zenshū: Kyōunshū* 一休和尚全集：狂雲集. vol. 1, Hirano Sōjō 平野宗浄, ed. vol. 2, Kageki Hideo 蔭木秀雄 ed. Tokyo: Shunjūsha, 1997.

SB   *Si Bu Bei Yao* 四部備要. Shanghai: Zhonghua shuju, 1936.

T   *Taishō Shinshū Daizōkyō* 大正新修大藏經. Tokyo: Taisō Issai Kyō Kankōkai, 1922.

ZZ   *Zoku Zōkyō* 續藏經. Hong Kong: Hong Kong Buddhist Association, 1946 (photo reprint of the original *Dainihon Zoku Zōkyō*).

Notes

Introduction

1. For a detailed treatment of the Ōnin War in English, see Paul Varley, *The Ōnin War*. For an overview of the Muromachi period, see George Samson, *A History of Japan 1334–1651*, and J.W. Hall and Toyoda Takeshi, eds., *Japan in the Muromachi Era*.
2. There are other firsthand accounts of the disaster that also remark on the disparity between those spared and those afflicted. See Varley, *Ōnin War*, p. 117, also Ikkyū's poem 203 analyzed on pp. 36–37.
3. References in parentheses are to poem translations relevant to the subject under discussion. When the reference is by poem number, it is a poem in the translation section. When the reference is by page number, then it is a poem cited in the Introduction.
4. See Samson, *History of Japan*, pp. 207–209 for a sample of that opinion.
5. Nagahara Keiji, *Gekokujō no Jidai, Nihon no Rekishi*, vol. 10, p. 6.
6. Ichikawa Hakugen, *Ikkyū: Ransei ni Ikita Zensha*, p. 15.
7. For this discussion, I am much indebted to Martin Collcutt's study of the institutional history of the Gozan system, entitled *Five Mountains: The Rinzai Zen Monastic Institution in Medieval Japan*. Any reader wanting to pursue this topic in more detail is advised to refer to Collcutt's work.
8. Ichikawa, *Ikkyū*, pp. 76–77.

9. Donald Keene, *Some Japanese Portraits*, pp. 15–27.
10. Yanagida Seizan, *Ikkyū: Kyōunshū no Sekai*, p. 10.
11. The standard text is available in the *Zoku Gunsho Ruijū*, vol. 9, part 2, beginning p. 749. Since the *Nempu* entries are organized according to the era year and the year of Ikkyū's age, the notes will cite Ikkyū's age for easy reference in any edition in the *Nempu*, including the English translation.

    Hirano Sōjō has translated the *Nempu* into modern Japanese in his *Ikkyū Oshō Nempu no Kenkyū*, and James Sanford has produced a complete English translation of it in his *Zen-man Ikkyū*. Sanford uses the *Nempu* as his base and sifts through information gleaned from a variety of sources, including the *Crazy Cloud Anthology*, and, with the judicial admixture of reasonable conjecture, has produced a coherent picture of Ikkyū's life which I recommend to the reader.

    There is one other general treatment of Ikkyū in English: this is Jon Covell, *Zen's Core: Ikkyū's Freedom*. While the work is to a certain extent based on primary sources, imaginative elaboration of the material gives the presentation a novelistic character. Nonetheless, the work is well illustrated and documents the little explored area of Ikkyū's paintings.
12. For translations of some representative Tokugawa tales about Ikkyū, see Sanford's *Zen-man Ikkyū*.
13. *Nempu*, first entry.
14. This Romanized text follows Yanagida Seizan, *Ikkyū 'Kyōunshū' no sekai*, p. 46.
15. *Nempu*, age 13. Only the last two lines of this poem are recorded in the *Nempu*, the entire poem is no. 999 in the *Ikkyū Tokushū*. The *Ikkyū Tokushū* is a catalog of an exhibition of portraits of Ikkyū held at the Yamato Bunkakan. Appended to the catalog is a text of the *Crazy Cloud Anthology* based on the collation of all extant manuscripts. Problems of the possibility of false attribution in later manuscripts aside, it remains the most complete version of the *Anthology* to date. The title of the poem indicates that Ikkyū was consciously composing the poem in the style of Sima Xiangru's "Changmen Fu" and Wang Zhangling's "Western Palace, Spring Lament."
16. Kōan, literally "case" in the legal sense. These are the topics assigned to Zen monks for meditation. Most of them are derived from anecdotes about former masters.
17. *Nempu*, age 25.
18. *Heike Monogatari, Nihon Koten Bungaku Taikei*, pp. 94–111. For an

English translation that renders the poetic quality of the original, see Royall Tyler, trans., *The Tale of the Heike*, pp. 15–28.
19. *Wumen Guan*, kōan 15, T 48, p. 294c.
20. *Nempu*, age 13.
21. Ibid., age 20.
22. Ibid., age 21.
23. Nearly all modern biographers of Ikkyū in Japan take this as evidence that he contemplated suicide. The subject of self-destruction comes up again on the occasion of troubles at Daitokuji. (See prose introduction to poems 100–108.) The *Nempu* states that Ikkyū, aged 54, resolved to starve himself to death in protest. It has thus come to be accepted that Ikkyū was as susceptible to the idea of suicide as many modern Japanese authors; witness Kawabata Yasunari's mention of it in his Nobel Prize acceptance speech *(Japan, the Beautiful and Myself,* p. 61). It bears mentioning, however, that the subject of self-annihilation never comes up in Ikkyū's own writings.
24. For a detailed study of Daitō's life, writing and contribution to the development of Japanese Zen, see Kenneth Kraft, *Eloquent Zen: Daitō and Early Japanese Zen*.
25. *Nempu*, age 22.
26. Ibid., age 27.
27. Ibid.
28. Murakami Tekken, ed., *Santaishi*, vol. 1, p. 64.
29. Yanagida, *Ikkyū*, p. 56ff.
30. *Nempu*, age 27.
31. Ibid., age 44.
32. Ibid., age 55.
33. In Ikkyū's "Last Testament," a document in his own hand preserved in Shinjūan, Ikkyū implies that no one would obtain a seal of enlightenment from him and that if any of his followers after his death let it be believed that he had received one from Ikkyū, that follower should be punished. (See *Ikkyū Tokushū*, p. 74.) Thus was his antipathy to the whole issue of seals expressed.
34. *Nempu*, age 39. Also, IZ, v. 1, p. 99.
35. *Chuan Deng Lu*, roll 9, T 51, p. 265c.
36. *Nempu*, age 42.
37. See *Ikkyū Tokushū*, plates 5 and 6; Sanford, *Zen-man Ikkyū*, plate 2a.
38. Sanford cites political reasons for the Sakai populace's support of Zen

schools outside the main Gozan line, *Zen-man Ikkyū*, pp. 31–32.
39. Ichikawa, *Ikkyū*, p. 183. However, attribution is a problem with Ikkyū's *kana hōgo*. Of the half a dozen or so works that have been attributed to Ikkyū, only *Gaikotsu* (Skeletons) has both a style and textual history that make its attribution quite certain. All the evidence has not been collected; they simply have not been studied enough to make judgments. Sanford, choosing to ignore the problem of attribution, has translated seven prose works believed to be Ikkyū's, so in his *Zen-man Ikkyū*, the reader may refer to those to get an impression of what *kana hōgo* are like. The translation of "Skeletons" alone makes the effort of the reading worthwhile.
40. *Nempu*, age 22.
41. Ibid., age 47.
42. It is noteworthy that this poem was not included in the *Nempu*.
43. Within the Rinzai school, *sanzen* refers to the meetings between student and master where the student demonstrates the quality of his understanding.
44. *Nempu*, age 61.
45. *Jikaishū*, in Nakamoto Tamaki's *Kyōunshū*, p. 354.
46. Ibid., p. 352.
47. *Nempu*, age 56.
48. Ichikawa, *Ikkyū*, p. 10.
49. *Nempu*, age 76.
50. The Chinese glyph with which this woman's name is written, which means literally "forest," can be read either as *shin* in the Sino-Japanese reading or *mori* in the native Japanese reading. Japanese scholars, if they provide a reading for the name, usually give *shin* primarily because she is often referenced with compound terms such as *shinjo* "Shin Woman" or *shinjisha* "Shin Attendant." However, since Donald Keene's chapter on Ikkyū in *Some Japanese Portraits* (1978), it has been standard for Western scholars to refer to her as Mori, perhaps because it is softer in sound and registers more clearly as a Japanese name. I follow that practice.
51. See frontispiece.
52. The poem in question is no. 1049 in the *Ikkyū Tokushū*, which is not based on the Okumura manuscript of the *Crazy Cloud Anthology* but gathers together all works appearing in any edition or manuscript of the *Crazy Cloud Anthology*. However, this poem appears only in the Tokugawa-period block edition of the *Gunsho ruijū*, so the attribution is not certain.
53. *Nempu*, age 75.

54. This poem is not included in the *Ikkyū Oshō Zenshū: Kyōunshū*. The text for this poem is no. 964 in the *Ikkyū Tokushū*, which includes the largest number of Ikkyū's poems based on a thorough collation of all extant manuscripts of the *Kyōunshū*.
55. The kundoku reading for this Romanized text is based on Nakamoto Tamaki's reading in *Shinsen Nihon Koten: Kyōunshū*, p. 322. Nakamoto's text for the poem, however, differs slightly from the text in the Ikkyū Tokushū with 二女 "two women" instead of 男女 "man and woman." "Two Women" also makes sense because the play *Matsukaze* has two women characters, the sisters, Matsukaze "Pine Wind" and Murasame "Passing Shower." Both women were lovers of the exiled courtier, and one could interpret Matsukaze's wild dance and monologue as expressing the suffering of them both. However, I prefer the text in the *Ikkyū Tokushū*.
56. Donald Keene, "The Comic Tradition in Renga," p. 272.
57. Tanchū Terayama, *Ikkyū Bokuseki, Ikkyū Oshō Zenshū: Bekkan*, p. 99.
58. For whatever reason, this poem was not included in the *Crazy Cloud Anthology*. Xutang is the Chinese patriarch of the Daitokuji lineage. For the text of this poem, see also Ikkyū Tokushū, p. 74.
59. For a good survey of Gozan poetry, see Marian Ury, *Poems of the Five Mountains*, and David Pollack, *Zen Poems of the Five Mountains*.
60. Ichikawa, *Ikkyū*, pp. 76–77.
61. For a detailed study of the wild fox kōan, see Steven Heine, *Shifting Shape, Shifting Text: Philosophy and Folklore in the Fox Kōan*.
62. *Wu Deng Hui Yuan*, roll 3, ZZ, v. 138, p. 44c.
63. *Heart Sūtra*, T 14, p. 540b.
64. Literally, this adage is, "Do none of the various evils, practice many forms of good." Thanks to the terseness of the Chinese language, this plurality can be expressed in a dense, rhythmic way; "shoaku makusa, shūzen bugyō" is the Japanese reading that Ikkyū would have been familiar with. The general singular has been used in this translation to attempt to capture some of the rhythm and compactness of the original.
65. *Chuan Deng Lu*, roll 4, T 51, p. 230b.
66. IZ, v. 1, p. 233. Not translated here.
67. *Vimalakīrti Sūtra*, T 14, p. 550c.
68. Fish, *Self-Consuming Artifacts*, p. 1.
69. For further information on Ikkyū and Chinese prosody, see Sonja Arntzen, "The Poetry of the Kyōunshū 'Crazy Cloud Anthology' of Ikkyū Sōjun," pp. 36–46.

70. Kijima Hajime, ed., *The Poetry of Postwar Japan*, p. xxvii. "Hadaka no Gengo: The Naked Language of Postwar Japanese Poetry" is the title to Roy Andrew Miller's essay in the preface to this book.
71. Murakami, *Santaishi*, pp. 165–166. Translation is my own as will be all others, unless otherwise noted.
72. *Wu Deng Hui Yuan*, roll 19, ZZ, v. 138, p. 370a.
73. *Daitō Kokushi Nempu*, pp. 33–34.
74. *Chuan Deng Lu*, roll 7, T 51, p. 254c.
75. Ibid.
76. Burton Watson, *Records of the Grand Historian of China*, v. 1, pp. 504–505. *Shiji*, SB, roll 84, pp. 4–6.
77. See the notes to poem 332 for a full citation of this poem.
78. There are conflicting legends about Tao Yuanming; some would have it that he was a Buddhist. He lived close to the famous Buddhist center of Lushan. Many of China's intellectuals were turning to Buddhism at the time, for the age was exceedingly disorderly and Buddhism offered at least peace for the mind, if not for the world. However, in the tradition of the Zen lineage Ikkyū belonged to, Tao Yuanming was certainly not thought of as a Buddhist. In the *Xutang Lu*, "Record of Xutang," a text crucial to the Daitokuji lineage since Xutang was its Chinese founder, he says in a poem, "Yuanming heard the bell and knit his brow" referring to Tao Yuanming's rejection of Buddhism. *Xutang Lu*, roll 7, T 47, p. 1034b. See also Hirano's commentary to this poem, IZ, v. 1, p. 65.
79. *Chuan Deng Lu*, roll 11, T 51, p. 284a.
80. *Blue Cliff Record*, kōan no. 47, T 48, p. 183b. There is a good translation of this text in English, Thomas and J. C. Cleary, *The Blue Cliff Record*. For that reason, it will be referred to in the body of the work by its English title. The kōan number enables one to find the cited passage whether in translation or in the original. For completeness sake, however, the notes will provide the reference for the Taishō Daizōkyō edition of the Buddhist canon.
81. See preceding note 72.
82. See notes to poem 121.
83. Although fūryū is a Japanese word, it has been left without italics since it will be used frequently in the poem translations. For a fuller explanation of the wide range of meanings of this term, see notes to poem 6.
84. The place name Xiang river has rich cultural associations in East Asia. For an excellent overview of this topic, see I Lo-fen, "The East Asian Cultural Image: A Study of 'Eight Views of the Xiao Xiang.'"

85. *Jin Shu*, SB, roll 80, p. 6b.
86. *Blue Cliff Record*, kōan no. 83, T 48, pp. 208–209.
87. *Wenxuan*, SB, roll 19, pp. 1–2.
88. IZ, v. 1, p. 60.
89. Katō Shūichi and Yanagida Seizan, *Nihon no Zengoroku: Ikkyū*, p. 222.
90. *Daitō Kokushi Goroku*, T 81, p. 224a.
91. For another analysis of this complex poem and an illuminating discussion of the metaphor of "cloud-rain" in Ikkyū's poetry, see Didier Davin, "Entre Étreinte and Éveil: La Métaphore du Nuage et de la Pluie dans le *Kyōunshū* d' Ikkyū Sōjun."
92. T. S. Eliot, *Collected Poems*, p. 77.
93. *Ikkyū Tokushū*, p. 15.
94. For a study of the differences between the *ge* and *shi* collections, see Nakamoto, *Kyōunshū*.
95. The Reverend Hirano was a Zen monk of the Daitokuji lineage and brought to his work not only an encyclopedic knowledge of Chinese and Japanese Zen texts but also an insider's knowledge of the tradition of kōan interpretation within the Daitokuji school.
96. Yanagida Seizan, professor of Kyoto University and long-term member of the *Rinzai roku* and kōan text study group centered around Ruth Sasaki Fuller at Daitokuji, exceled in textual analysis. His interpretations have philological rigour, historical depth and imagination. He collaborated with Shūichi Katō on one work, *Ikkyū*, in the *Nihon no Zengoroku* series. In his own *Ikkyū: Kyōunshū no Sekai*, he devoted a chapter each to thirteen poems, taking the time to explore the worlds of imagination each poem opens up.
97. Kageki Hideo, editor of IZ, *Kyōunshū*, v. 2, succeeded Hirano Sōjō in the project to provide commentaries for all poems in the Okumura manuscript copy of the *Kyōunshū*. He is author of *Gozan Shishi no Kenkyū* "Historical Study of Gozan poetry" and brought to the task a deep knowledge of Chinese poetry of the Tang and Song eras as well as of the vast production of poetry in Chinese by Zen monks throughout the medieval era.

Translations

1. For an excellent overview of the Chinese historical context for this term, see Peipei Qiu, "Aesthetic of Unconventionality: *Fūryū* in Ikkyū's poetry," *Japanese Language and Literature*, 35 (2001), 135–156.
2. Yanagida, *Ikkyū*, p. 165.
3. *Wu Deng Hui Yuan*, roll 19, ZZ, v. 138, p. 361b.
4. Yanagida, *Ikkyū*, p. 150ff.
5. *Xutang Lu*, roll 10, T 1063b.
6. *Linji lu*, T 47, p. 497a. Paul Demiéville, *Entretiens de Lin-tsi*, p. 51–54. Ruth Fuller Sasaki, *The Record of Linji*, pp. 7–9 and 150–153.
7. Didier Davin, "*Kyōunshū: Rinzai Shiryōkan shikishaku,*" pp. 116–117.
8. *Linji lu*, T 47, p. 506c.
9. Davin, "*Kyōunshū: Rinzai Shiryōkan Shikishaku,*" p. 125.
10. Ibid.
11. *Linji lu*, T 47, p. 497a.
12. IZ, *Kyōunshū*, v. 1, p. 21. Davin, "*Kyōunshū: Rinzai Shiryōkan Shikishaku,*" p. 126.
13. *Blue Cliff Record*, kōan no. 1, T 48, p. 140a.
14. IZ, *Kyōunshū*, v. 1, p. 21. Davin, "*Kyōunshū: Rinzai Shiryōkan Shikishaku,*" p. 126.
15. The summary of this episode is adapted from Didier Davin's English translation of this passage in "Between the Mountain and the City: Ikkyū Sōjun and the Blurred Border of Awakening," p. 57.
16. This summarizes the account in Watson, *Records of the Grand Historian*, pp. 298–300 and 330. The expressions in quotation marks are Watson's translations.
17. *Wu Deng Hui Yuan*, roll 7, ZZ, v. 138, p. 116a.
18. *Jin Shu*, roll 43, SB, p. 12b.
19. For a good explanation of the Six Courses as they were understood in medieval Japan, see William LaFleur's *Karma of Words*, pp. 26–29.
20. *Nempu*, age 61.
21. IZ, *Kyōunshū*, v. 1, p. 13.
22. *Blue Cliff Record*, kōan no. 60, T 48, p. 192c.
23. IZ, *Kyōunshū*, v. 1, p. 50.
24. *Zhouyi* (*Yijing*) SB, roll 3, p. 4b.
25. *Lotus Sūtra*, T 9, p. 15b. See also Leon Hurvitz, *Scripture of the Lotus Blossom of the Fine Dharma*, p. 75.

26. *Chanlin Leiju*, roll 15, ZZ, v. 117, p. 94a.
27. *Guzunsu Yulu*, roll 34, ZZ, v. 118, p. 304a.
28. IZ, *Kyōunshū*, v. 1, p. 58.
29. Ibid.
30. Ibid.
31. *Blue Cliff Record*, kōan no. 63, T 48, p. 194c.
32. Ibid., kōan no. 83, T 48, p. 209ab.
33. *Wumen Guan*, kōan no. 10, T 48, p. 294a.
34. *Lotus Sūtra*, T 9, p. 12bc. Hurvitz, *Scripture of the Lotus Blossom*, pp. 58–60.
35. IZ, *Kyōunshū*, v. 2, p. 166–167.
36. *Chuan Deng Lu*, roll 11, T 51, p. 286a.
37. *Blue Cliff Record*, kōan no. 64, T 48, p. 195a.
38. *Linji Lu*, T 47, p. 505c.
39. *Blue Cliff Record*, kōan no. 15, T 48, p. 155c.
40. IZ, *Kyōunshū*, v. 1, p. 74.
41. *Blue Cliff Record*, kōan no. 29, T 48, p. 169a.
42. *Hekigan Roku*, v. 2, p. 328.
43. *Blue Cliff Record*, kōan no. 29, T 48, p. 169a.
44. *Wu Deng Hui Yuan*, roll 19, ZZ, v. 138, p. 739a.
45. IZ, *Kyōunshū*, v. 1, p. 92.
46. Mochizuki Shinkō, *Bukkyō Daijiten*, v. 1, p. 629.
47. *Shishi Jigu Lüe*, roll 3, T 49, p. 833b.
48. IZ p. V. 1, 94. *Blue Cliff Record*, kōan no. 86, T. 48, p. 211b.
49. *Linji Lu*, T 47, p. 499c.
50. *Hai Long Wang Jing*, T 15, pp. 131–157.
51. *Jianghu Fengyue Ji*, part 2, p. 7.
52. *Blue Cliff Record*, kōan no. 96, T 48, p. 291b.
53. Ibid., kōan no. 83, T 48, p. 209ab.
54. *Wu Deng Hui Yuan*, roll 15, ZZ, v. 138, p. 276b.
55. *Hou Han Shu*, SB, roll 54, p. 2b.
56. IZ p. V. 1, 102.
57. *Shiji*, SB, roll 97, pp. 8–9.
58. *Blue Cliff Record*, kōan no. 42, T 48, p. 179b.
59. *Ren Tian Yanmu*, T. 48, p. 301a.
60. Sarah Messer and Kidder Smith, *Having Once Paused: Poems of Zen Master Ikkyū*, p. 34.
61. *Nempu*, age 49.
62. *Wu Deng Hui Yuan*, roll 3, ZZ, v. 138, p. 49a.

63. *Vimalakīrti Sūtra*, roll 10, T 14, p. 532ff.
64. *Du Gongbu Shiji*, SB, roll 9, p. 6b.
65. Yanagida, *Ikkyū*, p. 82.
66. *Nempu*, age 54.
67. Murakami, *Santaishi*, vol. 1, p. 149.
68. *Blue Cliff Record*, kōan no. 11, T 48, p. 151b.
69. *Chuan Deng Lu,* rolls, T 51, p. 235c.
70. *Guzunsu Yulu*, roll 9, ZZ, v. 118, p. 134b.
71. *Linji Lu*, T 47, p. 504b.
72. *Xutang Lu*, roll 1, T 47, p. 986b.
73. *Quan Tang Shi*, v. 2, p. 2164.
74. *Shiji*, SB, roll 117, p. 2a.
75. *Wenxuan*, SB, roll 1, p. 1.
76. *Shiji*, SB, roll 66, p. 4b.
77. Ichikawa Hakugen, ed., *Chūsei Zenka no Shisō*, p. 429.
78. *Chuan Deng Lu,* roll 30, T 51, p. 461c.
79. *Songyuan Yulu*, roll 1, ZZ, v. 121, pp. 289d–290a.
80. IZ, v. 1, p. 177.
81. *Xutang Lu*, roll 1, T 47, 996a.
82. *Dahui Wuku*, T 47, p. 956b.
83. *Wumen Guan*, kōan no. 41, T 48, p. 298a.
84. *Wu Deng Hui Yuan*, roll 6, ZZ p. 138c.
85. IZ, v. 1, p. 194.
86. For a full discussion of this topic, see Sonja Arntzen, "Chinese Community of the Imagination for the Japanese Zen monk Ikkyū Sōjun 一休宗純 (1394–1481)," in *Rethinking the Sinosphere: Poetics. Aesthetics, and Identity Formation*, 2020, pp. 67–94.
87. IZ, v. 1, p. 195.
88. Terayama, *Ikkyū Bokuseki*, pp. 23–29. Surprisingly, the vertical lines of Ikkyū's calligraphy on this scroll are written from the left to the right, rather than the usual practice of right to left. Terayama offers no explanation for this. One wonders if, given that the subject of the scroll is Indian, Ikkyū has written from the left as a nod to Sanskrit writing practice.
89. IZ, v. 1, p. 208. For Puhua's chant, see *Linji Lu*, T. 47, 503b.
90. IZ, ibid. See also Terayama, *Ikkyū Bokuseki*, pp. 76–77.
91. *Congling Shengshi*, roll 2, ZZ, v. 148, p. 47d.
92. Weinstein, "A Biographical Study of Tz'u-en," p.
93. *Wu Deng Hui Yuan*, roll 3, ZZ, v. 138, p. 46a.

94. *Diamond Sūtra*, T 8, 750b.
95. *Lotus Sūtra*, roll 7, T 9, pp. 50–51. Hurvitz, *Scripture of the Lotus Blossom*, p. 280.
96. *Songyuan Yulu*, roll 2, ZZ, v. 121, p. 301cd.
97. *Yunmen Guanglu*, roll 1, T 47, p. 547b.
98. *Guzunsu Yulu*, roll 34, ZZ, v. 118, p. 304a.
99. IZ, v. 1, pp. 273–274.
100. *Xu Chuan Deng Lu*, roll 22, T 51, p. 616b.
101. This kōan also attracted the modern author Kawabata Yasunari. In his Nobel Prize acceptance address he mentions how he often uses a version of it when requested for a sample of his calligraphy. *Japan, the Beautiful and Myself*, p. 59.
102. *Wu Deng Hui Yuan*, roll 12, ZZ, v. 138, p. 218a.
103. Burton Watson, *The Complete Works of Chuang Tzu*, p. 284. Zhuangzi, SB, roll 8, p. 26a.
104. *Wumen Guan*, kōan no. 11, T 48, p. 294b.
105. IZ, v. 1, p. 300.
106. *Jikaishū*, in Nakamoto, *Kyōunshū*, p. 354.
107. *Linji Lu*, T 47, p. 496b.
108. IZ, v. 1, p. 348–349.
109. *Zhouyi*, no. 26, SB, roll 3, p. 7b. Translation, Richard John Lynn, *The Classic of Changes*, p. 303.
110. IZ, v. 1, p. 357.
111. *Xutang Lu*, roll 8, T 47, p. 1045b.
112. Watson, *Chuang Tzu*, p. 295. Zhuangzi, SB, roll 9, pp. 1–2.
113. Burton Watson, *Chinese Lyricism*, pp. 94–95. Xu Ling, ed., *Yutai Xinyong*, v. 6, pp. 158–162.
114. IZ, *Kyōunshū*, v. 1, p. 358. See also, Murakami Tekken, ed., *Santaishi*, v. 1, p. 92. English translation by Richard John Lynn, unpublished, included with his permission.
115. Louis de la Vallée-Poussin, tr., *L'Abhidharmakośa de Vasubandhu*, v. 6, pp. 158–162.
116. James Hightower, *T'ao Yüan-ming*, p. 130. Wang Yao, *Tao Yuan Ji*, p. 63.
117. *Linji Lu*, T 47, p. 497a.
118. Ibid., p. 506b.
119. Rev. Coates and Rev. Ishizuka, *Hōnen, the Buddhist Saint*, p. 728.
120. *Wu Deng Hui Yuan*, roll 7, ZZ, v. 138, p. 115a.
121. *Bai Xiangshan Shiji*, SB, roll 13, p. 11b.

122. *Wumen Guan*, kōan no. 12, T 48, p. 294b.
123. Terayama, *Ikkyū Bokuseki*. pp. 58–59.
124. *Blue Cliff Record*, Thomas Cleary, trans., v. 1, p. 66; *Blue Cliff Record*, kōan no. 10, T 48, p. 150a.
125. Hirano, IZ, v. 1, p. 539.
126. *Linji Lu*, T 47, p. 505a.
127. *Nempu*, age 84.
128. Terayama, *Ikkyū Bokuseki*, pp. 50–51.
129. *Linji Lu*, T 47, p. 504a.
130. *Blue Cliff Record*, kōan no. 66, T 48, p. 196c.
131. Terayama, *Ikkyū Bokuseki*, pp. 72–73.
132. *Ren Tian Yanmu*, T 48, 310b. See also, *Wu Deng Hui Yuan*, Z 80, 351c.
133. *Bai Xiangshan Shiji*, SB, roll 12, p. 9a.
134. For an informative article on paper clothing and its connotations in literature, see Sukey Hughes, "Paper Clothing: A Brief History and Appreciation."
135. Yanagida, *Ikkyū*, p. 105–109.
136. Yanagida, *Ikkyū*, pp. 94–95.
137. Watson, *Chuang Tzu*, p. 49. *Zhuangzi*, SB, roll 1, p. 25ab.
138. *Nempu*, age 76.
139. IZ, *Kyōunshū*, v. 2, p. 118. For a fuller discussion of this line and the poem as a whole, see Arntzen, "Chinese Community of the Imagination," pp. 77–78.
140. See *Blue Cliff Record*, T. 48, 193b. The interpretation presented here rests on a detailed close reading of kōan no. 61; see Arntzen, "Chinese Community of the Imagination," pp. 78–81.
141. *Du Gongbu Shiji*, SB, roll 9, p. 15a.
142. See IZ, v. 2, p. 153, and *Blue Cliff Record*, kōan no. 9, T. 48, p. 149a.
143. Ibid.
144. *Linji Lu*, T 47, p. 497a.
145. *Nempu*, age 74.
146. Terayama, *Ikkyū bokuseki*, p. 24.
147. Thomas Cleary, *The Blue Cliff Record*, v. 1, p. 64, and kōan no. 9, T. 48, p. 149c.
148. Katō and Yanagida, *Ikkyū*, p. 254.
149. *Wakan Rōei Shū*, p. 67.
150. *Du Gongbu Shiji*, SB, roll 9, p. 14b.
151. *Jianghu Fengyue Ji*, part 2, p. 13.

Bibliography

Primary Sources

Bai Xiangshan Shiji 百香山詩集, SB.
Blue Cliff Record (Ch. *Biyan Lu* 碧巖錄), T 47. *See also* Hekigan Roku (Asahina) and Cleary, *The Blue Cliff Record*.
Chanlin Leiju 禪林類聚, ZZ, v. 117.
Chuan Deng Lu 傳燈錄, T 51.
Chūsei Zenka no Shisō 中世禅家の思想. Ichikawa Hakugen 市川白弦 et al., ed. Tokyo: Iwanami Shoten, 1972.
Conglin Shengshi 叢林盛事, ZZ, v. 148.
Daitō Kokushi Goroku 大燈國師語錄, T 81.
Daitō Kokushi Nempu 大燈國師年譜, Okuda Shozō 奥田正造, ed. Tokyo: Morie Shoten, 1933.
Diamond Sūtra (Ch. *Jin'gang Jing* 金剛經), T 8. *See also* Conze, *Buddhist Wisdom Books* and Price and Wong, *The Diamond Sutra*.
Du Gongbu Shiji 杜工部詩集, SB.
Guzunsu Yulu 古尊宿語錄, ZZ, v. 118.
Hai Long Wang Jing 海龍王經, T 15.
Heart Sūtra (Ch. *Xin Jing* 心經), T 8. *See also* Conze, *Buddhist Wisdom Books*.
Heike Monogatari 平家物語. *Nihon Koten Bungaku Taikei* 日本古典文學大系 v. 33. Tokyo: Iwanami Shoten, 1960. *See also* Royall Tyler, *The Tale of the Heike*.

Hekigan Roku 碧巖録, Asahina Sōgen 朝比奈宗源, ed. Iwanami Bunko edition. Third printing. Tokyo: Iwanami Shoten, 1975.

Hou Han Shu 後漢書, SB.

Ikkyū Oshō Nempu 一休和尚年譜, in *Zoku Gunsho Ruijū* 續群書類從, v. 9, part II, Tokyo: Zoku Gunsho Ruijū Kanseikai, 1927.

Ikkyū Oshō Zenshū: Kyōunshū 一休和尚全集：狂雲集. vol. 1, Hirano Sōjō 平野宗浄, ed. vol. 2, Kageki Hideo 蔭木秀雄 ed. Tokyo: Shunjūsha, 1997.

Ikkyū Tokushū 一休特輯, Itō Toshiko 伊藤敏子, ed, Yamato Bunka Monograph no. 41. Nara: Yamato Bunkakan, 1964. Originally published as a catalog to an exhibition of portraits of Ikkyū.

Jianghu Fengyue Ji 江湖風月集 (J. *Gōko Fūgetsu Shū*). The most available modern edition of this work is a Japanese one: *Gōko Fūgetsu Shū* 江湖風月集, Shibayama Zenkei 柴山全慶, ed. Second printing. Osaka: Sogen Sha, 1975.

Jikaishū 自戒集, in Nakamoto Tamaki 中本環, *Kyōunshū* 狂雲集. Hiroshima: Gendai Shichōsha, 1976.

Jin Shu 晉書, SB.

Kuzōshi 句雙紙 Only available in manuscript form, Hōsa Collection, Manuscript number 123-15, Nagoya, Hōsa Bunkō. See also Victor Hori, *Zen Sand*.

Lian Deng Hui Yao 聯燈會要, ZZ, v. 136.

Linji Lu 臨濟錄, T 47. *See also* Demiéville, *Les Entretiens de Lin-tsi*.

Lotus Sūtra (Ch. Miao Fa Lian Hua Jing 妙法蓮華經), T 9. *See also* Hurvitz, *Scripture of the Lotus Blossom*.

Quan Tang Shi 全唐詩. Taipei: Photo reprint of 1706 Kangxi edition Hongye Shuju, 1977.

Ren Tian Yanmu 人天眼目, T 48.

Shiji 史記, SB. *See also* Watson, *Records of the Grand Historian of China*.

Shishi Jigu Lüe 釋氏稽古略, T 49.

Songyuan Yulu 松原語錄, ZZ, v. 121.

Śūraṅgama Sūtra (Ch. Leng Yan Jing 楞嚴經), T 19. *See also* Luk, *The Śūraṅgama Sūtra*. *Dahui Wuku* 大慧武庫, T 47.

Vimalakīrti Sūtra (Ch. Weimojie Suo Shuo Jing 維摩詰所説經), T 14. *See also* Thurman, *The Holy Teaching of Vimalakirti* and Lamotte, *L'Enseignment de Vimalakīrti*.

Wakan Rōei Shū 和漢朗詠集, Kawaguchi Hisao 川口久雄, ed., *Nihon Koten Bungaku Taikei* 日本古典文学大系, v. 73. Tokyo: Iwanami Shoten, 1965.

Wenxuan 文選, Xiao Tong 蕭統, ed, Wuzhang: Chong Wen Shuju Block Edition, 1896.

Wu Deng Hui Yuan 五燈會元, ZZ, v. 138.

Wumen Guan 無門關, T 48. *See also* Blyth, *Zen and Zen Classics*, vol. 4.
Xu Chuan Deng Lu 續傳燈錄, T 51.
Xutang Lu 虛堂錄, T 47.
Yunmen Guanglu 雲門廣錄, T 47.
Zhouyi 周易 (Yijing), SB.
Zhuangzi 莊子, SB. *See also* Watson, *The Complete Works of Chuang Tzu*.

Secondary Sources

Arntzen, Sonja. *Ikkyū Sōjun: A Zen Monk and His Poetry*. Bellingham: Western Washington State College Press, 1973.
——. "The Poetry of the Kyōunshū 'Crazy Cloud Anthology' of Ikkyū Sōjun." Ph.D. thesis, University of British Columbia, 1979.
——. "Chinese Community of the Imagination for the Japanese Zen monk Ikkyū Sōjun 一休宗純 (1394-1481)." In *Rethinking the Sinosphere: Poetics, Aesthetics, and Identity Formation*, Nanxiu Qian, Richard J. Smith and Bowei Zhang, eds. Amherst, NY: Cambria Press, 2020, 67–94.
Blyth, Reginald Horace. *Zen and Zen Classics*, vol. 4. The *Mumonkan*. Tokyo: Hokuseido, 1960.
Cleary, Thomas, and J. C. Cleary, *The Blue Cliff Record*. 3 vols. Boulder and London: Shambala Publications, 1977.
Coates, Rev. H., and Rev. R. Ishizuka. *Hōnen, the Buddhist Saint*. Kyoto: Chion In, 1925.
Collcutt, Martin. *Five Mountains: The Rinzai Zen Monastic Institution in Medieval Japan*. Cambridge: Harvard University Press, 1981.
Conze, Edward. *Buddhist Wisdom Books, Containing the Diamond Sutra and the Heart Sutra*. London: G. Allen and Unwin, 1958.
Covell, Jon Carter (in collaboration with Abbot Sobin Yamada). *Zen's Core: Ikkyū's Freedom*. Elizabeth, New Jersey; Seoul: Hollym International Corp., 1980.
Davin, Didier. "*Kyōunshū: Rinzai Shiryōkan Shikishaku*"『狂雲集』臨済四料簡試釈. *Indo Tetsugaku bukkyō kenkyū* インド哲学仏教学研究 15 (2008) 117–129.
——. "Entre Étreinte and Éveil: La Métaphore du Nuage et de la Pluie dans le *Kyōunshū* d' Ikkyū Sōjun." *Journal Asiatique* 200 (2012): 841–854.
——. "Between the Mountain and the City: Ikkyū Sōjun and the Blurred Border of Awakening." *Studies in Japanese Literature and Culture* 2 (2019): 45–60.

Demiéville, Paul. *Les Entretiens de Lin-tsi*. Paris: Librairie Fayard, 1972.
Eliot, T. S. *Collected Poems: 1909–1935*. London: Faber and Faber, 1936.
Fish, Stanley. *Self-Consuming Artifacts*. Berkeley: University of California Press, 1972.
Hall, John Whitney, and Toyoda Takeshi, eds. *Japan in the Muromachi Era*. Berkeley: University of California Press, 1977.
Heine, Stephen. *Shifting Shape, Shifting Text: Philosophy and Folklore in the Fox Kōan*. Honolulu: University of Hawaii Press, 1999.
Hightower, James K. *T'ao Yuan-ming*. Oxford: Clarendon Press, 1970.
Hirano Sōjō 平野宗浄. *Kyōunshū Zenshaku* 狂雲集禅釈. Tokyo: Shunjūsha, 1976.
——. *Ikkyū Oshō Nempu no Kenkyū* 一休和尚年譜の研究. Kyoto: Hanazono University Zen Bunka Kenkyūjō, offprint no. 7, n.d.
Hori, Victor Sōgen. *Zen Sand: The Book of Capping Phrases for Kōan Practice*. Honolulu: University of Hawaii Press, 2003.
Hughes, Sukey. "Paper Clothing: A Brief History and Appreciation," *Chanoyu Quarterly* 30 (1982): 41–52.
Hurvitz, Leon. *Scripture of the Lotus Blossom of the Fine Dharma*. New York: Columbia University Press, 1976.
I Lo-fen. "The East Asian Cultural Image: A Study of 'Eight Views of the Xiao Xiang." In *Rethinking the Sinosphere: Poetics. Aesthetics, and Identity Formation*, Nanxiu Qian, Richard J. Smith and Bowei Zhang, eds. Amherst, NY: Cambria Press, 2020, 67–94.
Ichikawa Hakugen 市川白弦. *Ikkyū: Ransei ni Ikita Zensha* 一休：乱世に生きた禅者. Tokyo: Nihon Hōsō Shuppan Kyōkai, 1970.
Kageki Hideo 蔭木秀雄. *Gozan Shishi no Kenkyū* 五山詩史の研究. Tokyo: Kasama Shoin, 1977.
Katō Shūichi, and Yanagida Seizan 加藤週一，柳田聖山. *Nihon no Zen Goroku: Ikkyū* 日本の禅語録：一休. Tokyo: Kōdansha, 1977.
Kawabata Yasunari. *Japan, the Beautiful and Myself*. Edward Seidensticker, trans. Tokyo: Kodansha International, 1969.
Keene, Donald. "The Comic Tradition in Renga." In *Japan in the Muromachi Era*, John W. Hall and Toyoda Takeshi, eds. Berkeley: University of California Press, 1977.
——. *Some Japanese Portraits*. Tokyo: Kodansha International, 1978.
Kijima Hajime, ed. *The Poetry of Postwar Japan*. Iowa City: University of Iowa Press, 1975.
Kitagawa, Hiroshi and Bruce Tsuchida, tr. *The Tale of the Heike*. Tokyo: University of Tokyo Press, 1975.

Kraft, Kenneth., *Eloquent Zen: Daitō and Early Japanese Zen*. Honolulu: University of Hawaii Press, 1992.

LaFleur, William. *Karma of Words: Buddhism and the Literary Arts of Medieval Japan*. Berkeley: University of California Press, 1983.

Lamotte, Etienne. *L'Enseignment de Vimalakīrti*. Louvain: Publications Universitaire, 1962. La Vallée-Poussin, Louis de. *L'Abhidharmakośa de Vasubandhu*. Brussels: Institut Belge des Hautes Etudes Chinoises, 1971.

Luk, Charles. *The Śūraṅgama Sūtra*. London: Rider, 1966.

Lynn, Richard John. *The Classic of Changes*. New York: Columbia University Press, 1994.

Mazanec, Tom J., "The Medieval Chinese Gāthā and Its Relationship to Poetry," *T'oung Pao*, 2017, Vol. 103, pp. 94–154.

———. *The Invention of Chinese Buddhist Poetry: Poet-Monks in Late Medieval China (c. 760–960 CE)*, PhD dissertation, Princeton University, 2017.

Messer, Sarah, and Kidder Smith. *Having Once Paused: Poems of Zen Master Ikkyū (1394–1481)*. Ann Arbor: University of Michigan Press, 2015.

Minakami Tsutomu 水上勉. *Ikkyū* 一休. Tokyo: Chūkō Bunko, 1978.

Miura Isshū and Ruth Sasaki Fuller. *Zen Dust: The History of the Koan and Koan Study in Rinzai (Linji) Zen*. Melbourne and Basel: Quirin Press Updated Edition, 2015.

Mochizuki Shinkō 望月信亨. *Bukkyō Daijiten* 仏教大辞典. Kyoto: Sekai Seiten Kankō Kyōkai, 1954.

Murakami Tekken 村上哲見. *Santaishi* 三体詩. 2 vols., *Chūgoku Koten Sen* 中国古典選 series nos. 16 and 17, Tokyo: Asahi Shimbunsha, 1975.

Nagahara Keiji 永原慶二. *Gekokujō no Jidai* 下剋上の時代, *Nihon no Rekishi* 日本の歴史, vol. 10. Tokyo: Shibundō, 1952.

Nakamoto Tamaki 中本環. *Kyōunshū* 狂雲集, *Shinsen Nihon Koten* 新選日本古典 no. 5. Hiroshima: Gendai Shichō Sha, 1976.

Pollack, David. *Zen Poems of the Five Mountains*. Decatur, GA: Scholar's Press, 1985.

Price, A. F., and Wong Mou-lam. *The Diamond Sutra and the Sutra of Hui Neng*. Berkeley: Shambala Publications, 1969.

Protass, Jason. Buddhist Monks and Chinese Poems: Song Dynasty Monastic Literary Culture. PhD Dissertation, Stanford University, 2016.

———. "Returning Empty-Handed: Reading the *Yifanfeng* Corpus as Buddhist Parting Poetry." Journal of Chinese Literature and Culture, 4:2, November 2017, pp. 383–418.

Qiu, Peipei. "From *Kuang* 狂 to *Fūkyō* 風狂." In *Rethinking the Sinosphere: Poetics, Aesthetics, and Identity Formation*, Nanxiu Qian, Richard J. Smith,

and Bowei Zhang, eds. Amherst, NY: Cambria Press, 2020, 95–135.
———. "Aesthetic of Unconventionality: *Fūryū* in Ikkyū's poetry," *Japanese Language and Literature*, 35 (2001), 135–156.
Samson, George. *A History of Japan, 1334–1615*. Stanford: Stanford University Press, 1967.
Sanford, James. *Zen-man Ikkyū*. Harvard Studies in World Religion, no. 2. Chico, Calif.: Scholars Press, 1981.
Sasaki, Ruth Fuller. Thomas Yūhō Kirchner, ed. *The Record of Linji*. Honolulu: University of Hawaii Press, 2009.
Steininger Brian. *Chinese Literary Forms in Heian Japan: Poetics and Practice*. Cambridge, MA, and London: Harvard University Press, 2017.
Terayama Tanchū, *Ikkyū Bokuseki* 一休墨跡, *Ikkyū Oshō Zenshū: Bekkan* 一休和尚全集・別巻. Tokyo: Shunjūsha, 1997.
Thurman, Robert A. F. *The Holy Teaching of Vimalakirti: A Mahayana Scripture*. University Park: Pennsylvania University Press, 1976.
Tyler, Royall. *The Tale of the Heike*. New York: Penguin Books, 2014.
Ury, Marian. *Poems of the Five Mountains*. Tokyo: Mushinsha, 1977.
Varley, Paul. *The Ōnin War*. New York: Columbia University Press, 1967.
Wang Yao 王瑶, ed. *Tao Yuanming Ji* 陶淵明集. Beijing: Zuojia Chuban She, 1956.
Watson, Burton. *Records of the Grand Historian of China*. New York: Columbia University Press, 1961.
———. *The Complete Works of Chuang Tzu*. New York: Columbia University Press, 1968.
———. *Chinese Lyricism*. New York: Columbia University Press, 1971.
Weinstein, Stanley. "A Biographical Study of Tz'u en." *Monumenta Nipponica* XV (1959), nos. 1–2.
Xu Ling 徐陵, ed. *Yutai Xinyong* 玉臺新詠. *Shijian Wenku, Wenxue Congshu*. Shanghai: Shi Jie Shuju, 1931.
Yanagida Seizan 柳田聖山. *Ikkyū: Kyōunshū no Sekai* 一休：狂雲集の世界. Kyoto: Jinbun Shoin, 1980.
———. "Ikkyū no Shisō to Sono Shōgai" 一休の思想とその生涯. Daihōrin special edition 大法輪特輯, *Zensō Ikkyū no subete* 禅僧一休のすべて. August 1976.
Zengetsu Myokyo, ed. *words have no meaning: poems and translations from the 2007 Montreal Zen Poetry Festival*, Montreal: Enpukuji Press, 2009.

Index to Poems

Most poems are indexed under their titles. Those without titles have been provided with one based on the content of the poem or are indexed under their first lines. Multiple poems under a single title are noted under the joint title.

A Beautiful Woman's Dark Place Has the Fragrance of a Narcissus, 168
A Cup of Rice in a Bent Foot Cauldron, 38–9
A Layman Reciting a Poem Before the Gate of a Brothel and Then Returning, 139
A Vow Taken to Repay My Deep Debt to Lady Mori, 173
About Disturbances at Daitokuji, 133
Account List of Nyoian Property, Appendix, 20
Acts of Grace, 143
Addressed to an Assembly on the Winter Solstice, 76–7
Addressed to a Monk at Daitokuji, 124
Addressed to a Monk in the Hall of Long Life, 119
Addressed to a Monk Who Burned Books, three poems, 157–8
Addressed to a Monk Who Killed a Cat, 132–3
Addressed to Reverend Yōsō upon My Retiring from Nyoian, 20–1
Arhat Chrysanthemums, 43
Bai Letian, 177
Baizhang Fasting, 125
Blind Girl's Love Songs at Yakushidō, 171
Calling My Hand Mori's Hand, 168–9
Cause and Effect for a Lustful Monk, 177–8
Changmen Spring Grass, 10
Chrysanthemums: An Arhat and Yang Guifei in the Same Vase, 95

Composed When Ill, 29
Composed When Ill, 137
Composing a Poem and Trading It for Food, 130
Congratulating Daiyūan's Monk Yōsō upon Receiving the Honorary Title of Zen Master Sōe Daishō, 123
Congratulating Elder Ki on the New Construction of Eagle Tail Monastery and Inquiring after His Leprosy, 134–5
Congratulations for Yōsō, 109–10
Death Poem, 28
Deluded Enlightenment, 156
Do No Evil, Do Much Good, 31–2
Dream Chamber, four poems, 187–8
Du Ling's Sprinkling Flowers With Tears, 179
Earth House, 107–8
Enlightenment Poem, 14
Face to Face with the Beautiful One on the Eve of Daitō's Commemoration Ceremony, 56
Fisherman, 132
Fisherman, 175
Frogs, 93
From the Mountains, Returning to the City, 100
Gathering Horse Dung to Cultivate the Mottled Bamboo, 46
Gathering Horse Dung to Cultivate the Mottled Bamboo, 162–3
Half a Cloud, 107
Hearing a Crow, Attaining Realization, 16
Hell, 159
Humorous Composition on Becoming Abbot of Daitokuji, 176
I Hate Incense, 160
I Recall the Old Times Living at Takagi, 172
In the Morning at Tiantai, in the Evening at Nanyue, 48
Inscription for Yōsō's Daiyūan Hermitage, 124
Instructing the Cook in the Mountains, 99
Lady Mori Rides in a Cart, 167
Lady Mori's Afternoon Nap, 174
Living in the Mountains, two poems, 97–8
Master Songyuan Rose to Lecture and Presented This Case, 127
Mori Refusing to Eat, two poems, 164–5
Mourning Soldiers Dead in the War, 159
Muddy *Sake*, 41
Night Conversation in the Dream Chamber, 174–5
Nirvana Hall, 188
No One Sees It the Same, 148

Index to Poems 225

Nō Play: Matsukaze "Pine Wind," 25–6
Old Woman Kōan, 101
On Tiger Mount, the Snow Falls on Three Grades of Monks, two poems, 116
On a Brothel, 118
On a Spring Outing to the Mausoleum of the Retired Emperor Go Komatsu at Unryūin in Sennyūji, 186
On the Topic of *The Venerable Master Daitō's Conduct*, 60
Ox, 17
Pain in Pleasure, 82
Paper Sleeves, 170
Peach Blossom Waves, 75
Picture of an Arhat Reveling in a Brothel, two poems 138
Pleasure in Pain, 80–1
Praising Master Rinzai, 164
Praising Monk Xutang, 59
Praising Puhua, 111
Praising Saint Hōnen, 152
Praising the Dharma Master Ci'en Kuiji, 121
Praising the Fish-Basket Kannon, 87
Presented to a Gathering, 126
Promise to Be Born in the Time of Maitreya, 169
Quietly Singing Beside the Lamp, 153–4
Reading Du Fu's poetry, two poems, 140
Remorse over Sins for which My Tongue Should Be Pulled Out, 142
Recollecting the Past, 154
Reduce Desires and Know Contentment, two poems, 145–6
Retreating from Mikanohara and Going to Nara, 178
Reverend Songyuan, two poems, 161
Ridiculing Literature, 153
Rinzai Burned the Meditation Plank and Desk, 84
Rinzai's Four Propositions, four poems, 61–3
Śākyamuni Practicing Ascetic Discipline, 120
Sea Cloud, 184
Self-Appraisal, 113
Self-Appraisal, 120–1
Shakuhachi, 94
Shameful Today, a Purple-Robed Monk, 27
Snowball, 96
Sonrin, Forest of Venerability, 185
Straw Raincoat and Hat, 108–9
Straw-Sandal Chen, 69
Taking a Metaphor for Reality, 151

Tettō's Sermon, 72–4
Thanking a Man for the Gift of Soy Sauce, 136
The Buddha's Nirvana, 78
The Correct Skill for a Disorderly Age, 145
The Correct Skill for Great Peace, 144
The Gentleman's Wealth, 149
The Great Master Yuanwu Strikes a Harmony with the Cosmic Organ, 86
The Last Chrysanthemum in the South Garden, 149
The Plum Ripened, 39–40
The Scriptures Wipe Away Filth, three poems, 88–9
The Second Year of Kanshō—Starvation, three poems, 180–1
The Stick, 155
The World at War, All Heaven, All Earth, Battle, 182–3
Three Poems to Show the Monks of My Circle, three poems, 114–15
Three Reflections of Master Foyan, 129
To Hear a Sound and Awaken to the Way, 45
Tortoise Around Dasui's Hermitage, 83
Troubles at Daitokuji, two poems, 102–3
Two Pieces of Skin and One Set of Bone, 150
Typhoon and Flood in 1460, 36
Under One's Feet, the Red Thread, 112
Utterly Absorbed in the Dream of Wushan, 154
When Ikkyū Was Old, 190–1
Wind Bell, two poems, 104–5
With a Poem About a Brothel, Putting to Shame Those Brothers Who Obtain the Dharma, 142–3
Xutang's Three Pivot Phrases, three poems, 70–1
Yantou's Old Sail Kōan, 78–9

Glossary-Index

Ankokuji 安國寺, 11
Arhat (rakan) 羅漢, 14, 15, 16, 43, 44, 95, 96, 138, 146
Ashikaga 足利, 2, 5, 6, 8, 9, 13, 123

Bai Juyi 白居易, 31–3, 158, 170, 177, 197
Baizhang Huaihai 百丈懷海, 64, 74, 84, 125–6, 165–6
Ban (Lady) 班婕妤, 10, 14–15, 135, 147
Bing 拌, 62, 65
Bird Nest. *See* Niao Ke.
Biyang (Marquis) 辟陽侯, 95–6
biwa hōshi 琵琶法師, 10
Bodhidharma, 38, 65–6, 68, 87, 95, 117
Bokkei 墨溪, 24, 161
Bokusai 墨齋, 7, 24–5, 113
bōyomi 棒讀み, 198

Caoshan 曹山, 81
Chang'an 長安, 141, 179, 189–90
Chu Sizong 儲嗣宗, 103
Ciming 慈明, 56, 58, 131, 135–6
cloud-rain, 1, 48, 49–50, 56, 57, 59, 87, 91, 98, 118, 166, 178, 188, 189

Daguan 達觀, 133
Dahui 大慧, 116–17
Daiō 大應, 13, 23, 60, 61, 79
Daitō 大燈, 13, 27, 39, 50–1, 56–9, 60–1, 74, 98, 109, 124, 176
Daitokuji 大德寺, xiii, 7, 13, 19–21, 23, 26–7, 57, 58, 60, 71, 79–80, 102–3, 113, 121, 123–4, 133, 176
Damei 大梅, 40, 42
Dasui 大隨, 83, 85
Deshan 德山, 69, 100–1, 111, 158, 183
Dōgen 道元, xii, 195
Dongshan 洞山, 10–11, 14, 16
Donne, John, xiii, 194
Doushuai 兜率, 131
Du Fu 杜甫, 100, 137, 140–1, 179–80, 189
Du Mu 杜牧, 155
Du Ling 杜陵. *See* Du Fu.

Eguchi 江口, 25

Fen 汾, 63, 65
Fojian 佛鑑, 98
Foyan Qingyuan 佛眼清遠, 79, 80, 129
Fu (Master) 孚上坐, 45
Fujiwara 藤原, 8
Fujiwara no Teika 藤原定家, 27
fūryū 風流, 46, 56, (definition) 57–8, 62, 83, 98, 116, 118, 132, 135, 138, 149, 167, 168, 170, 175, 188, 191

Gaoqiu 高丘, 49
Gaotang Fu 高唐賦, 49
ge 偈, 53
gekokujō 下剋上, 2–3
Giō 祇王, 10
gō 號, 53
Go Daigo 後醍醐, 8, 13
Go Komatsu 後小松, 8, 9, 186
Gongsun Shu 公孫述, 94
Gozan 五山, 5–7, 11, 13, 18, 22, 27, 28, 123–5
Gozan Jissatsu 五山十刹, 5
Great Chiliocosm, 84–5, 96, 109
Guizong 歸宗, 99–100
Guyin 谷穩, 133

hadaka no gengo 裸の言語, 35
haikai 俳諧, 25
haiku 俳句, 25
hajun 波旬, 153, 157, 158
Heike monogatari (Tale of the Heike), 10
Higashiyama 東山, 11, 130–1
Hōnen 法然, xii, 152
Hotoke 佛, 10
Huang Shan'gu 黃山谷, 155

Huangbo 黃檗, 84, 163
Huanglong Huinan 黃龍慧南, 169
Huineng 慧能, 105
Huisi 慧思, 50

Ikkyū Sōjun 一休宗純: birth, 8; death, 27–8; different characters for name, 176; and Mori, i, 16, 24, 119, 165–75; and Yōsō, 19–22, 25, 74, 109–10, 113, 123–4, 135, 176; Zen training, 9–17

Jasoku 蛇足, 24
Jianhe 監河, 146
jie 偈. See *ge*.
Jikaishū 自戒集, 21–2
Jōdoshū 淨土宗, 152
Jōdo Shinshū 淨土眞宗, 22

kalpa (gō) 劫, 74
kana hōgo 假名法語, 19
Kan'ami 觀阿彌, 25
Kannon 觀音, 12, 87–8
Kasō 華叟, 12–14, 16–17, 19–21, 109, 110, 113, 176
Katada 堅田, 13, 110
katsu 喝, 100, 164
Katsuroan 瞎驢庵, 22, 23, 183
Kenninji 建仁寺, 5, 11, 131
Ken'ō 謙翁, 12
kōan 公案: first mention, 16; defined, 205n16
Kokyūan 虎丘庵, 183
Komparu Zenchiku 金春禪竹, 24, 25
kundoku 訓讀, ix, 197–9
kunten 訓點, 198

kyō 境, 63

Lancan 懶殘, 46, 47, 58, 110
Li Bai 李白, 155, 172
Li Jian 李監, 100
Li Yi 李益, 36
Lingyun 靈雲, 87, 115
Linji. *See* Rinzai.
Liying 李郢, 147
Liyuan 李源, 171
Louzi (Pavilion Master) 樓子, i, 118–19, 139, 165, 166, 167
Lushan 盧山, 209n78

Ma Yuan 馬援, 94
Maitreya (Miroku), 113, 169–70
Mahākāśyapa, 66
Mañjuśrī, 66, 138, 139
Matsukaze 松風, 25
Mazu 馬祖, 40
Mori 森, i, 16, 24, 119, 165–75
Mumu Issei 無夢一清, 189
Murata Shukō 村田珠江, 25, 26
Musō Soseki 夢窓疎石, 188
Musū Ryōshin 夢嵩良眞, 189

Nanpō Jōmyō 南浦紹明. *See* Daiō.
Namu Amida Butsu 南無阿彌陀佛, 152
Nanquan 南泉, 79, 80, 83
Nanyue 南嶽, 48, 50, 51
Nanzenji 南禪寺, 5
Niao Ke 鳥窠, 32–3
nin 人, 63
Nō 能, 4, 24, 25

Ōei 應永, 8
Okumura manuscript 奧村本, 53, 182, 199, 208n52, 210n97
Ōnin War 應仁の亂, 2, 6, 24, 26, 121, 161, 166, 176, 178, 181, 183, 184

Pang (Lay brother) 龐居士, 97
pāpīyān. *See hajun*.
Pavilion Master. *See* Louzi.
Puhua 普化, 105–6, 111, 121

Qingsu 清素, 130–1
Qu Yuan 屈原, 41–3, 56, 132

renga 連歌, xi, 4, 24
Rinzai (Master) 臨濟, xvii, 22, 54, 59, 69, 84–5, 89, 100, 105, 111, 137, 150, 152, 162–3, 164, 183; Four Propositions (of), 61–8, 98, 104, 196
Rinzai Zen 臨濟禪, xi–xii, xvii, 5–7, 28, 90, 125, 195
rokudō 六道, 74
Ryōzen. *See* Tettō Ryōzen.

Sakai 堺, 3, 18, 19, 20, 22, 23, 27, 28, 167
Śākyamuni, 78, 82, 120, 185
Sansheng 三聖, 64
sanzen 參禪, 21
sanzen daisen sekai 三千大千世界, 85
Sen no Rikyū 千の利休, 25
Shen Yiji 審食其, 96
shi 詩, 53
shichigon zekku 七言絶句, 35
Shida-dera 尸陀寺, 99
shigin 詩吟, 199
Shinjuan 眞珠庵, 27, 74, 113, 173

shoaku makusa, shūzen bugyō 諸惡莫作衆善奉行, 31, 208n64
Shōkokuji 相國寺, 5
Shūon'an 酬恩庵, 7, 23, 24, 27, 60, 161, 183
Shun (Lord) 舜君, 47, 48, 51, 163
Sima Xiangru 司馬相如, 63, 66–7, 68, 108
Sōchō 宗長, 4, 24, 25, 27
Soga painting school 曾我流, 24, 25, 161
Sōki (Elder Ki) 宗熙, 135–6
Song Yu 宋玉, 49
Songyuan Lingyun 松源靈隠, 112, 113, 119, 127–8, 161–2
Sōrin 宗臨, 121
Su Dongpo 蘇東坡, 155
Sumiyoshi 墨吉, 23, 167, 171, 172, 173, 178

Takigi 薪, 23, 24, 161, 172, 173, 178, 183
Tamagaki 玉垣, i, 167
Tao Yuanming 陶淵明, xiii, 35, 43–4, 45, 149–50
Tenryūji 天龍寺, 5, 188
tetralemma, 63
Tettō Ryōzen 徹翁靈山, 21, 74, 113, 176; Ryōzen Sermon, 72–3
Tianbao (Era) 天寶, 95, 96, 140, 141
Tiantai 天臺, 43, 48, 50, 51, 191
Tianze 天澤, i, 71; see also Xutang
Tōfukuji 東福寺, 5, 189
tokusei (act of grace) 德政, 3, 143

unsui 雲水, 1
un'u 雲雨. See cloud-rain.

Vimalakīrti, 32, 99–100, 117

Wakan rōei shū 和漢朗詠集, 189, 197
Wang Changling 王昌齡, 14–15
Wang Huizhi 王徽之, 47, 48, 51
Weishan Lingyou 潙山靈裕, 18, 61, 64, 67, 87, 151
Wenjun 文君, 66–7, 108
Wu Zixu 伍子胥, 110
Wushan 巫山, 49, 57, 107, 155, 166, 178, 188
Wuzu 五祖, 37–8, 86, 137

Xiang river 湘水, 46, 47, 132, 163
Xiangru 相如. See Sima Xiangru.
Xiangyan 香嚴, 45, 87
Xu Zhongya 徐中雅, 106
Xuanzong 玄宗, 96, 141, 170
Xubaitang 虛白堂, 147–8
Xuedou 雪竇, 90, 92, 97
Xutang 虛堂, i, 13, 28, 50, 59–60, 70–2, 74, 79, 102, 106, 113, 115, 119, 146

Yakushidō 薬師堂, 23, 171
yang 陽, 7
Yang Guifei 楊貴妃, 95–6, 170
Yangqi 楊岐, 58
Yangshan 仰山, 151
Yangtai 陽臺, 49
Yantou 岩頭, 79
Yaoshan 薬膳, 97
yin 陰, 77
Yoshino 吉野, 8, 13
Yu Shun 虞舜, 140, 141
Yōsō 養叟, 19–22, 27, 74, 109–10, 113, 123–4, 124–5, 135, 176

Yuanwu 圓悟, 37–8, 85, 86–7, 90
Yuanze 圓澤, 171
Yue Guang 藥廣, 72
Yunmen 雲門, 10–11, 48–9, 50–1, 59, 75–6, 88, 91, 92, 128, 129
Yuzuriha 譲羽, 99

Zeami 世阿彌, 25
Zhao Zhaoyi 趙昭義, 15
Zhaozhou 趙州, 57, 83, 121, 156
Zhiyi 智顗, 50
Zhuang Zhou 莊周, 146, 174
Ziyang 子陽, 93, 94

Notes

ABOUT QUIRIN PRESS

Established in 2012 Quirin Press is a small independent publisher specializing in: Asian Studies; Cultural Studies; Poetics; and Aesthetics.

The first titles of the press have concentrated on re-issuing classical works in the field that have been out of print for some time. These are new editions that update and revise established titles in line with current scholarship and practices (e.g. the older Wade-Giles transliteration of Chinese words is updated to the current Pinyin standard).

For details on any of our present or forthcoming titles visit:
www.QuirinPress.com
and follow us on Twitter @QuirinPress

www.ingramcontent.com/pod-product-compliance
Lightning Source LLC
Chambersburg PA
CBHW021824300426
44114CB00009BA/310